MERRY Christmas
1997

Be of Good Cheer

M. Ba

FRIENDS
IN
HIGH
PLACES

FRIENDS IN HIGH PLACES

Our Journey from
Little Rock to Washington, D.C.

WEBB HUBBELL

WILLIAM MORROW AND COMPANY, INC.
New York

It is the policy of William Morrow and Company, Inc., and its imprints and affiliates, recognizing the importance of preserving what has been written, to print the books we publish on acid-free paper, and we exert our best efforts to that end.

Library of Congress Cataloging-in-Publication Data

Hubbell, Webb.
Friends in high places : our journey from Little Rock to Washington, D.C.:
/ Webb Hubbell.
p.   cm.
Includes index.
ISBN 0-688-15749-1
1. Hubbell, Webb. 2. Clinton, Bill, 1946– —Friends and associates—Biography. 3. Clinton, Hillary Rodham. 4. United States—Politics and government—1993– 5. Arkansas—Politics and government—1951– I. Title.
E840.8.H8A3 1997
973.929'092—dc21   97-32401
                                                              CIP

Printed in the United States of America

First Edition

1 2 3 4 5 6 7 8 9 10

BOOK DESIGN BY BERNARD KLEIN

www.williammorrow.com

To
Suzy, Walter and Missy, Rebecca,
Caroline and Kelley

Contents

Part III: THE AFTERMATH

FRIENDS
IN
HIGH
PLACES

Prologue

As Good as
It Gets

In the first ten days, Washington had all but swallowed us whole.
The inaugural celebrations were just a blur now, and the reality
of grinding work had set in. The President was busy fighting the
furor over gays in the military. The First Lady was caught up in
health care reform. My old buddy Vince Foster, now the deputy
White House counsel, was holed up with his boss, Bernie Nussbaum, trying to find an attorney general nominee who didn't have
the "nanny problem" that had just sunk Zoe Baird. And over at
Justice—where I was suddenly the one permanent political employee in management—I was trying to get up to speed on all
sorts of strange new subjects, such as HIV-infected Haitians at
the Guantanamo military base in Cuba and A-12 Stealth fighters.
It seemed as if every hour George Stephanopoulos was calling me
to make sure the handful of Republican holdovers at Justice
weren't torpedoeing the administration. More than once I told
him everything was just fine.

I hadn't actually talked to Bill or Hillary since before he was
sworn in. So when Hillary phoned on Monday, Feburary 1, asking me to stop by the White House for an after-work drink, I was
more than ready. I just hadn't figured out when the "after-work"
part of the day was in this city.

Washington really sparkles on late winter afternoons, when the sky becomes a dark marbled haze to the west and all the monuments are lit up like diamonds. The artist Walter Anderson called that the "magic hour." I hadn't seen the city much at that time of day since the inauguration. It was usually dark by the time I left the office, which gave the city a different mood.

I walked the six blocks from Justice to the White House and Vince was waiting for me at the southwest gate. Good old Vince. It was great to see a friendly face. We shook hands and headed up the drive. I remember seeing the light burning on the south portico, and thinking, *They really live here.* I had been to the White House once before, over a decade ago when I was mayor of Little Rock and Jimmy Carter had invited some of the nation's mayors. But that had been a working trip, a meeting with a lot of others in the public rooms. Now I was invited for a social call. My friends called this place home now.

Vince showed me through the West Wing, where I saw many faces that I still associated with the small transition headquarters back in Little Rock. Now here they were in the White House. This impromptu tour felt like a scene out of the *Twilight Zone*—I was walking through the most famous house in America, and I knew everybody working in it. I said hello to Bruce Lindsey, former partner at the Wright, Lindsey and Jennings law firm and Bill Clinton's right-hand man during the campaign. I stopped and chatted with Deb Coyle, once an assistant at the Rose Law Firm, whom I had recommended to Mickey Kantor during the transition. Now here was Deb in the White House. It was almost eerie.

Vince took me upstairs to show me his office. I was surprised at how small it was. Mine at Justice was laughably large. Even *I* looked small in it, and I'm six foot five. When I kidded Vince about his office, he explained that at the White House, office size wasn't the crucial thing—proximity to the President was. In the White House caste system, the West Wing, with its smaller offices, was a much better place to be than the more distant Old Executive Office Building with its larger ones. George Stephanopoulos had a couple of White House work spaces. One of them was nothing but a cubbyhole, but it was right outside the Oval Office, and was thus a very coveted room. Vince's little second-floor office had a single window that looked out over the West Wing parking lot. But it was right across the hall from Hillary's office, so it too was a prime spot. As Vince talked, I thought how embarrassing it was to be talking about such trivial things—the right office, the wrong location, who's important, who's not. But I soon learned that those very concerns were what everyday life in Washington was mostly about.

Vince led me to the small, ornate brass elevator that took us to the President's residence on the second floor. We stepped out onto a white wall-to-wall carpet that covered the entire floor like snow. The room was essentially a hall, but it was wide and comfortable like a sitting room, with chairs and tables and sofas lining the rich yellow walls. In the center was a beautiful octagonal burl table with an enormous vase of flowers on it. As we turned right toward the family quarters, Vince motioned in the other direction, through an arched doorway with an elegant spiderweb window above it. "The Lincoln Bedroom is down that way," he said.

The First Family's private domain was at the opposite end of the hall, through an arched door that mirrored the first one. Vince and I waited on an overstuffed sofa and chair. But just as soon as we sat down, people were swarming around Vince peppering him with questions. Maggie Williams, Hillary's chief of staff, handed him papers to look at. Someone else pulled him aside to get his advice. Watching all this, I thought back to the Vince Foster I had worked with every day for twenty years at the Rose Law Firm. He'd always had a presence about him, a reassuring self-containment. When he gave his opinion, people felt comforted by it. Now he was having that same effect in the White House. He couldn't even take a moment to talk with an old friend, but Vince didn't really mind—more than anything, he loved to be counted on. It occurred to me that this was exactly what he had wanted—for all of us to come up here and be a team, the way he and Hillary and I had been at the Rose firm. Now that the team had taken the field, he was determined to play with his usual brilliance. He had a considered answer for every question, and people trusted his word implicitly.

Suddenly, Hillary appeared from a door off the sitting area. For fifteen years I'd worked with her every day, but I hadn't seen her much in the past year of the campaign. Not to talk to, anyway. She looked radiant, and we hugged hard and laughed as we always had. I held her at arm's length and studied the new Hillary. She *was* a new Hillary, of course. New hair; new makeup; new, more fashionable clothes. Vince and I had noticed the incremental changes during the campaign—first on magazine covers, and then in person on the rare times she would pop into town and call to meet us for our traditional lunch getaways. During those lunches, we didn't quite know what to make of the differences in her. She looked beautiful, of course, but we kidded her about when she'd first come to the Rose firm with her frizzy hair, dowdy clothes, no makeup, and Coke-bottle glasses. Soon she started representing a jewelry sales company, a group made up primarily of very down-home southern women with elaborate beehive hairdos. Hillary won their lawsuit, and the beehive ladies revered her as their hero. Every one of them volunteered to give her a makeover. Even then, Vince and I kidded her about it. She said she loved those ladies but didn't want to look like them. Today, she looked like something out of a New York fashion magazine. Her happy laugh told me she was enjoying it. I pulled her close and hugged her again.

She sat down next to me and asked how Suzy was, how my kids were doing. Hillary always did that. Then she asked how things were going at Justice. "We hear you're doing a great job," she said. Vince was beaming. For a minute, it seemed like old times.

Then the President came in and he gave me a hug, too. I still hadn't gotten used to my old golfing buddy now being addressed as "Mr. President." Mickey Kantor had told many of us just before election night that no matter how well we'd known Bill before, once he was elected he was to be called Mr. President. It showed respect for the office, and for what he had sacrificed to achieve it. The first time I addressed him that way was just days after the election, as we headed to the golf course in the backseat of his limousine. It was the first time we'd been alone since he was elected. "Well, congratulations . . . Mr. President," I said. He looked at me and I looked at him. Then he slapped me on the knee and we both broke out laughing. It reminded me of two boys giggling over some prank we had pulled at school.

A white-coated White House waiter brought us drinks and everybody wanted to hear how things were going at Justice. I was about to tell them when Harry and Linda Bloodworth-Thomason showed up. Most Americans think of the Thomasons as Bill and Hillary Clinton's glamorous Hollywood friends, the producer-writers of *Designing Women* and *Evening Shade.* Those who knew Harry back in Arkansas think of him as just a high school football coach who made good. Linda, due to her upbringing in southern Missouri, has become accepted as an honorary Arkansan. The Thomasons brought their showbiz flair to bear on both the past summer's Democratic convention and the recent inauguration, and they had a gift for the President. It was one of those little glass scenes that "snows" when you shake it—except in this case, the snow was the silver confetti that Harry had come up with for the convention. The President loved it.

The Thomasons were dressed to go out, and I got the feeling the President and First Lady were going with them. When the party was breaking up, Hillary tugged at my sleeve and pulled me aside. "I want you to come to dinner next Sunday. It's Mary Steenburgen's birthday. Just you and Vince and me and Bill and Mary." My first thought was, My kids are going to *kill* me. Mary Steenburgen, another Arkansan, was one of their favorite actresses. I had met her on several occasions, usually with Bill and Hillary. She was a friend of Vince's, too, from the days when he headed up the Arkansas Repertory Theater and Mary had been caring enough to come home to perform. But my second thought went right to my own insecurities: I'm still in the inner circle, I told myself. Everybody I knew was working here at the White House, and I was over at Justice all alone. I was glad to know I hadn't been forgotten.

As Vince walked me out, I told him about Hillary's invitation. "She needs to see you," he said. "She *needs* her friends." I knew exactly what he meant. The three of us had survived the Rose firm wars together—survived *because* of one another. Hillary didn't have many people in this world whom she could be herself around, and Vince and I were two she felt comfortable with. Now she needed us more than ever. We shook hands and promised to talk the next day. Then, passing through the gate and the small crowd of sightseers, I reentered the anonymity of the Washington night.

I hadn't expected to play golf with the President quite so soon. It was the dead of winter and we had just started these overwhelming new jobs. But during the inauguration ceremonies, Nancy Hernreich, his loyal executive assistant, came up to me and said, "Webb, did you bring your clubs?" When Bill Clinton was governor, Nancy was the one who would call and say, "Can you play Friday? Pencil it in."

"Are you serious?" I said.

"Oh yeah—we've got to get him out even more now than before."

The morning after that conversation, I phoned a friend in Little Rock and had my golf clubs sent via Federal Express. And sure enough, I got a call from Nancy that week, asking if I could play with the President and Vernon Jordan on Saturday, February 6. "I'll clear you through the southwest gate," Nancy said.

Just before the appointed hour, the plans changed. The President was running late, so Vernon picked me up in his red Cadillac convertible and we were to meet the President at the golf course. I had been wondering how I was going to get my clubs over the guard-station turnstile at the southwest gate, and whether I would actually lug them through the West Wing up to the residence. Later, I would do just that.

Thankfully, the top on Vernon's caddy wasn't down, though I wouldn't have put it past him. I had met him only during the transition, but already I could tell that he was a man who enjoyed life.

The President met us at the spectacular Robert Trent Jones course in Manassas, Virginia. The day was clear, but the air was bitterly cold. The Secret Service men followed us in carts of their own. I was used to that by now—Bill and I had played many times since the election. I had learned a lot about the Secret Service. Although these serious young men watched us with their usual cool detachment, I had detected a glimmer of humanity in them. I had learned that they weren't allowed to help with the golf clubs because then their hands would be occupied. I had learned that they wouldn't help me find a ball in the rough, because their eyes were to be trained for potential threats, not golf balls. But I noticed they might help the President. I had learned that they sometimes got tired of sitting outside in the freezing cold. "If he asks if you want to play longer or go in," one of them once told me, "please say, 'Go in.' "

Before the round was over, I offered my jacket to the President. I might not have done that in Little Rock, but here was the President of the United States shivering while he tried to putt.

"Here, take my jacket," I said.

"No, no, you'll be cold."

"I've got plenty of insulation," I said. He laughed and gladly accepted. One of the perks of his new job.

Most people think we must talk serious politics on the golf course, and nothing could be further from the truth. But on this day, he did say, "Webb, I'm going to have to get you involved in choosing your own boss." His second candidate for attorney general—Judge Kimba Wood—had had to withdraw as well. Like Zoe Baird, she had a "nanny problem." It was an epidemic the Centers for Disease Control hadn't warned us about. The President asked if I could stay and meet with him and Vince and Bernie that afternoon at the White House. Vernon stayed, too. We went up to the third-floor solarium and talked for hours. By this time, the stakes were dangerously high. The President wanted to appoint a woman, but we were having a hard time finding one. We had a sense of being painted into a corner. "You think I *have* to appoint a woman, don't you, Webb?" said the President. I told him that after two false alarms with women candidates, if he bailed and gave the job to a man, he would be killed politically. "The right person is out there," I said. "We just have to find her."

The next afternoon Bernie, Vince, Bruce Lindsey, and I picked up again in Bernie's office. Later Bruce left for an appointment, but the rest of us kept talking. Eventually the President came in and we all went over to the Oval Office to continue the discussion. We lost track of time. Outside, the light faded until the Rose Garden was in deep shadows, but we didn't notice. When the phone rang at about 7 P.M., it was almost a shock—a jolt back to reality. It was Hillary calling. "Have you guys forgotten?" she said. "It's time for dinner." She had already invited Bernie as well.

By now we were a bedraggled bunch. My head was foggy from the intensity of our discussions, and I wanted to go splash water on my face and maybe change my shirt. I mentioned this to Vince, but I knew we had to go up right away. This was the dinner for Mary Steenburgen. Fortunately, it was a casual dinner, so I re-tucked my shirt and brushed myself off and gave my hair a quick lick with my hand. Glancing in the mirror, I thought my sideburns looked a little grayer than I'd remembered.

When we got to the second floor, a butler led us into a private dining room in the family quarters. A small antique table was set with elegant china and silverware and flowers. It was quite a con-trast to the impromptu eat-fests we used to have at the Governor's Mansion in Little Rock. That's where I first got to know Mary—all of us sitting in the kitchen on high stools, laughing and telling stories about the outrageous characters we all knew, and raiding the refrigerator when we wanted more to eat. Now here were these people in white coats and gloves, serving us. How on earth had we gotten to *this* place?

Hillary came in looking happy to have her oldest friends around her. We hugged again, and I could tell she was relaxed because the hug lasted just a little bit longer. Vince held her chair for her, and I remember hoping the candle glow would mask how exhausted I felt. *Mask,* what an appropriate word. At times like this, when I was very tired, I sometimes had a hard time keeping my mask on straight. I wondered if the others were fighting sim-ilar battles. Everybody in this room wore a mask of one kind or another. Except Bernie, maybe. I didn't know him well enough to say.

Suddenly Mary Steenburgen breezed in wielding a camcorder. "Webb! Vince! Smile!" She was positively bubbling, as thrilled as

I'd ever seen her. It was her fortieth birthday and she was having dinner in the White House! This Arkansas girl was sleeping in the Lincoln Bedroom! Her friends were the President and First Lady of the United States! She was as excited as a child.

Mary's openness filled the room that night. It made the candles burn a little brighter and the flowers smell a little sweeter. Before long the rest of us had caught her spirit. Vince and I talked about it later. In mere weeks we'd been sucked into Washington's mire. We had almost lost sight of what had happened, where we were, *who* we were. Less than three months earlier, when Bill was elected President, we had seen it as in some ways a vindication of where we'd come from. No more Arkansas inferiority. For the first time ever, we could openly dare high hopes and big dreams.

Whenever I remember those first visits to the White House, I can't help thinking of Vince's eloquently ironic words, spoken just months later to the graduating class at the University of Arkansas Law School. "When we leave work at night," he said, "we pull up to a large heavy gate that surrounds the White House complex. While the Secret Service guards slowly open the gate, I always look to my right and inevitably there are dozens of people aligned along the iron fence that runs along Pennsylvania Avenue, holding on to the bars, peering through intently at the White House lit in the background. When I look into their faces, I can tell that each has hope for something from their government. It is a wonderful reminder of why we are there."

We told ourselves we had to remember that, and in that speech Vince was doing his best to keep the thought from slipping away. Like all of us, he was trying to remember that we had come to Washington together, all good friends, all of us playing our parts in something grand and historic, something important, something bigger than we were.

We had yet to learn just *how* much bigger.

Part I

THE
RISE

1

Law School
and Love

There have been many moments during my Washington years when I've thought back to the first time I ever saw Bill and Hillary. All three of us were at a mental institution.

In the late spring of 1973, I had graduated from the University of Arkansas Law School in Fayetteville—graduated with honors, actually—and had been lucky enough to land one of two associate positions that year with the prestigious Rose Law Firm in Little Rock. My dad thought I was crazy to have given up a good job with the phone company to become a lawyer. But I was idealistic back then. I was twenty-five years old, had a wife and a son, and I was going to earn $900 a month once I passed the Arkansas bar exam. That's what Bill and Hillary and I—and about two hundred others—were doing at the auditorium of the Arkansas State Hospital on that summer day in 1973.

I'll never forget my first image of Bill. We had filled our blue books for the morning session and had come outside for a break, even though the Little Rock humidity was enough to wilt us. There was a grassy area with big rocks that people congregated in, and that's where Bill was holding court. He was tall and lean, with a bushy mop of dark brown hair that swooped down and covered his ears like he was wearing a helmet, and he was standing in the center of a circle of people who were listening to him talk. I wasn't close enough to hear what he was saying, but he seemed intense and charming at the same time. He would gesture with his hands, furrow his brow—and then he would cock his head and smile a kind of off-center smile that would make the people listening smile and laugh with him. He seemed to *have* them, his audience, and he could do anything he wanted with them.

Hillary was sitting next to him on a big rock. She wasn't listening to him; she was studying. He was talking; she was thinking. I remember she had frizzy hair and thick, round glasses, and she was wearing jeans and a light blue sweatshirt with the word YALE on the front of it. Under the wild hair and behind the glasses, there was something oddly attractive about her. She was quiet, and there was a power in that. At one point she reached over and gently tugged at Bill's sleeve. She didn't look up, didn't implore— she simply tugged at his sleeve as if to say, *Okay, time to stop talking and start studying.* In a minute or so, he did just that.

I was standing with a couple of friends. "Who is that?" I asked, nodding toward the boy with the bushy hair. One of my friends was Bobby Hargraves. "That's Bill Clinton," he said. "He's from Yale, he's a Rhodes scholar, he's going to go up to Fayetteville and teach. He's brilliant."

"Who's *she*?" I said, meaning the girl on the rock.

Hargraves laughed. "Well," he said. "The rumor is, she's his brains."

Leading up to that crossroads were three lifetimes, three lives led day by day and year by year until the stars aligned and the three of us came together. On that day at the mental institution, I of course knew nothing more than I had just been told about the lives of Bill Clinton and Hillary Rodham. In fact, when I first saw and heard about them, I did what so many of us do: I projected my own fears and insecurities onto them. I had a great many fears and insecurities to project. I assumed not only that they probably had a life of the mind that I could never comprehend, but that they also came from a background of wealth and privilege. I looked at the handsome Bill and imagined that he had grown up in an imposing home with a paneled library full of leather-bound books. I looked at the enigmatic Hillary and imagined an unapproachable intellectual brought up in a stuffy family whose metier was the razor-sharp dinner-table discussion.

In later years I would learn just how wrong I was—how much the three of us had in common. But back then I couldn't fathom such a thing. I was simply the son of an engineer and a librarian, and I had a deep inferiority complex. I never felt attractive as a man, and that started early, when I was six and overheard my father telling guests that he didn't know how it could have happened, but "Webb has nigger lips."

I also felt I had to constantly prove myself intellectually just because I played football. Sometimes I let other people's doubts get to me. I had been a "jock" at a state university, so how could I possibly compete with someone who had walked the hallowed halls of Yale or Georgetown—much less the timeless stones of Oxford? Not that I hadn't enjoyed success in school. When I thought about my talents objectively, I guessed that I possessed a combination of analytical ability and people sense that was somehow special. I could make good grades and still have fun. I remember one day in Torts class under Dr. Robert Leflar, a daunting law-school legend. He called on you but once a semester, and you'd better be ready.

One Monday morning he looked down at his book and rumbled the words, "Mr. Hubbell." I had read the assigned chapter only once a few days back and hadn't gotten around to taking notes. I froze. The rest of the class sighed, almost audibly, in relief.

"Mr. Hubbell," the professor said, "will you recite the facts in this case?"

My memory kicked in and I began to describe the case.

"Okay, Mr. Hubbell, now will you tell me what the appellate court held?"

Somehow I knew, although it wasn't in the textbook.

Now he was having fun. "Well, Mr. Hubbell," he said, "what would be your instructions to the jury?" We hadn't studied jury instructions—that was for next semester. Everybody in class craned his neck to see how I would handle *this* one.

But there's a certain combination of legal knowledge, logic, and get-along-with-people sense involved in jury instructions, so I took a stab at it. Dr. Leflar later told me I was the first football player he'd ever given a passing grade to—in my case, a B+. On some level, that kind of backward compliment was also intended to undermine confidence, not build it. When I felt good about myself, such comments just made me mad. The next semester I made an A in Leflar's class—just to show him I wasn't a dumb jock.

I was very clearly a product of my two parents. My father was a big, quiet man who had no hobbies. Work was his recreation. He did like sports, and he took pride in claiming a distant kinship to the baseball great Carl Hubbell. His family had come from New England, but as a boy he had gone to military school in Virginia, where he played football. It was there that he was spotted by a scout of the legendary General Robert Neyland, coach of the Tennessee Volunteers. I grew up hearing the stories of my father's football heroics. The scout recruited young Webster, and he went on to become a star offensive tackle at Tennessee during the team's heyday in the late 1930s and early 1940s. They called my father "Moose" Hubbell.

He and my mother met at UT. She was Virginia Erwin, from Memphis, and in the way these things so often happen, they were almost exact opposites. Where he was quiet, she was outgoing. Where he didn't drink, she poured a bourbon every afternoon at the stroke of five. Where he abhorred cigarette smoke, she inhaled three packs of Salems a day. Somehow it worked. They never fought. That was something my father insisted on in our house while my two sisters and I were growing up. Nobody was allowed to raise his voice. Confrontation was not okay. I saw him lose his temper only three times in my whole life—once when he threw my eighteen-year-old sister Patty's eighteen-year-old husband out of the house after an argument; another time when he slapped Patty for sassing our mother; and a third time, many years later, when my wife's father gave my son a shotgun for his sixteenth birthday.

My dad hated guns, though we never knew exactly why. I

wasn't allowed any kind of gun at all, from toys to BB guns to rifles. My dad had been in both World War II and Korea, and he once told my younger sister, Terry, that he had "seen enough people killed in Korea by guns to ever risk having one in our house."

My parents married a week before his final football game, in the Sugar Bowl against Duke on New Year's Day, 1941. Shortly after that, he left to join the Army as a lieutenant in the Corps of Engineers. My mother stayed with her parents in Memphis while he was gone, and my sister Patty was born in Memphis in 1942. After the war Daddy took a position as an industrial engineer for a company that built power plants throughout the South. He was overseeing the construction of one in Little Rock, Arkansas, when I was born there on January 18, 1948.

We moved around a lot in my early years, but then Mother and Patty and I went back to Memphis when my father had to go off to war again. Later he took a job in Memphis, and I lived there until I was fourteen. That summer we moved to Montgomery, Alabama, where I would spend my tenth-grade year. It was 1962, and the Selma marches occurred while we were in Alabama. As one who would someday be in charge of the civil rights division at the Justice Department, I wish I could say that the racial injustice that existed all around me galvanized me to action. I saw it, of course, but at that age and at that time, I didn't have any idea that something could be done about it. I heard the word "nigger" being used by people who weren't even angry. The word bothered me back then, and it's not a word my children have ever heard in our house. But when I was growing up, it was just another word in the white person's lexicon. I saw the separate bathrooms for "whites" and "coloreds." Like most southern boys of that time, I was practically raised by a black maid. Fanny Taylor was her name. I sat in her lap, curled into the folds of her ample flesh, even spent the night at her house sometimes. But on the counter in our kitchen was a water glass the rest of us weren't to drink from. That was Fanny's glass. I remember when Fanny asked my grandparents for a raise from $1.00 to $2.00 a day.

They loved Fanny, and they were appalled. They didn't quite see her as a person. Until I moved to Little Rock, I never attended school with, played sports with or against, or went to church with an African American—except when Fanny babysat me in her tiny home. Those times I viewed as an adventure into a foreign world.

When we moved to Alabama, I was an awkward, skinny kid— five feet eight inches tall and 140 pounds—barely enduring puberty and wrestling with the heartache of having to leave my friends behind in Memphis. Like most teenagers, I was self-absorbed. I wished I felt handsome; I wished I was tall. I wished I could be a football hero like my father had been. Not that I complained. By that time, a certain pattern was showing itself. I didn't see it then, but in hindsight I do. My sister Terry and I often talk about the fact that we inherited a need to please. Patty didn't. She went her own way early, stumbling many times. Maybe it made her healthier than Terry and me. We didn't dare stumble. We had a great deal invested in our parents' approval.

In his own life, my father operated according to a body of truths derived from his years in engineering and football. His was a world of low tolerances. You didn't fudge the rules or get loose with the measurements, because if you did, a building might come crumbling down. Even if you fudged and *won,* he didn't approve. I remember one time when Ole Miss was playing Tennessee and the Ole Miss quarterback dropped back to pass from his own end zone. The pass connected with the receiver, who ran it the length of the field for a touchdown. My father was furious. "You *never* pass on your side of the field," he said, "much less from the end zone." That had been one of General Neyland's tenets, and it was now my father's. Doing that kind of stunt was "bad football."

And "bad life," I suppose. You didn't let yourself get in that situation in the first place. You gained ground methodically, a yard at a time. You watched your flanks and didn't take chances. That way, you were always safe. You didn't get thrown for a loss. If you played right, there was no need for grandstanding.

When I was fifteen, we moved back to Little Rock. By then I had shot up to six feet four and weighed a grand total of 175 pounds, and my father was convinced that the only way I would meet people and adjust to yet another change was to go out for football. Daddy had been in Little Rock four months before the rest of us moved, and he set up the whole thing before I got there. Within two hours of my arrival, I had a phone call from the coach at Hall High School, saying he was expecting me to try out for football the following day. One of my father's friends had a gorgeous daughter who was a Hall cheerleader. She was apparently dispatched to tell me that the only way to be cool at Hall was to play ball. I had never played tackle football, except for a brief time in Memphis when I was an utter failure. I didn't really like the contact. But my father wanted me to play, the coach wanted me to play, and most of all a pretty cheerleader wanted me to play. So I went out for football.

The wonderful thing was, my father was right. I played defensive end in high school, and although I wasn't very good at the beginning, I improved. As I did, I met more people and made more friends, many of whom I have to this day. It was my first taste of the vaunted Arkansas "interconnectedness" that has been so vilified by the outside media. At Hall, I played football with a boy named Chris Piazza, who later became Pulaski County prosecuting attorney and is now a circuit court judge in Little Rock. Bruce Lindsey was two years behind me at Hall. One of our cheerleaders was a girl named Marsha Scott, who is now a White House deputy—as well as one of my most loyal friends. Chosen by my teachers to go to Boy's State, the American Legion's annual mock government program put on for high-achieving seniors in states all over the country, I met there a charismatic boy from Hope, a boy everyone already predicted would go on to great things. He had been governor of Boy's State the year before, and the person elected governor always returns the next year to preside over the new delegates. When I met him I could immediately see the energy and charm that everyone talked about. His name was Mac McLarty.

That was just the start of it. When it came time for me to go to college, I was slightly surprised to have so many choices. My mother had stressed grades and I'd done well, so I was offered academic scholarships to Dartmouth and the Air Force Academy.

What I didn't expect were football scholarships. But both the University of Arkansas and Arkansas State were interested in me. So was my father's alma mater, Tennessee.

Daddy didn't take a stand on this issue. "Do what you think is right for you, son," he said. What he never told me was that Jack East, Sr., one of the most powerful insurance men in the state—the man who provided bonding for my father's construction business—was putting pressure on *him* for me to go to Arkansas. East was a rabid Razorback fan, of which there were, and are, many throughout the state. As I later heard about the conversation, it went something like this:

"Webster, I hear young Webb has been offered a full scholarship to play ball for Arkansas."

"That's right, Jack. I'm real proud of him."

"Webster, I hear he hasn't signed yet—and that he's thinking of playing ball for Tennessee."

"Yes, that's right. You know, Jack, my brother and I both played ball at Tennessee."

"But Webster, if young Webb goes to Tennessee, how are you going to get bonded?"

That's the *other* side of the vaunted Arkansas interconnectedness.

In the end, I chose Arkansas—not just the school, but the state. Several of my teammates from Hall were going up to Fayetteville, and that played into my decision. But the final straw was that I felt my life had turned around when I moved to Little Rock. I'd started playing football, started making friends, started enjoying a certain level of popularity. In twelfth grade I'd run for class representative to the Student Council—and won. I liked that feeling. On Friday nights after I made a crucial tackle, I liked looking up at the stands and seeing a wall of people cheering for *me*. I liked knowing my father was in that crowd. I liked being part of a winning team. In my mind's eye, Arkansas had worked magic on a shy, lonely kid and made him a happy and admired young man. How much better would it become when I moved to the home of the national champions—the Arkansas Razorbacks.

*   *   *

In Arkansas, old Razorback games flicker like home movies through the state's collective memory. Once a Razorback, always a Razorback, and in later life I found that having played football opens doors. No one ever mentions that I have a degree in electrical engineering. Through many years of law practice, and even when I was working at the Justice Department in Washington, I was often introduced as offensive tackle on the great team that beat the undefeated University of Georgia 16–2 in the 1969 Sugar Bowl.

Or as a man once drafted by the Chicago Bears.

That I never played a single game on a frigid day at Soldier Field—never even put on a Bears uniform, in fact—becomes another pivotal point, another crossroads story in a long line of them that set me inexorably on the path to law school, to the Rose Law Firm, to friendship with the Clintons. The life-changing moment happened in the first game of my senior year, against Oklahoma State. At the start of the second half, I was running down on a punt. My eyes were focused on the receiver, when out of the corner of my eye I saw an opposing lineman zeroing in on me. A hundred times before in this situation I had absorbed the blow and bounced back up, sometimes to make the tackle. This time I didn't get up.

My memory of the next moment comes from the film I watched the following morning. The O-State player's helmet had crashed directly into the outer part of my right knee. I fell to the ground. On the film I saw myself try to raise my body to make the tackle, but I couldn't. Instead, I passed out from the pain. I came to a minute later with trainers and ballplayers surrounding me. Before they carried me off, I do remember, I was praying—as most players do under such circumstances—that my mother would not come out onto the field.

We came from behind in the fourth quarter to win the game, and during the postgame celebration Coach Frank Broyles came to me in the locker room. "Webb," he said, "are you going to be able to get back on the field and play?"

Two considerations went through my mind. One, the coaches had told me that the Rams, the Packers, and the Cowboys were all interested in drafting me when the season was over. And two, I couldn't stand to let people down. "Coach," I said, "wild horses couldn't keep me off that field."

I began practicing again the following Monday. They kept me out of the next game, but I continued to work out. From time to time, I would feel a pain so sharp and blinding that I wouldn't be able to walk, or to keep from crying out. They examined my knee again, stuck a long needle in it and drained out a cup of blood. The trainer and doctors explained that I had two choices: I could either have surgery, in which case my college career would be over; or they could continue to drain the knee and shoot it full of cortisone, and I could have surgery after the season. They stressed that we had a chance for a great season and that I was needed very badly, but the decision was up to me.

There was no decision.

The next winter I was drafted in the seventh round by the Bears. A running back from USC named O. J. Simpson was the top draft pick that year.

I was thrilled and honored to be drafted by the Bears. To me, the Bears meant Dick Butkus, Doug Atkins, Mike Ditka, Gale Sayers. It was a team of men. But I think I already knew that I would never be one of them. After the Sugar Bowl, I had gone in for the surgery. The doctor gave me sobering news. The cartilage had been torn and retorn, and it was that way throughout the knee. "If you play pro ball," the doctor told me, "you'll end up crippled for life." Later, I had talked to my coaches about my future. Several had a hard time looking me in the eye. "If only we had known what *you* were doing to your knee . . ." one told me wistfully.

That summer I reported for Bears camp, hoping for a miracle. I met all my heroes—Butkus, Sayers, Brian Piccolo. It was his last camp, and I still cry when I watch *Brian's Song*. After I took the physical, I got a call to go see Coach George Halas. "Webb," he said, "your knee hasn't healed—but over the next year, it might. If you'll let us put you on injured reserve, we'll give you a first-class plane ticket home and a thousand dollars." The engineering program at Arkansas was five years then, and I was trying to graduate in four and a half. A thousand dollars would be enough for me to finish college.

I flew home to Little Rock and took Western Civilization that summer, and played golf in the afternoons. My knee never healed. After graduation, instead of moving to Chicago, I accepted a job with Southwestern Bell and soon found myself managing the local phone office in the minuscule town of Mena, Arkansas.

Many, many years later, when I gave speeches during my time in Washington, I would tell a joke about my aborted pro football career that always got great laughs. "Probably the best thing that ever happened to me was not having the knees to play for the Bears," I would say. "If I had, I'd probably have had ten knee operations and be punch-drunk and running a bar in Chicago."

The audience would chuckle appreciatively, and then I would hook them with the punch line. "But after being in Washington for all these months, that bar sounds pretty good right now."

It was guaranteed to bring down the house. Even people who love Washington know it's a more brutal game than football.

My seven-month stint as Wire Chief in Mena, Arkansas, can be summed up in one sentence. I was twenty-one, single, and in a town so small it had two movie theaters—an indoor and a drive-in—but only one projector, which traveled from one theater to the other according to the season.

My work was uninspiring. On Easter Sunday, 1970, I had to track down the selfish person who took the phone off the hook and tied up an entire eight-party line. The most exciting moment was when a train crashed south of town and I had to work all night restoring long-distance service. I channeled my spare time in Mena toward reading, and whenever I could I jumped in my car and drove to Fayetteville to visit friends. Many of them were becoming upset over the country's involvement in Vietnam, and I found my own consciousness raised by listening to them. I even wrote to the chairman of AT&T complaining about the company's position, or lack thereof, on Vietnam. To his credit, Chairman H. I. Romnes wrote me back. Somewhere in the files of Southwestern Bell in Mena is a thoughtful response by Mr. Romnes to a young and idealistic employee.

My high school friend Marsha Scott had gone to work for Senator J. William Fulbright, and I started paying attention to the things the senator was saying. He thought our involvement in Southeast Asia was a serious mistake, and I admired him for speaking out. Meanwhile, I sat there on my couch in my lonely apartment in Mena, reading Herman Hesse and listening to Simon and Garfunkel. My friends were taking part in marches and demonstrations. They were supporting causes they believed in. I couldn't escape the growing feeling that life was passing me by.

One of my favorite uncles was a lawyer, and he'd often talked to me about going to law school. I began thinking that maybe law was exactly the outlet I needed. It was a way to help people, to fight on behalf of those less powerful. It was a way I could help change the world. But such a lofty notion ignited a conflict in me. At the phone company I was making $900 a month, and since there was nothing to spend my money on, I was saving half of it. Was I prepared to trade that for three more years of school and living in a smelly apartment with a roommate? It was the old internal battle between the practical son of an engineer and the idealistic son of a librarian. For most of my life, the practical side had won out.

One day I devised a test to help me make up my mind. My one bit of rebellion was my love for sporty convertibles. My dad didn't care at all about cars. When I was growing up, he drove a plain blue Ford sedan with no chrome, no leather, no excitement whatsoever. Now that I was on my own and had my own money, I wanted a nice car. A *really* nice car. I had bought a used Austin-Healy, and that was a lot of fun. In fact, it had been my salvation in Mena. On a cool night, I would put the top down and go for a drive that brought me a peace surpassing anything my friends gained from drugs or Eastern meditation. But peace aside, the car I had always lusted for was a Porsche 911.

So I decided it would come down to that—a Porsche or law

school. So much for my budding idealism. Looking back on it, I have to admit it was a ridiculous way to make such an important decision, but it made perfect sense to me at the time. I've always been a believer in fate—I guess I was looking for a sign.

One weekend when I was visiting my parents in Little Rock, I drove over to Riverside Motors, in whose lot sat a beautiful dark blue Porsche 911. I parked my Healy and a salesman appeared. I told him I wanted to take that Porsche for a test drive, and he promptly went and got the key. I guess he could tell he didn't have to do much selling.

When he came back, he placed that precious key in my hand. Being an aficionado, I knew that Porsche ignitions were always on the left of the steering column, so I took the key with my left hand. The salesman escorted me to the car, held open the door, and waited expectantly while I slid my six-foot-five-inch, 230-pound frame into the . . .

No, that's not what happened. What happened was, I didn't fit. No matter how hard I tried, I couldn't manage to squeeze my bulk behind the steering wheel of that beautiful car. At the time, it was one of the most disappointing moments in my life, and I'm sure the salesman felt the same.

On the other hand, it made my decision easy. For one of the few times in my young years, I was resolved to go against my father's wishes. I was leaving the sure thing, the safe yard-by-yard grind, and dropping back for the old Hail Mary.

I had arranged to work during law school, a concept that appalled most of my fellow students and professors. "Are you nuts?" one friend said to me. "My wife's taking a second job just so I don't *have* to take one." Before orientation I was sent to see the dean, who tried to discourage me but said my scores on the LSAT were high enough that he'd be willing to try it. He didn't hold out much hope, though.

So after finishing orientation, I drove the forty miles to my draftsman job in the little town of Bella Vista. I was preoccupied that day, disturbed by all the fuss about my working. Nothing seemed to be clicking for me—just as I got my drafting table set up, it was time to go back to Fayetteville. I wondered if I had made a big mistake.

On the way home, a fine drizzle started falling, but I didn't bother putting up the top. Maybe I thought the water would help clear my head. I just put on my hat and kept going, my mind a million miles away.

Just outside Fayetteville, I came to a stop sign I had dealt with dozens of times before. Only this time, when I applied the brakes, I realized I had misjudged just how slick the road had become. In a split second I decided to gun it and shoot through the intersection. The only problem was, when I glanced to my left, I saw a Mack truck full of chickens barreling toward me.

The truck broadsided the little Healy. Chickens flew everywhere, and my beloved car ended up wrapped around a telephone pole. I suppose it's true that God looks after fools and drunks, and occasionally kids in sports cars. Because that's the only explanation for my having survived. The one injury I sustained was a cut on my head when I banged into the steering wheel and broke it.

Food has always been a therapy for depression for me. That night at a friend's house, I ate everything she could dish up. School hadn't started yet and I had worried my teachers (and missed my first day of class), totaled my car, and lost my only way to get to work. I hated calling my father, but I had no choice. He and Mother had always disapproved of my Austin-Healy, assuming that sooner or later I would kill myself in it. So when I bought it, Daddy kept my six-year-old sensible car, my 1965 Ford Fairlane. Now *that,* to my father, was the car of a responsible man. I had come to loathe it. It was turquoise, and my friends and I had named it the Turquoise Turd. Like it or not, however, this time *it* was my salvation. I ended up driving it for years.

Despite that rocky start, I found myself increasingly comfortable with law school. The logic appealed to me, and so did the rich history of human affairs that's filtered through each and every case. I enjoyed the intellectual challenge of writing briefs, and the adrenaline rush of arguing before a judge and jury. That feeling reminded me of old ball games, except now I wasn't just an offensive lineman—I was quarterback and blocker and wide receiver all in one. Some still questioned my academic credentials because of football, and I resented that, though characteristically I tried not to show it. (I can tell you what position someone played by their personality—offensive linemen are steady and good-natured, and accept blows; defensive linemen are aggressive and don't tease easily; wide receivers are individualists and flashy dressers; safeties are lovers; all kickers are oddballs.) But before long, more and more classmates started coming up to me and asking questions about the cases we were studying. I enjoyed that, and gave them as much time as they wanted. I finished the first semester in the top ten of my class.

My only real problem was that I was lonely. I had always had female friends, though not girlfriends. As long as there was that distinction, I could talk to them, tell them my dreams. But I guess there was a reason I didn't play safety. I was shy and awkward around girls I wanted to date. Calling a girl was a major trauma. Fortunately, I had some friends at the Kappa Alpha Theta sorority house, and they were good about fixing me up. For someone like me, that was a godsend. In fact, I owe my greatest happiness in life to them, because one day one of the Thetas called and said, "Webb, Suzy Ward wants you to ask her out."

I knew who she was. Actually, Suzy had graduated from Hall High School too, but she was two years younger and so we only overlapped my senior year. But lately I had caught myself thinking about her. The law school was on a corner of the campus across the street from the Theta house, and many afternoons I had stood at the window of the law library and watched her come and go from class. She was short and blond, with piercing blue eyes. She drove a brown Thunderbird.

I called, and to my surprise she was open for Saturday night. My old turquoise Ford—which around girls we discreetly called the Hubmobile—wasn't working, so Suzy and I double-dated with my friend William Ketcher and his date, Margo. William still laughs about that evening—the beauty and the beast. I was a guy who never cared much about clothes. Being six feet five, I had a hard time buying clothes off the rack, but I didn't know there were any other options open to me. My shirts would sometimes be three inches too short in the sleeves, and they wouldn't stay tucked in no matter how stiffly I stood. In college, my wardrobe mostly consisted of several pairs of jeans, a few sweatshirts, and moccasins with no socks. That's what I was wearing on my first date with Suzy, except I had really dressed up—instead of a sweatshirt I had on my best light blue shirt. Suzy came out in a long skirt, white blouse and vest, with her hair perfectly done. No wonder she still buys my clothes for me.

William and Margo couldn't stop laughing, but I thought we had a good time. I called Suzy the next day and asked her out for the next weekend. She accepted—and then, a couple of days later, called and broke the date. I asked her out again and she said yes—and then called back and said she had to decline because her "old boyfriend didn't have a date for his fraternity formal." Any other boy would have gotten the hint—she obviously had a lot of guys after her, and I was nice . . . *but*. That thought never occurred to me. In those days I took people at their word. I'm glad I did, because the next week I phoned her again and we dated every night for the next three weeks—at which time we got engaged. It was May 2, 1971. We had no idea what we were doing, how we were going to live, but we were in love and didn't want to face the world without each other.

The next weekend we drove to Little Rock to break the news to our parents. Mine were a snap—my mother cried, and my father just wondered why I was always attracted to short girls. Suzy was a little over five feet tall. She won him over by promising to grow.

Her parents, on the other hand, were a much different matter. Her parents required *strategy*. And lest you think I'm simply indulging in some cute but irrelevant bit of nostalgia, I urge you to read on. This is the story of a journey, and every crossroads plays its part.

Suzy's strategy went like this: We would go tell her mother first, then go tell my parents while her mother "kinda breaks it to Dad." Then we would drive to the Wards' lake house in Hot

Springs where I would ask her father for his permission to marry his daughter. Suzy directed me to a beautiful home in West Little Rock, the newest area of the city. She showed me around, and then her mother came in and we were introduced. Mrs. Ward, a short, blond woman with more than a hint of her Swedish ancestry about her, was nice but seemed preoccupied—she was buzzing about trying to get ready to leave for Hot Springs. Finally, Suzy uttered nine words that stopped her in her tracks. "Mom, Webb and I are going to get married," she said.

Some silences are calming, but this one had a portentous edge. Mrs. Ward's face went white, and her mouth wouldn't seem to close. Then she spoke: "But . . . but . . . But, Suzy, what about all those *other* boys?"

Suzy pushed her out of the room and for the next hour I was left sitting in the kitchen wondering, *What other boys?* An hour later my future mother-in-law came back into the kitchen. Though she had pulled herself together, I didn't derive much comfort from her words: "I will try to prepare Seth," she said. I nodded grimly, trying to manage a smile.

The Wards' lake house sits on the eastern shore of Lake Hamilton, a huge body of water south of downtown Hot Springs. For a century or more, Lake Hamilton and its less-crowded sister, Lake Catherine, have helped draw visitors to the "Spa City." Such notables as Alf Landon and Pretty Boy Floyd and Bill Clinton have fished on Lake Hamilton, though in different parties, of course.

I confess that my idea of a lake house is a big old rambling cabin with a porch or deck and a pine-shaded grounds that never needs mowing. That's not the Wards' house. Made of stone and glass, it sits far back on a manicured lawn that rises gently from the lake wall. There are pines, but not a pine needle in sight. A sidewalk meanders from the boat dock to the patio, and Old Glory waves from a tall flagpole by the water.

Obviously Suzy needed some time with her parents, because right away I was invited on a boat ride with her younger brother. His real name is Seth II, but all his life he has answered to "Skeeter." We took off across the water with an abandon that in future years I would come to associate closely with my brother-in-law. While he drove, he told me that no boy would *ever* consider marrying his sister if that boy knew what Skeeter Ward knew. I tried to get him to tell me what he was saying, but all I plumbed from his responses was a murky layer of sibling rivalry mixed with real devotion.

When we got back to the house, Suzy introduced me to her father. At the time, Seth Ward was in his early fifties. I would have known from his manner that he was a former Marine—even if Suzy hadn't already told me that she and her siblings knew the "Marine Corps Hymn" before they knew their ABCs. Seth was trim and straight, and his blue eyes were hawklike. His red hair was cut close to his head. Suzy has his chin, but her jawline is streamlined while his jaw juts like somebody flexing hard from deep anger. He offered to show me the lake property, and then he took off like a man on a mission. I followed a steady two steps behind and was never able to break into his staccato monologue. Finally, as we were coming back inside, I saw my moment and took it: "Mr. Ward," I said, "I love your daughter and would like your permission to marry her."

He glanced at me, but hardly broke stride. "Will you get your damn hair cut?" he said.

I was taken aback. "Sure," I said, trying to keep up.

"Well, okay. Let's go tell the girls."

They had already cracked open the champagne. As the discussion turned toward wedding arrangements, Suzy gingerly told her mother that we were planning a wedding in a park with hot dogs, beer, casual clothes, and pets. "What do you think, Mom?" Suzy said.

"No," said Mrs. Ward.

I was soon dispatched to the den to find a ball game on TV. Occasionally, Suzy would come in and talk softly to me, promising that everything would turn out okay. We would caress for a second or two, and then her mother would stick her head in. "Suzy, your dad wants to remind you," she said sweetly, "that you aren't married yet."

Mr. Ward came down with a case of hives within one hour of my asking for Suzy's hand. He had to be given a shot and put to bed. He blamed it on the barbecue sauce.

After our marriage, Suzy and I lived in a house in Fayetteville that her father bought and rented to us. We had virtually no money, even though she worked and I picked up all the part-time jobs I could. I made four dollars an hour as a campus cop, but it was hard work for me because I didn't have the heart to give people tickets. As an ex-Razorback player, I also picked up ten dollars a ball game serving as an usher, and they gave me a free game ticket that I could sell for cash. Suzy had a secretarial job at a local manufacturing company I'll be kind enough not to name. When we discovered she was pregnant with Walter, she went to her boss and told him she would have to leave in five months. He said fine, but they needed to get started training her replacement. In order to do that, he said, he was moving her desk to a place with more room. It turned out to be right on the lead-paint line. She did exactly what he knew she had to do—she quit.

I arrived at law school driving an Austin-Healy loaded with my golf clubs and TV. I left in an old turquoise Ford carrying a wife and son and pulling a U-Haul trailer full of hand-me-down furniture. But I had a future. Law firms didn't recruit then the way they do now, but as one of the top five students in my class, I had a good shot at the plum jobs. We wanted to move back to Little Rock, so I asked an older friend where I should apply. He named four firms, starting with Rose.

The Rose Law Firm had only one associate position available when I interviewed. I liked the firm, but there was another one that I liked, too. After my second interview, Herb Rule, the Rose recruiting partner, called and offered me the job. I thanked him— and told him I would get back to him. "What?" he said. He was incredulous. In Little Rock in the 1970s, the Rose Law Firm was *the* prestige firm. If you were lucky enough to be offered a position there, you took it.

Eventually, I did. And that's how I found myself at that mental institution in Little Rock taking the bar exam in the summer of

1973. I had no idea what roads I would travel in the future, but I was facing a major detour if I didn't pass this bar exam. "No one in the history of the Rose firm has ever failed," I was told by one of the partners. The very thought brought back all of my "dumb jock" insecurities.

I was nervous during the breaks, playing back the part of the test just taken and worrying about the part to come. But across the way, standing by the quiet girl on the rock, the handsome boy with the thick curly hair seemed to have all the confidence in the world. I envied him.

Maybe Bobby Hargraves noticed me watching Clinton hold court, because at one point he said, "Bill Clinton is somebody you ought to know. Let me introduce you." He led me over and got Clinton's attention. "Bill," he said, "you need to meet this guy. This is Webb Hubbell. He's just joined the Rose firm." We shook hands, and he introduced the girl on the rock: "My friend, Hillary Rodham." We talked for a few minutes, mainly about one of Rose's senior partners who was Bill's Rhodes scholar adviser. Then the break was over and we all went back in.

There's no grainy super-8 film of that momentous meeting. There's no brass plaque at the spot. Like most chance encounters, only time would document its true meaning. Meanwhile, somewhere in a record book at the Arkansas Supreme Court, there's a notation that in September 1973 William Jefferson Clinton, Hillary Rodham, and Webster Lee Hubbell each passed the exam and were admitted to the Arkansas bar.

2

A City of Roses

Even now, life in Arkansas is like a stroll down Main Street. One reason for this is Fayetteville, home of the state's major university. If Arkansas is an hourglass, then Fayetteville is the narrow center. All these young people grow up all over the state in towns like Mountain Home and Bald Knob and De Valls Bluff and El Dorado (here pronounced El Do-*ray*-do), and then at a certain point the kids all leave those hamlets and go off to the University of Arkansas at Fayetteville.

There, the continuity of the statewide bond is forged. For four years these people from all corners eat together, drink (a lot) together, sleep with one another, cheer for the Razorbacks together, and in so doing they form alliances, marital and otherwise, that will affect the future of the state for years. Because, after college, having all passed through that unifying filter, they disperse once again back into the wider (but still not very wide) geography, taking with them an expanded field of acquaintances, loyalties, and bonds.

As a result, everything in our state—including its business and politics, which you can't separate from everyday life—is intensely personal. That's why it's like Main Street. Everybody's on a first-name basis. And that means that political talk is personal talk, and business deals are personal deals, and personalities are more important than issues. Furthermore, they don't want this system to change. When Suzy Ward expressed an interest in Wellesley, Seth put his foot down: "You'll just end up marrying a damn Yankee and never coming home again. You're going to the University."

I bring this up because it's a good background to have when you try to understand the culture of the Rose Law Firm. The Rose firm is *not* on Main Street, neither literally nor figuratively. It's changed a lot since I joined, but when I got there the firm was located high in an ivory tower, so high that the dust of daily commerce rarely formed a billow outside its tinted windows.

In the book-lined conference room, our illustrious forefathers stared down like stern pilgrims over the firm's proceedings. There was a palpable sense of history at the Rose firm. It was, we heard time and again, "the oldest law firm west of the Mississippi." New associates were expected to steep themselves in that rich tradition, much like pledges in a fraternity. Stories were told about U. M. Rose, the man from whom the firm got its name. He was a delegate to The Hague Peace Conference and is one of two Arkansans in Statuary Hall at the U.S. Capitol. We heard how founder Chester Ashley ran Stephen F. Austin out of Arkansas and on to Texas, where the latter eventually lent his name to that state's capital. The older partners told these stories as though the events had happened yesterday. We younger associates picked them up and passed them on ourselves.

Every morning at precisely 9 A.M., the members of the firm gathered around the massive glass-covered oak conference table. I don't mean just the partners—all the associates were expected to be there, too. There were sixteen of us when I joined—ten partners and six associates. Democracy wasn't just a word; it was a principle at Rose. Except for firm membership, which required unanimous approval, all other matters were decided by a majority vote. There was no distinction between the most senior and junior members—everybody's vote counted equally.

When I joined the Rose firm, I had no concept of the culture I had become a part of. I was more of the Main Street mentality—

open, accessible, easygoing, simple in the best sense of that word. I had never even been a fraternity member—*football* had been my fraternity. But I soon gathered, from other people's responses, that where I worked made them think of me in a certain way. "Suzy's doing real well," somebody told Seth. "Her husband got that plum job at the Rose firm." My father, who understood the Rose culture less than I did (all he cared about was how much I was making), said a friend told him, "So Webb got the job at the Rose firm. He's set for life."

"We'll see," said my dad.

I enjoyed hearing such compliments, of course, but I still didn't understand them fully. All I knew for sure was that I was suddenly among these men—these gentlemen—who seemed to operate by a code both older and more indirect than any I had ever imagined. It was as though that big glass-top table was the tip of some unfathomable iceberg, and as these men sat in their morning meetings in their fine suits and cufflinked shirts, their hands on that cool surface connected them to something very deep and broad and hidden.

Despite the Rose firm's current reputation as a political hothouse, politics was actually frowned on back in those days. It was seen as a pastime for the hoi polloi, and not suitable for a conservative old silk-stocking club like ours. Rose's most senior partners were Gaston Williamson, William Nash, and Phil Carroll. Gaston, who was fifty-nine when I arrived, was a Rhodes scholar and tax lawyer extraordinaire. He had married into one of the oldest and wealthiest families in Little Rock, the Worthens, who owned one of the state's largest banks. When the courtly Gaston spoke, you could almost hear the moan of riverboats along the Mississippi. For him, the word "firm" had three syllables.

Where Gaston was as smooth and comfortable as one of the club chairs at his beloved Country Club of Little Rock, his partner William Nash projected an impression of rigidity. Also a Rhodes scholar, Mr. Nash—which is what most of us always called him— was a bond lawyer and the head of all Arkansas Masons. He was sixty-five, tall and thin, and he neither smoked nor drank. He wrote in a tight, precise hand that conveyed far more than the words on the page. Once, he arrived at the office very early and heard strange sounds emanating from one of the closets. He opened the door to find the married janitorial couple engaged in love among the brooms. At the morning meeting, Mr. Nash asked to speak first, saying he had to bring up a matter of utmost urgency. When he told what he had seen, the rest of the members began trying to stifle their laughter. "Well now, Bill," said Archie House, the then-senior partner, "they *are* married."

"Yes," said Mr. Nash, "but if they'll do *that,* they'll *steal.*" The janitors were asked to henceforth keep their amorous urges confined to the home front.

Phil Carroll, then forty-eight, was known to be a thorough, articulate litigator with an undying and incorruptible sense of ethics and loyalty to his case. He was also as tight with a dollar as anyone I've ever met. He complained when the firm stopped using carbon paper and began making photocopies of letters and pleadings. He also, like many World War II veterans, returned home with a heart that couldn't quite forgive the enemy. In Phil's case, he had escaped from a German POW camp, and he always voted against buying any office equipment manufactured by any of the former Axis countries.

When I joined Rose, the firm was situated in a decidedly non-silk-stocking building on the northeast corner of Third and State. It was then a two-story blond-brick self-consciously modern structure that I later found out had been designed by an architect client of ours. Eventually a third story was added. At Rose, it was tradition for each lawyer to be responsible for decorating his own office, and Gaston, Bill, and Phil had each chosen dark paneling for their too-modern walls. They also sat behind big, wood-grained, traditional desks and greeted their clients on dark carpets as rich as old money.

I mention those details for a reason. In 1973, thirty-eight-year-old Joe Giroir wasn't yet the powerhouse he would become within the Rose firm, but he had already glimpsed the future and started nudging the rest of us along his chosen path. A securities whiz, Joe was part of that generation at our firm between Gaston's group of elders and my group of young up-and-coming associates.

Joe's interior decorator wife, Janine, outfitted his new third-floor corner office with modern lamps and a sleek glass desk. Against that contemporary decor, Joe carefully positioned his bronze Frederic Remington sculptures.

You could make the case that Joe's office was a symbol of the conflicts the Rose firm itself would soon face—very much at his instigation. For Joe Giroir had come to see the role of the law firm very differently from the way a partner like William Nash did. Mr. Nash, who was rumored to have once refused to represent Stephens Inc. in a bond issue because he didn't agree with the use of municipal bonds to build a particular project, seemed to regard the Rose firm as a social stabilizer, a force for doing right in the community. Joe, on the other hand, saw the modern law firm as a place for making a great deal of money.

As a new associate, I spent my first few months doing research and small projects for the partners. I worked on a personal bankruptcy case, drafted discovery motions for small workers compensation files, and handled traffic tickets issued to Mr. Nash's Mason friends. As I went about these menial chores, I tried to understand just what it meant to be a Rose firm lawyer.

In school, I had been managing editor of the *Arkansas Law Review* and graduated with honors. The idealism kindled during my Mena year had gradually been channeled into devotion to a concept I thought of as the Law, as opposed to simply winning or losing in a courtroom. My capital-L notion of Law embraced the concept of Justice. I thought by being a lawyer I could fix the world.

I had imagined a law firm to be a team, like when I played ball, but as I passed the bar and got more acclimated I realized that wasn't the case. I was the only one of the six associates who didn't have a specialty. I liked what I was learning—how to get things filed at the courthouse, how to keep your client from waiting in traffic court to have his case heard, where all the courthouses were in the rural counties. Sometimes I had to drive a hundred miles to a small town simply to announce that the case was or wasn't ready for trial. Almost always, whatever town I was in, I would know somebody from school. After court we would have a cup of coffee and shoot the breeze. Later on, knowing those people around the state was a tremendous help.

But all of my experience was practical, even pragmatic, and I began to figure out that that's largely what everyday law is. I began to see how pragmatism also applies to the lawyers themselves. Two of the other associates had staked out securities and banking law as their specialties, and they were working very closely with Joe Giroir, whose practice was growing incredibly fast. In a sense, *they* were a team, but it wasn't a team that I, or others, was part of. Another associate, a quiet, smart man named Vince Foster, worked closely with Phil Carroll. Vince was senior to me in time at the firm. He was well on his way to becoming a star. Phil trusted him completely, and he was already trying his own cases. So Vince and Phil were a kind of team, too. But while the Rose firm was seen as a team to the outside world, inside we were sixteen different lawyers with sixteen different practices.

Rose's billing policies both reflected that free-for-all and added fuel to it. In most firms, all partners share in the profits of the firm; at Rose, the billing partner decided how to share the money he brought in. Also, while other firms across the country had begun billing quarterly and even monthly, at Rose, most clients were billed only once or twice a year—and some only when the case was over. That was the "gentlemanly" way to practice law.

The first of these policies caused associates and young partners to gravitate to the billing partners who could share the wealth by associating them on cases. The second policy created cash flow problems that required some of us in the less lucrative areas to take out personal loans to get by on. The two together created an enormously tense dichotomy within the law firm. In time, it would grow into an all-out war between the old guard and the young turks.

Suzy and I had settled into a rent house owned by her father, and she worked at his sheet aluminum company, Ward Supply. The company had been bought by National Aluminum, a subsidiary of National Steel, and Seth had been asked to stay on and run the business as before. It was a sweet deal, and Seth received a small fortune in National Steel stock.

In those very early days, we socialized mostly with friends we'd made in law school. Far away in Washington, D.C., the Watergate mess was spilling out of the media daily, but all of that seemed so remote, so unreal to us. None of our circle of friends was that interested in politics. We were consumed by our work and our new lives. When we did have friends over, we talked work and houses and babies over hands of bridge. Out by the patio grill, we men tried to impress one another with tales about how hard we were working. After a few beers, we confessed how excited we were about law and how great it was all going to turn out for us.

None of us had much money, but Suzy and I were able to live on a higher plane early because of her parents. We furnished our house from the Wards' attic. Seth bought us a dishwasher and Suzy a car. I remember feeling slightly uncomfortable accepting this largesse, but Suzy wouldn't have understood any protest. For her, it had been a way of life. I didn't want to fight about it, so I just smiled and said, Thank you. It became easier and easier.

The Wards liked having their children around. More precisely, they *didn't* like *not* having them around. Seth was one of those old-line southern patriarchs who overwhelmed his family with his forcefulness. When Suzy got pregnant with Walter, she wrote her father a letter to inform him. "I knew he was going to be furious that we'd done something without his permission," Suzy says. If we wanted to take a vacation to the Gulf Coast, Seth would be outraged. "Why would you do that when you can go to our lake house?" he would say. We were invited to dinner at the Wards' a couple of nights a week. The big bar was always open, though Seth talked more than he drank. The rest of us loaded up and listened to him. On most weekends we all went to the lake—Suzy and me, Mr. and Mrs. Ward, Skeeter and sister Sally. I actually enjoyed those times at first, though as the years rolled by I felt more and more out of place there. My idea of a weekend at the lake consisted of a good book, a shady hammock, and a long nap. Naps are foreign to the Wards. Seth and Skeeter were always mowing and raking and fixing things, to the point that I felt uncomfortable napping. "Is he okay?" they'd say to Suzy, who was cleaning house with her mother. "He's taking a *nap*."

In my first year out of school, my father and Seth both began giving me some of their law business, and encouraging their friends to do the same. My dad and Seth were pro bono, of course. It's a custom of the southern culture for lawyers to provide advice and services free to family and close friends. There are times when a bill is a breach of etiquette. Seth was officially represented by the Friday firm, one of our main competitors, but he began asking me for some piece of legal advice almost every time we were together. I was flattered by his confidence in me, and happy to oblige.

Over time, our social life shifted away from old law-school friends toward other Rose associates and their wives, the ones we could most safely talk shop with. That's how we first became friends with the Fosters.

Vince was only two years older than I, but in many ways he seemed like a man who had never made the stop at childhood. There was a seriousness about him that made him old beyond his years. In the office, he kept his suit coat on while other associates were wandering the halls in shirtsleeves. Very often he worked behind closed doors. What the rest of us saw emanating from that inner sanctum were briefs meticulously considered and brilliantly written, cases anticipated and organized to the nth degree. The only people who didn't admire this attention to detail were the secretaries who had to type his work. More than one quit after redoing a letter five or six times—"to get it right." Vince couldn't be swayed by the mediocrity of others. Deep inside him was a taskmaster he could never say no to.

Reading back over the last paragraph, I wonder if I've made him seem priggish and dour. He was anything but that. His charm—with both men and women—derived largely from his kind of enigmatic self-containment. He never talked much at office get-togethers, but that didn't relegate him to the social sidelines. People gravitated to him because he was also a world-class listener. His eyes would twinkle when you talked. Marsha Scott tells me that after he went to Washington, an informal poll was taken at the White House asking the women there whom they would most like to have an affair with. Vince won going away. George Stephanopoulos wasn't even in the running. I think women were drawn to Vince not just because he was smart and handsome, but because he seemed to keep secrets. I have a photograph of him in conversation with two women in Washington. They're eyeing him admiringly, and Vince is striking the classic Vince Foster pose—right arm folded protectively across his chest and tucked into the crook of his left arm, which is raised so his thumb rests under his chin and his forefinger is gently pressed against his smiling lips. It's as if to say, *I'll never tell*. His eyes are dancing.

I suppose it was our children who first enabled Vince and me to bridge that chasm between my easygoing nature and his buttoned-down facade. His son Vincent was just a little older than our son, Walter. My daughter Rebecca and his son Brugh have been lifetime friends. Vince was devoted to his children, sometimes almost laughably so. In later years he would crawl all over the soccer stands videotaping his kids' ball games, or he would unabashedly shuffle out of the middle of a row at ballet recitals to get a better angle for his camera. He could be almost excessive in that single-mindedness about his kids.

Suzy and I first met Lisa shortly after the birth of their second child, Laura. Like Vince, Lisa was, and still is, physically attractive and very photogenic, but her energy was the polar opposite of his. Hers flowed outward as ferociously as his flowed inward. She was the life of the party, and sometimes you could see Vince wince at something she'd said that violated his stringent sense of propriety. Lisa was from Nashville, Tennessee, and they had met when Vince was in his first year of law school at Vanderbilt. Later, having enlisted in the Army National Guard because of Vietnam, he transferred to the University of Arkansas so he could commute to the National Guard unit in Hope.

We soon learned that Lisa was passionate in expressing her opinions and her beliefs, many of which were colored by her devout Catholicism. Family was everything, and she guarded that principle with every ounce of her considerable strength. She was very jealous of her Vince, and talked openly about how other women better not even *think* of trying to snag him. She didn't like for him to work late at the office or go out on the road.

I noticed that Vince didn't tell Lisa much about the office or the people in it, not even the everyday gossip or the funny stories that I didn't think twice about sharing with Suzy. He felt that such talk was professionally improper, I suppose, but I think he also didn't want to say anything that would give the slightest glimpse behind his veil. Years later, after he died, it occurred to me that Vince was maybe as much of an enigma to Lisa as he was to the rest of us.

By the mid-1970s, Suzy and I began moving to bigger and better houses. In 1974 we left Seth's rent house (he had given us the equity and we were making mortgage payments, but the house remained "Seth's house" in everyone's mind) for a small two-bedroom cottage in The Heights, the best section of old Little Rock. Seth thought we were fools to buy it. "Nobody but a blind man will ever buy it from you," he said. The truth is, Seth resented our moving to The Heights. That was the old-money section of Little Rock, the area in which the Country Club of Little Rock was located. Seth had always yearned to be a member of the country club, but he couldn't get in. No matter how much money he had, the Country Club of Little Rock crowd didn't cotton to his combative entrepreneurial style. So he lived in West Little Rock and joined the Pleasant Valley Country Club. I'm sure he thought we had betrayed him by moving to The Heights.

Our little house was on the corner of Country Club Boulevard and North Taylor, an address that I felt had a certain resonance in spite of the size of the house. On some deep level, I was beginning to absorb the unwritten rules of the Rose firm. That showed in the automobile I bought when I traded in the turquoise Fairlane.

Mr. Nash rose early and walked to work, arriving on the dot at 6 A.M. I had gotten into the habit of getting up early myself. Suzy would say it was so I could avoid feeding Walter, but the truth is I wanted to get to the office to impress my employers with my diligence. One morning I was working in my little office when I noticed that I wasn't alone. Mr. Nash had a presence you could feel even if you weren't looking. "Good morning, Mr. Nash," I said, clambering to my feet. "Good morning, Webb," he said. "Is that *your* car in the parking lot?"

By now the Fairlane had a huge dent on the driver's side, the legacy of a deer that was trying to cross a country road at the same time I was. "Um, yes sir," I said.

"Oh," said Mr. Nash. "I thought somebody had abandoned it in the parking lot. I was about to have it towed."

I went home that night and told Suzy it was time for me to get a new car.

I haunted the used-car lots until I found a car I instinctively knew would *fit*. It was a 1961 Mercedes 190 SL. It was sporty, but it was classic. It was new to me, but it was fourteen years old. It was black-and-white with red interior. I thought it was the perfect car for me at that time of my life and career. We already had a family car, so this couldn't say anything about my lack of priorities. It didn't cost much, so it couldn't say anything about profligacy. On the positive side, it attested to my affinity for quality and luxury, which spoke tacitly of my ambition to succeed. The car had an undeniable old-money patina. I named my Mercedes the General, though it drove like a bad truck.

It was about this time that Seth got mad and retired from his company. Even then, I could have predicted it. The only flaw in his arrangement with National Steel was that Seth Ward was incapable of being an *employee*. He couldn't deal with the corporate mentality. He was an entrepreneur. Like many successful men of his generation who grew up in the Depression, he had built his company by sheer force of will. He simply outworked and outwitted his competition. This type of personality just couldn't exist in an atmosphere of reports, meetings, and asking for approvals for whatever he wanted to do. So one day he stormed out and suddenly he had too much time on his hands.

This affected us in two ways. First, Suzy also quit her job at his old company. Second, Seth used most of his free time phoning me. He wanted to find another business to buy; and he wanted to be appointed to the Airport Commission. In Little Rock, the government is run by boards and commissions. The seven-member Little Rock City Board is elected by the people; that seven-person body then elects a mayor from its ranks. They also appoint people to the various boards and commissions, such as the Art Center Board, the Water Commission, the Port Authority, and the Airport Commission. These become old-boy networks. If you're on the Airport Commission, you basically run the Little Rock airport. You decide everything from what kind of gas to buy to when and how to expand. Seth had flown airplanes in World War II, and in fact had learned to fly before he learned to drive. Flying must have been connected in his mind to being in control of the world.

From the beginning, despite any personal agenda he might have had for wanting to be on the Airport Commission, I never doubted his love for aviation and his desire to help the industry he loved. It was the city directors who appointed members to the commissions, and suddenly Seth was calling and saying, "Don't you know so-and-so? Will you call him and ask him to appoint me?" He also wanted to introduce me to various city directors *he* knew, such as Jim Dailey and Dwight Linkous. Like a good son-in-law, I went along with it. He set up lunches, invited us all for drinks. It was fascinating, hearing how the city worked from the inside. But I had no idea that any of this conversation would eventually affect me in the way it did.

Seth did get on the commission in 1975. Immediately he started doing what he always does—trying to take over.

In November 1975, Suzy gave birth to our second child, Rebecca. We responded by buying a bigger house. (Ironically, a blind man *did* buy our old one.) That would become our pattern. We owned six houses between 1974 and 1980. "Suzy must be pregnant," people would say, as Caroline came along in 1977, and then Kelley in 1981. "The Hubbells just bought another house." Suzy never found any humor in that at all.

*   *   *

Meanwhile, inside the Rose firm, Joe Giroir succeeded in persuading the members that we should divide into sections. Joe could see that the practice of law was changing—that, as in medicine, specialties were the coming thing. Of course, his specialty of securities law was about as coming as you could get. Corporations were building fabulous wealth by going public, and Joe wanted as much of that business as he could sweet-talk in his direction. But he knew that if a law firm got a company's business, it was only natural for that company to hire the firm for other things, such as litigation. Rose, unfortunately, was mostly a collection of generalists, and Joe knew he couldn't hold on to his securities clients if he didn't have a support base in other specialties.

The sentiment within Rose was that we had a nice little firm, so why add more lawyers and all the headaches that would entail? An undercurrent of that sentiment was a widespread resentment of the large fees that Joe and the associates working with him were generating. For the first time in the history of the firm, it was possible for lawyers who had started at basically the same time to be earning wildly disparate sums of money. Joe was aware of that undercurrent, and he used it to his benefit. "What if Joe leaves?" various partners would say to one another behind closed doors. The unspoken implication was that if Rose didn't placate Joe Giroir, he could walk away with any number of the firm's clients. Joe was our rainmaker, and everyone knew it.

A year after I joined the Rose firm, we divided into specialty groups: the Tax and Probate Section, headed by Gaston Williamson; the Securities Section, headed by Joe Giroir; the Bond and Commercial Section, headed by Bill Nash; and the Litigation Section, headed by Phil Carroll. I had a choice—Gaston's group, or Phil's group? I chose to work with Phil and Vince in Litigation. It seemed most purely like what I had imagined as the Law.

I moved my office next to Vince's, and we shared a secretary until Hillary came. And that was the other thing that happened in the mid-1970s. In 1974, Bill Clinton ran for the congressional seat of the Arkansas legend John Paul Hammerschmidt. Nobody really gave this upstart a chance of winning. In this state of J. William Fulbright, John McClellan, Wilbur Mills, Dale Bumpers, David Pryor, Jim Guy Tucker, and Ray Thornton, Bill Clinton wasn't even in the first tier of politicians. And yet he almost beat Hammerschmidt. He was suddenly being talked about all over the state, even in the staid offices of the Rose Law Firm. When I read about his near win, I remembered what Bobby Hargraves had said outside the state hospital that day: "He's brilliant. You need to know him."

Bill and Hillary were married in October of 1975, and the next year he announced his candidacy for attorney general. Even then he could read the political tea leaves. Most people know that Bill Clinton is a masterful politician, but what most people may not realize is that he's also one of the luckiest. He came along when Arkansas was going through a political sea change. First, the canny old congressman Wilbur Mills ended his illustrious political career with an ignoble romp in Washington's Tidal Basin with the stripper Fanne Fox. Then the state's attorney general—a handsome and ambitious young man named Jim Guy Tucker—decided to go after Mills's seat. That left Clinton as a virtual shoo-in for the AG job.

And in that campaign fall of 1976, Vince Foster embarked on one of those road trips that Lisa so hated for him to take. He worked in Fayetteville off and on for several weeks, chairing the Arkansas Bar Association's attempt to set up a legal aid clinic in northwest Arkansas. He came back to the Rose firm raving, uncharacteristically, about a smart female law professor he had worked with up there, a Yale graduate named Hillary Rodham. Many people think Vince's contact was mainly with Bill, since both grew up in Hope. But Bill left Hope in grade school, and the two didn't stay in touch. As Bill Clinton began emerging in statewide politics, Vince never once told me they were friends as boys. I feel sure they reconnected at a reception or two during one of Bill's campaigns, but Vince's initial and strongest relationship was with Hillary. He came home from Fayetteville saying we should be thinking about hiring her—that surely they were moving to Little Rock, and surely she would be looking for a job. At the time, the Rose firm had no women lawyers. Vince argued vehemently that it was time for a change.

3

"Webb, Could You Talk to Hillary?"

Hillary could have gone anywhere, of course, but she chose to follow Bill Clinton to darkest Arkansas. One of the questions people persistently ask about Hillary is, Why did she come? Was it ambition? Did she know her future husband was going to be President, and did she want to live in the White House so much that she was willing to sidetrack her own career? She certainly had a sense that Bill was destined for greatness. In January 1974, she had gone to Washington to work with John Doar, the special counsel for the inquiry into the impeachment of President Richard Nixon. One of her colleagues there was Bernie Nussbaum. In September, when she left Washington to teach at the University of Arkansas, Bernie asked why she would do something as crazy as go off to Arkansas. Hillary told him, "Bill Clinton will be President someday."

But she never said anything like that to me. In our heart-to-heart talks, she revealed a dream not of political power but of a life partnership. She loved Bill Clinton, and so she followed him home. And if somebody had intercepted her at the state border and said, "You know, don't you, that by crossing this line you're going to give up your self?" she wouldn't have believed it. It's the kind of thing you have to experience for yourself.

So she moved, first to Fayetteville, a beautiful but insulated little college town tucked into the Ozark Mountains. Then they moved to the state capital, and I'm sure Hillary had hopes for something that meshed with her meaning of the word city. What she found was an insulated *big* town, a place that ran according to unwritten rules. Rule 1 might well have been: Little Rock women don't have careers. To be fair to Little Rock, she would have found that in cities of similar size all over the country back then—especially in the South.

In the Rose Law Firm, most of the partners seemed to assume that the world would just continue on the way it always had, with the men doing the work and the wives taking care of the home and family. Wives of successful lawyers engaged in certain charity jobs, but aside from that they spent their days playing tennis and eating lunch and shopping. I'm appalled to see these words flashing on my computer screen, but that's the way it was in Little Rock twenty years ago.

Hillary was an explorer. We use that word to describe men like Meriwether Lewis and William Clark, but there's room in the definition for Hillary Rodham. She came to Arkansas and redrew the maps. Not the physical ones, but the social and business ones. She paid a tremendous price for that, and she's still paying. The light shone too *much* on her. The only place to hide was within herself.

In November 1976, Bill Clinton won the election to become the state's attorney general. As his wife, Hillary was suddenly a very high-profile person.

Vince was afraid some other firm would snatch her up, and he began lobbying very hard on her behalf. He had made partner already, so he was working the partners and dispatched me to convince the associates that hiring Hillary was a good idea. It was like backroom campaigning for a bill in Congress. Vince wanted all the votes in his pocket, but I wasn't sure I could deliver. With the associates, the problem wasn't Hillary so much as her husband. One associate, Bob Banks, had some run-in with Bill years before and didn't trust him. Another associate, Charlie Owen, was a staunch Republican who worked for the Winthrop Rockefeller family. He didn't have any use for Bill.

The partners had more subtle, and telling, objections. "How will we introduce her to our clients?" one asked at a morning meeting. All our clients were male. "What if she gets pregnant?" said another. That naturally led to the pillow talk problem. "What if the attorney general has a case against our client?" someone said. Everyone sat there glumly imagining Bill and Hillary spilling secrets all over the sheets. Vince had me research the question of spousal conflicts. There wasn't much written on it, because there weren't many lawyer couples back then.

Actually, conflict was one of Hillary's main concerns, but not in the pillow talk sense. She could readily see the problems that might arise with her husband the state's top lawyer. Assuming she would be interviewing with others, we used their client lists to our benefit. The attorney general's major two roles were to handle criminal appeals and to be a consumer advocate in rate cases before the Public Service Commission. We didn't do any criminal work, and we didn't represent any utilities. Our big clients were Worthen Bank, the *Arkansas Gazette,* and the Hussman media family from southwest Arkansas. Gaston had estate planning clients, and we represented a big chicken producer in the central part of the state. Joe had an oil distribution company in West Memphis. Those were the kinds of clients we had.

On the other hand, the Friday firm basically controlled the state business. This was thanks to its partner Judge Bill Smith, who had been Governor Orval Faubus's major adviser. The other top Little Rock firm was the Wright firm, whose clients included the Rock Island Railroad. Wright also defended a lot of insurance companies.

Vince persuaded the partners to send him and Herb Rule, a Yale grad and former recruiting partner, to meet with Hillary in Fayetteville. Herb was impressed, too. He and Vince stressed the Rose firm's client list, and Hillary agreed we had the fewest potential conflicts. She liked our 160-year history, our Rhodes scholars, our refusal to sully the dignity of our tradition with politics. The next step was for her to come to Little Rock for interviews.

In Hillary's usual way of turning the existing world upside down, I think all the members of the Rose Law Firm were the nervous ones on the day she visited. Though our unanimous-vote rule would later be amended to three-fourths majority (after a few episodes such as the one when Mr. Nash said he couldn't vote for an otherwise-popular candidate because the man wore a mustache), Hillary's hiring required approval by everyone in the firm. She was scheduled to meet with each one of us for approximately ten minutes. We each sat silently waiting, trying to work but inevitably straightening our ties and checking our shoeshines, while Vince escorted her around from office to office.

We all found her charming. Even Bob Banks and Charlie Owen were taken with her. (Charlie later told her, "I don't have anything good to say about your no-good husband, but I love you.") I would learn that Hillary's strength as a lawyer was the one-on-one discussion with a judge as opposed to dealing with a jury, and on interview day as each one of us judged her, she managed us beautifully. When she was ushered into my small office, I reminded her of that day we'd met at the State Hospital and how the image of her studying in that YALE sweatshirt stood out in my mind. I told her she didn't need to spend any time with me—I was already in her camp.

Earlier I said all of us at the Rose firm were nervous. Maybe I was exaggerating—or maybe I *under*stated the depth of the disturbance Hillary's coming caused. It must have been a Saturday when she visited, because Joe Giroir interviewed her in his tennis shorts—with a cigar in his mouth and his bare feet in her face. He had leapt over a couple more senior partners to get his name included in the firm name—then Rose, Nash, Williamson, Carroll, Clay and Giroir. When Hillary was introduced to Joe, he was sitting behind his desk dictating and blowing smoke, with his sweaty feet on his glass desk. He and Hillary had their talk looking over Joe's toes.

I'm sure that was offensive to Hillary—it would have been to me. But it wasn't her manner to get upset about such affronts. Later, once she became a partner, she told that story whenever any member of the firm got too haughty about the Rose Law Firm's recruiting abilities. "Oh, yeah," she would say. "Joe Giroir made me look at his smelly feet during my interview."

Down at the other end of the table, Joe would chuckle. "Well, it worked," he might say. They kidded each other about that for years.

Hillary joined the Litigation Section the month I made partner— January 1977. Her arrival gave all the disparate elements of this old-shoe firm a focus for their frustrations.

They never said anything to her directly, of course. At Rose, indirectness had been elevated to an art form. No one ever critiqued anyone's work to that person's face. But behind closed doors, the partners would joust at a problem with oblique thrusts. "Do you think he knows his work is unsatisfactory?" they would say of a partner or associate with whom they were displeased. The usual, comforting response was, "He must." At that point, partners would simply begin freezing out the unlucky one. They wouldn't refer work to him. No one was ever fired. At the very most, they were asked to "look elsewhere."

With Hillary's arrival the indirectness struck the way lightning often does, hitting one spot but burrowing beneath an open space to emerge and singe something somewhere else. No matter where Hillary stood, she soon became the prime destination for most of the bolts from on high. It would happen like this. On a Thursday or a Friday, Mr. Nash might be strolling through the halls and would catch a glimpse of Hillary turning into her office. He would go pale when he saw that on this particular day she wasn't wearing her lawyerly dark suit, but instead was dressed in jeans.

Mr. Nash would go directly to Vince's office, or he would come to mine. "You've got to say something to Hillary," he would demand.

This happened over many, many issues. Either her clothes weren't light and frilly like southern men were used to their women wearing, or else they weren't lawyerly enough. Her hair wasn't soft and shiny, her glasses were bulky and unfeminine, and she didn't wear makeup. In our morning meetings she didn't hold her tongue. At firm functions Hillary didn't "show enough deference" to a partner's wife. Later, when Governor David Pryor named a respected attorney named Kaneaster Hodges to fill the unexpired term of the late Senator John McClellan, Senator Hodges gave a speech supporting the Equal Rights Amendment. Having consulted with Hillary on the issue, he signed the page of the *Congressional Record* containing his speech and sent it to her. She had it framed and mounted on her office wall. Some partners were concerned that some of our more conservative clients might walk by and see it.

I want to be careful not to give the impression that she was aggressive in any way. People think that about her, but that's not Hillary. She was never "in your face." The problem for a lot of partners was that she was simply never intimidated by anyone, partner or client, and that in itself is often intimidating to others. She had the confidence in herself to *be* herself. Outside the office, she didn't play by the rules. It sounds absurd now, but it used to be that if your spouse was out of town and another couple called to invite you to go to a movie with them, you would say, "Oh, thanks, but Allen's out of town. Maybe next time." Hillary was the first woman I knew who said, "Bill's out of town, but I'd love to go." People criticized her for that. But she was just being herself. I think her core of self-confidence came from her father, from her educational experiences, and from her superb intelligence. It's very hard for me to express just how frighteningly smart Hillary is.

I suppose Vince and I became the conduits to her because we had become her confidants. That was obvious to most people in the firm, who saw us talking among ourselves and later going out to lunch together. It was natural that the three of us would become friends. We were all in Litigation, so we worked in close proximity. We were near in age and in seniority at the firm. And finally, we enjoyed one another's company. Hillary could actually get Vince to talk.

When the older partners said, "You need to talk to Hillary," more often than not Vince would say, "No thanks. If you want to say something to her, tell her yourself." We felt a little silly complaining about blue jeans to this former Watergate Committee attorney, this member of the National Legal Services Corporation Board, this former law professor. My tack was to use humor— to laugh with her about the utter stupidity of the comments others had asked that I pass on. Usually she would take it, laughing along with me even though it meant someone out there wanted to keep her from being who she was. She was becoming increasingly used to that.

The Litigation Section took over the first floor of the Rose firm building. There were five of us now, plus a couple of secretaries. Phil Carroll's office was at the left end, mine was near the entrance, and that of Bill Kennedy, a former staffer for Senator McClellan, was close to mine. Vince and Hillary were in the center of the floor, their offices across the hall from each other. They shared a secretary.

Hillary was never the typical associate. She wasn't sent to the courthouse to deal with traffic tickets, and she didn't have to drive out into the state to announce that a Rose firm partner needed a continuance in a case. Instead, she worked with Vince a lot in the beginning. I was still junior enough so that I couldn't ask her to help me with my cases. Eventually she and Bill Kennedy or she and I would work together on various combinations of projects. She was smart, articulate, usually very funny. Having her around made us men look at life in a whole different way.

I don't remember the first time she and Vince and I went to lunch together. It was probably several months after she started, and I imagine it was at what was then the Lafayette Hotel (now The Legacy). The Lafayette was just across the street from the Federal Building, about a three-block walk from our office. I've never been one to eat at my desk. For one thing, I like a *meal* at lunch. But also I need a break. Before Hillary, Vince and I would occasionally have lunch together, though he was more likely to hole up in his office with a sandwich in one hand and a legal pad in the other. He began to open up more when Hillary came.

The day we three first went to lunch, I came home about six and Suzy said, "I hear you went out to lunch today." Vince got the same thing from Lisa, though I imagine with considerably more force. Someone—I still don't know who—called each of them and said, "Did you know your husband is having lunch with a *woman*?" Maybe I was more progressive than I thought—I no longer considered Hillary "a woman." She was a fellow lawyer, another litigator, albeit one who brought a new dimension to our usual lunchtime discussions.

Vince, for all his reserve, loved to talk with me about sports. He was a big basketball fan. We spent a lot of time discussing the Razorbacks, assessing their strengths and weaknesses. This kind of talk relaxed Vince, made him forget his pressures. We also, from time to time, took advantage of a late-seventies trend called the "lingerie style show." Fancy lingerie stores were just getting started then, and the proprietors of such places hit on a surefire way to get attention to their wares: They hired models to show off their nightgowns and robes at restaurants. They would parade around from table to table, and the idea was that the female lunch customers would see something they liked for them-selves and the male customers might buy a gift for a wife or girl-friend. The fact, of course, was that there were many more male customers on style-show days, and they were ogling the models as much as the lingerie.

I hasten to stress that Vince and I didn't go to these shows often, but we enjoyed them. There was a deep-seated wild streak in Vince. It came out on rare occasions when he was drinking, though we never drank at lunch in those days. President Jimmy Carter was railing against the three-martini lunch, but that was something that happened only in big cities. Vince's wild streak could show up at the oddest times, probably triggered by some internal overload of his internal coping system. It was always sig-naled by a sly, devilish smile.

Sometimes Hillary would go with us to the style shows. She would go just to laugh at us and tell us what Neanderthals we were. But for the most part, Hillary improved the level of dis-course at our lunches. She would talk about the Panama Canal and other news stories. She would ask how we felt about various social movements. The truth is, I usually hadn't given them much thought. Later, I would see that the subjects Hillary floated by us at lunch often became the issues Bill Clinton championed in government. Vince and I were mesmerized by her. She was like nobody we had ever been around before.

Bill wasn't much of a presence in our lives.

The month I was made partner, Seth lost his position on the Airport Commission. It was actually sad to see, this grown man so hurt and lost without having the slightest inkling of how he had created the situation. He began a campaign to retake the commission the way the Marines took Iwo Jima. I think he increasingly saw me as the figure at the very front of that famous photograph and statue, the one spiking the flag of victory in the bloody dirt.

Seth was hard to tolerate that winter and spring. He would show up at my office unannounced. The phone would ring and I would answer, and with no preamble, no soft, southern "How are you," Seth would tell me to do this or that, call this person or that person, get him information on this subject or another one. I'm still trying to figure out why I let him do that to me. I had been reared not to have conflict. I had been reared to please. I had been reared to believe that loyalty to family was all-important. It's taken me my entire life to learn that first should come loyalty to your own deepest values.

In addition to his quest for the Airport Commission, Seth was worried about his finances. Most of his assets were in National Steel stock, and the stock wasn't doing well. He owned two warehouses and an office building that he'd been leasing to National Aluminum. As part of his estate planning, Seth's accountant suggested it would be smart to sell his interest in these buildings to his children.

I don't know what Seth would have done had any of us said we weren't interested, but we wouldn't have dared. The emotional fallout was too toxic. Besides, I needed cash flow and Seth's buildings all had tenants. The plan was this: Initially he would put all the buildings into a trust for the children, along with a forty-acre ranch he owned west of town. That way, if one of the buildings came up empty, the rental income from the other properties would offset the loss.

At the last minute, Seth changed his mind. Here was the new plan: Suzy would get the smaller warehouse, Skeeter would get the larger one, and Sally would get the ranch. Seth would keep the office building. And because Skeeter's warehouse was so much bigger than Suzy's, Suzy would get two thirds of a lot that fronted Skeeter's warehouse. Seth had already given the three children equal interest in the family's Hot Springs lake property, so suddenly Suzy looked pretty prosperous on paper.

All we had to do was take out a $50,000 bank loan as a down payment to Seth. That was a bit frightening, since I was already maintaining a personal line of credit for normal monthly expenses. But the rental income covered the payment to Seth and the bank. Income taxes were covered by interest and depreciation deductions. All was fine as long as the building was leased and the tax laws didn't change.

I asked Seth about the tenant, Falcon Jet. It was a very reputable manufacturer of high-quality private aircraft—but how did it happen that an aircraft company was leasing a warehouse fifteen miles from the airport? Seth said not to worry. Falcon Jet "needed" a warehouse, and he provided them one. When he was on the Airport Commission, he abstained from voting on Falcon Jet matters.

Much later—after I'd taken the $50,000 loan, the warehouse was empty, and I was up to my ears in debt to the bank and Seth—I would hear Falcon Jet's version.

No sooner had Hillary joined the firm than we had a major case pitting us against the state—in other words, her husband. The General Motors Corporation had been one of Rose's clients for many years. GM retains attorneys in every state. Mostly we defended it in product liability cases.

Phil Carroll, the car manufacturer's main Rose firm contact, called me into his office one day and told me GM was gearing up

for consumer lawsuits around the country arising from the discovery that Chevrolet engines were being put in Oldsmobiles. Phil
was afraid this was too big a case for him alone, and maybe even
for the firm. But if I wanted to take it on it, we would give it a
try. I couldn't believe it—this was a major piece of national business that Phil was handing over to me.

The only problem was that GM expected the various state attorneys general to take the lead against the car company. In fact,
a nationwide steering committee of AGs was being formed, and
our state's new young star was taking a high-profile role in it.

This, of course, was the very scenario everyone dreaded. I had
to deal with it in two ways—first, I had to discuss it with Hillary.
Second, I had to explain the situation to GM. Hillary was in an
awkward position. She was a new associate at an old firm, and
this was a lucrative case. She really wasn't in a position to say
we shouldn't take it on because of *her*. I covered all this with
GM. They were skeptical, but agreed to let us remain as counsel—
provided that all files were locked in a cabinet in my office, no
conversations about the case took place in front of Hillary, and
GM had an ongoing right to reevaluate the situation. Ultimately,
the case was settled on a national level, so no real problem arose
for the firm. I can't say the same for Hillary.

With that case I began to see what a box she was in. I have a
coffee cup featuring a cartoon from *The Far Side,* showing the
devil prodding some poor soul to choose one of two doors. The
doors are marked DAMNED IF YOU DO and DAMNED IF YOU DON'T.
That's how Hillary must have felt at the Rose firm. For a world
of reasons, she could never be who she wanted to be. That person
was fading further and further behind an accommodating mask.

Vince and I didn't feel Bill's presence much personally in those
days. He was always on the road, out doing his AG work, but
also laying the groundwork for grander things. Sometimes he
would come to the few social get-togethers the firm had, but when
he did he usually got off in the corner and talked with Gaston
about Rhodes scholar days. Bill didn't seem to be much interested
in the Rose firm issues. He burned with ambition. Hillary, I think,
was afraid he would burn out, would kill himself with his energy.

She tried her best to give him as normal a life as possible. Whenever he was going to drop by the office, she would ask Vince and me to stay around and say hello to him. She wanted him to have friends. He and Vince would chat a little about Hope, and the people such as Mac McLarty whom they knew in common. Bill and I might compare views on the chances of the latest Razorback team, and then he would be gone.

In early 1978, her situation got even more complex. Scarcely a year after he had taken over the AG office, Bill Clinton announced his candidacy for governor. It was the usual small-state musical chairs game that sparked his opportunism, except this was stage two of that political sea change I mentioned earlier. Dale Bumpers had taken the senatorial seat of William Fulbright. Senator McClellan had recently died and most of the young up-and-comers were going after that seat—Congressman Jim Guy Tucker, Congressman Ray Thornton, and Governor David Pryor had all entered the race. Clinton looked around and said, Hey, *I'll* be governor. It was almost that easy. People thought he was awfully young. But there was nobody left who could beat him.

That year's Senate race was a tough three-way fight, however, with Jim Guy Tucker edging out Ray Thornton for a runoff with David Pryor, who then beat Tucker. Besides the election of a fine senator, that race had other, less obvious ramifications in Arkansas's interconnected political-business-social world. The powerful Stephens family—whose investment bank was long the largest off Wall Street, and whose owners were the uncles of Ray Thornton—began to hate Jim Guy Tucker for beating their blood kin. For years, that fact alone would affect most of the politics and much of the business in Arkansas.

When Bill was elected the nation's youngest governor later in 1978, the mostly conservative Rose firm partners saw dollar signs. (How wrong they were about that.) They also congratulated themselves on their foresight in hiring Hillary. It never occurred to them that they had treated her badly. Now it was *prestigious* to have the state's first lady as a member of our firm. They chortled over the Wright firm's and the Friday firm's loss.

The Bill Clinton era was ushered in with a pomp that foreshadowed the coming splashy inaugurals of his Washington years. Bill's and Hillary's friends from the East Coast and from his Rhodes scholar days flew to Little Rock to help celebrate his ascendancy. The ball itself spoke of the rise to power of a new generation—it was called "Diamonds and Denim," and the new young establishment danced to the beat of such home-grown musicians as Levon Helm of The Band, and Charlie Rich, the Silver Fox. I had never been to a governor's inaugural in my life, and never expected to. To us, governors had always represented the pinnacle of power of our grandparents' and parents' generation. Now here was Hillary telling Vince and me we should come to the ball, the speech, the whole shindig. "It'll be fun," she said. The Fosters and Hubbells, good friends of the new first lady of the state, went to the festivities together. Bill, she later told us, was still rewriting his inaugural speech getting out of the car on the way to the hall. Watching him deliver those stirring words, I realized that the new governor was only two years older than I was. It was my ascendancy as well.

Once the euphoria died down, the Rose firm began to flip-flop on the benefits of having the first lady as a partner. What if Governor Clinton's politics rubbed one of our clients the wrong way? What if Hillary says something in her public role that conflicts with something the firm is doing? The paintbrush, it seemed, slathered both ways. Also, when Bill became governor and Hillary took on the duties of first lady, she began the on-again, off-again law practice that would shadow her all the way to Washington. "Hillary's not billing enough," someone would inevitably say. When she did go into the courtroom, she carried baggage. How did the jury feel about Bill Clinton, and would that affect their perception of her? I remember the first case Vince gave her to try, defending a canning company against a claim brought by a consumer who had found a mouse's rear end in his can of pork and beans. Vince later described her defense as "flawless," but she was amazingly nervous facing that jury. She won the case, but began steering her practice toward nonjury matters.

The first case Hillary and I worked on together was a strange one for two people who had gravitated to law to "make a difference." Instead of defending poor people and righting wrongs, we found ourselves squarely on the side of corporate greed against the little people. In the late 1970s, a group called Arkansas Citizens Organization for Reform Now (ACORN) formed to become an advocate for the poor. Their first target was utility rates—they wanted residential rates reduced by one third and industrial rates *raised* by a like amount. At first the Little Rock business community didn't take ACORN seriously. But through smart positioning and effective grassroots politicking (not to mention high utility rates), the group managed to pass an initiated measure for the change they wanted.

The business community was flabbergasted. Who *were* these upstarts? How would we ever attract another industry? The law firm that was the epitome of the Little Rock establishment was handed the task of quashing the ACORN measure. Herb Rule took the lead, dealing with the clients. I was to prepare the witnesses and get the case ready for trial. And the brilliant young lawyer Hillary Rodham would come up with the research and theories to combat this obvious "unconstitutional" bleeding of the wealth of the city's industries.

Because all local judges used Little Rock electricity, a judge was imported from out of town. He turned out to be Robert Dudley from the little northeast Arkansas hamlet of Pocahontas. Bob and I would later become close friends when we served together on the Arkansas Supreme Court, but until the ACORN case I'd never had any dealings with him. He brought to the Little Rock bench, in addition to his keen sense of jurisprudence, a particularly small-town tradition called inns of court. Opposing Little Rock lawyers weren't used to socializing with one another during a case, but that was exactly what Judge Dudley had in mind. At 5 P.M. after a day of trial, he would declare, "Inns of court will be held at the hotel bar starting at 6 P.M." Then he would bang down his gavel.

Hillary's interest was the law, not drinking with the good old boys. Usually she begged off and went back to the office to prepare for the next day. But since it was considered bad form not to go drink with the judge, I was designated our inns of court representative. After an hour of swilling liquor and swapping stories, I would excuse myself and go to the office to help Hillary. Right before the end of the trial, Judge Dudley announced that trial briefs were due *when the trial ended*—and then he promptly declared inns of court.

When I got back to the office, Hillary was up to her frizzy hair in law books. We ordered pizza for dinner, and then, as these two onetime idealists struggled for a legal theory to question the constitutionality of consumer-friendly electric rates, the combination of pizza and drinks apparently inspired me. Here was the scene: We were in the Rose firm library, Hillary sitting in a chair taking notes while I lay resting my aching back on the floor under the conference table, espousing stream-of-consciousness constitutional law. I really suspect it was Hillary's interpretation of my ramblings that resulted in our winning brief, but from that day forward I never underestimated the weight of pizza on the scales of justice.

One month before Bill Clinton was elected governor, I accidentally became a politician.

Seth had succeeded in regaining his seat on the Airport Commission earlier that year, and I suppose I helped him with a few phone calls. Now I thought the subject of the Little Rock City Board was closed. Then on a summer day in 1978, Jim Dailey and Dwight Linkous, the city directors I had met through Seth, called me at my office. They told me that one of the directors had died and they needed to select someone to fill his unexpired term. When I started to object, they said not to worry—they were being pressured by the black community to name a black to the position (at that point, the city board was all white), but they still needed a good list of candidates to choose from. They painted a strong upside—raising my profile in the community and giving me an inside track if I ever wanted to get on a commission. Seth encouraged me to throw my hat into the ring. My law partners didn't seem to care as long as there was no chance I would be appointed.

After joining some thirty applicants in the first round, I got a call from Dwight saying that six of us were being invited in for individual interviews. He told me of course they still had to select a minority, but that everyone was impressed by my application. "Enjoy the publicity," he said. I was thirty years old and proud of myself. I took it as a free shot. In my interview I was totally honest about issues I didn't even know *were* issues, such as sidewalks and water policy. That night I got a call from Dwight. "Come down to City Hall and be sworn in," he said.

"*What*?" I said. I wasn't really sure I wanted to be on the city board.

Dwight spun a sketchy story, the bottom line of which was that another opening had become available and they had elected *two* board members. I remember suspecting my father-in-law's hand in this somehow.

My partners at the Rose firm were stunned. Suddenly I was in a position similar to Hillary's—what conflicts would arise between my new city duties and my old law firm? The phone started ringing, the press asking me those very questions. I quickly said that I would recuse on any issue involving Rose. Little did I know that hatching in the dark corners of the firm were two of the most explosive issues the city board would ever face, residential housing bonds and cable TV. The partners called down to my office. "Webb, we need to meet."

I won't bore you with the details of either issue. What's important for this story are the effects of my accidental political career on my relationship with my partners, and my relationship with my bank account. Very quickly, I developed numerous conflicts with my partners because they inevitably represented clients whose interests were counter to the city's. Also, city board positions are nonpaying and all-consuming, so suddenly I was spending at least 50 percent of my time doing work that brought me pleasure and satisfaction, but no money. At the same time, my firm billings dropped drastically because I was working so much on the city board. My partners began to grouse because I wasn't contributing to the firm's profits. "Is Webb a lawyer or a politician?" they snarled.

In hindsight, I wish I had risen to those ethical dilemmas by leaving the Rose firm. But it was more complicated than simply resigning. To a small extent, my conflict was similar to Hillary's conflict with the firm. We both tried to accommodate our partners. Law was no longer black and white; it was compromise and accommodate. I wish I had said those were rules I couldn't live with.

But I didn't quit my practice. I didn't go out on my own. I liked the celebrity my city board work brought me. I liked seeing my picture in the paper. I also felt that my city work tapped into some of that idealism I had all but lost working as a day-to-day lawyer. So I stayed at the firm and I stayed on the city board. And as my cash flow slipped and my expenses mounted, I began borrowing more and more to make ends meet.

Our Italian lunches started as just meals, but eventually they became escapes for all three of us.

I think Vince and Hillary became such friends because each recognized that the other was battling to find a viable life. Hillary, assailed from all sides, drew into herself. Vince, assailed from inside, drew ever deeper into himself. At Rose firm parties, Hillary couldn't win. Bill often wasn't in attendance, and if Hillary followed her instinct and spent time talking to her partners, their wives would cut her to shreds. The wives wanted to quiz her about working in an office full of men, but they also wanted to enlist her support for their particular charitable cause. But if she spent time talking with the wives, the partners would be reinforced in their suspicion that she was, after all, a woman, not a real lawyer. And the wives would *still* cut her to shreds.

In Little Rock, we had never seen this dynamic so familiar now to working women everywhere. I felt for Hillary, and I know it hurt her. But she couldn't win either way, so she kept trying to be herself. She wanted a career separate from her husband's. She wanted to have her own friends and pursue her own interests. She didn't want to have to fit her expectations to a place that usually asked women, "And who were you, dear, before you were married?"

These were intelligent and efficient women who were carping about her, and yet they were women who kept house and raised children, drove in carpools, went to charity teas, and cooked dinner for their families. They were envious. They made fun of her hair and clothes and criticized her refusal to take her husband's name. Some complained that Hillary didn't engage in small talk. Lisa Foster hated that Vince would talk to Hillary, tell her things that Lisa didn't know. In 1978 we had our first firm retreat at the Red Apple Inn on Greer's Ferry Lake in Heber Springs. Several of us, including Suzy and Lisa, drove up together in a big van. On the way, Vince, Hillary, and I were talking about the major issue coming up for vote—Watt Gregory, Joe's right-hand man in the securities section, had been floating the notion of renaming the firm Rose and Giroir. I'd told Suzy about the pending battle, but this was the first Lisa had heard of it. She hated it. And though it had nothing to do with Hillary and everything to do with Vince, I think Lisa's jealousy was mainly aimed at Hillary.

At the same time, many of the wives—especially the ones in our general age group—admired Hillary and began seeing her as a kind of role model. They wanted their daughters to become like her, but that wasn't all. They wanted to be like her, too. They wanted to pick her brain and find out the secret—how they, too, could escape the lives to which their place and time had bound them. The real secret was that Hillary hadn't escaped either.

Vince must have felt as volatile inside as Hillary did. Day in and day out, he drove himself to perfection in his work, then went home to be the perfect dad and husband. In the early days, back when it was still okay to send bottles of good whiskey to judges and court clerks, the Pulaski County Courthouse would be full of good cheer at Christmastime. Everybody would be there—the colorful old lawyers, the secretaries, the clerks, all tipsy and telling stories about outrageous courthouse romances. Vince always looked forward to those parties. He liked sipping his Scotch and hearing the war stories. He liked the attention of the female clerks, all of whom thought he was the best-looking and nicest attorney in town. And I believe there was a part of him that thrilled to rub shoulders with what we considered the other side—the divorce lawyers, the ambulance chasers, the you-don't-owe-me-a-dime-unless-we-collect crowd. I don't know whether they reinforced his need to feel superior, or whether he felt he could let down his guard in their presence. He would say, "Hub, I have to be home by such-and-such a time. Make me leave." If I was successful at prying him out into the brisk December night, he would ramble on about the party all the way to his car. "You and I, Hub," he'd say, "we're the only ones at the firm who'll ever appreciate that." He sounded melancholy, like Sinatra singing about the wee hours.

The publisher Walter Hussman always threw a big weekend party at his Hot Springs lake house during Arkansas Derby week at Oaklawn Park. Vince, having known Walter's family since boyhood, seldom missed the festivities, and he always came back and regaled Hillary and me with stories of the wild weekend escapades. One story he didn't tell, but which I heard from my friend William Ketcher, was about the night Vince disappeared from the party. There was a little bit of the devil in Vince, and sometimes he just couldn't be as good as he always tried to be. When people at the party noticed they hadn't seen him, several went looking for him—went to his hotel room, to some of the nice restaurants, to the hotel piano bar, down by the lake. The places you might expect Vince Foster to be. Eventually somebody found him in a country-and-western bar, by himself, wearing jeans and boots and drinking beer and smoking cigars, and flirting with the waitresses.

As for me—well, on the surface, I seemed to be the untroubled one. I laughed and told stories. I was their touchstone of normalcy. But my life was heading step-by-step toward a precipice.

There was an old red-checked-tablecloth Italian restaurant called The Villa down on University Avenue, and sometime in the late 1970s the three of us began going there to get away. Part of it was that Hillary was now the first lady of Arkansas, and downtown restaurants were too crowded. We couldn't eat without her being interrupted—not to mention our wives being bombarded with calls from the local gossips. Also, things were uncomfortable inside the Rose firm. Joe Giroir's group was pulling away from the field financially, and there was a lot of whispering behind closed doors. I sometimes felt alienated because of my city work. The office was a good place to leave behind for a couple of hours.

In Arkansas, days start early so lunches usually begin around 11:30 A.M. We drove to The Villa at one o'clock to minimize our chance of running into anyone. One of the attractions of that restaurant was that we could get a carafe of red wine and that made the lingering all the more enjoyable. If the three of us had been seen drinking wine in downtown Little Rock, the busybodies would have had a field day.

Hillary was of course aware of all the jealousies, criticisms, double standards, and resentments within the firm, and she was beginning to develop the same relationship with the people state-wide. They talked about her fashion sense, her failure to fit the stereotype of the southern belle first lady. She hated it, didn't know how it had happened, and didn't know what to do about it. Vince and I became her sounding boards, her confidants. We couldn't do much for her relationship with her public, but we could be her emissaries to the firm just as we were the firm's emissaries to her. The office secretaries often came to Hillary with horror stories about the behavior of the partners, and Hillary passed those stories on to us. "He told her that if she'd wear tight jeans more often, she'd get a raise. Webb, you need to talk to him." Hillary had been the first lawyer in the firm to post a THANK YOU FOR NOT SMOKING sign in her office. "Help me on this one, Webb," she would say. "Herb keeps lighting up his Camel in my office—and then flicks the ashes in my trash can." She talked to us about the gap in compensation between men and women, treatment of the office staff, the ethics of various part-ners. She knew she couldn't raise those issues, so she encouraged us to. Vince and I began to feel protective of her, as though she were our little sister.

Meanwhile, after a glass or two of Chianti, the three of us could imagine that we were someplace far away—not in Little Rock, not in Arkansas, not even in America, but in a dim trattoria in the hot boot heel of Italy. There, by the endless sea, our troubles didn't exist. There *we* didn't exist. Hillary even gave Vince a new name to reflect our mutual fantasy: *Vincenzo Fosterini.*

4

Politics and Polite Company

Governor Clinton irritated a lot of Arkansans during his first term. One of them was my father-in-law.

Most of the complaints about the new Clinton administration concerned the governor's immediate staff and how they handled their business. Determined to lift this backward state into the twentieth century, Bill had swept in with an ambitious agenda. To carry it out, he had surrounded himself with some of the bright young people he had met during his college years. To a man, they were bearded, brusque, and busy—too busy to consult with everyday Arkansans about everyday Arkansas issues. It's grating enough for *Arkansans* to act like know-it-alls, but most of these people were outsiders. In the coffee shops and watering holes across the state, people began grumbling that Bill Clinton and his bearded bunch needed to be taught a lesson.

Seth Ward was constitutionally wired to agree with such sentiments, of course, but his main problem with Bill Clinton was much more personal. Seth wanted something and Bill wouldn't give it to him. To Seth, that's the definition of an enemy.

It started soon after Suzy and I moved to Little Rock, long before Clinton became governor. Actually, I guess it started years and years before that—*generations* before that, even. Seth grew up in a home dominated by his mother, Helene Irma Ward, and

Suzy says she pronounced the first name El-*lay*-na. She was very ambitious, very social. She took great pride in the fact that she could trace her family back to the time of the Magna Carta. Her husband, Suzy's grandfather, was named Seth *Walter* Ward. Helene hated that, because in all that long lineage of Seths he was the only one with a middle name. Had it not been for him, she used to say, there would be thirteen uninterrupted Seth Wards.

Helene didn't make that mistake with her son. He was christened Seth Ward, and his unspoken job was to get the lineage back on track. In the Ward family, sons were king. When Skeeter—whose real name, of course, is Seth—came along, Seth set out to pass that legacy on to him.

When he quit National Aluminum and began phoning me about various business opportunities, Seth's real goal was to buy a business for Skeeter. That had been going on since the day Skeeter graduated from college. Seth had first set him up selling static vacuum cleaners called "Hokeys." Then Seth created a burglar alarm business for Skeeter to run—Triple S Burglar Alarm, named for the Ward children, Suzy, Skeeter, and Sally. Skeeter was never allowed a goal of his own, and to my knowledge he never dared to dream one. Seth had an idealized view of being in business with his son, and Skeeter couldn't say, "Dad, I don't want to work with you." Seth Ward is a hard man to say no to—assuming Skeeter wanted to say no.

In the fall of 1976, Seth bought the Datsun dealership in downtown Little Rock. It seemed like a smart move, since the Japanese car market was booming. Seth gave Suzy and Skeeter each one third of the business. Suddenly everybody in the family got Datsuns, and Seth sent me a certain amount of legal work involving repossessing cars. Not surprisingly, he also began to have conflicts with the people at Nissan headquarters. Seth wanted more cars than they would allocate to him. Even more disturbing was Nissan's notion to perhaps open another Datsun dealership in Little Rock.

One day during Governor Clinton's first legislative session, Seth called and asked me to write up a bill that he could have submitted to the Arkansas legislature. What he wanted was a bill making it difficult for a car manufacturer to award more than one franchise in an area. I looked into the issue and drafted a bill requiring manufacturers to go through certain steps—to prove need, and so on. With such a law, a manufacturer would have a hard time giving a franchise to anyone other than an existing dealer. Seth loved it.

He took it to a senator friend of his and said, in that time-honored Arkansas you-scratch-my-back-and-I'll-scratch-yours way, "Senator, I have this little old bill. Let's just run it through." The Arkansas legislature runs on money. In three days, Seth's bill had passed both the House and the Senate. Now it was sitting in the governor's in-box.

Then Seth's senator called and said there was a problem. "The governor believes it's unconstitutional." Seth went out of his mind. He wanted me to walk the bill into Hillary's office and *demand* that her husband sign it. By then I knew how Seth operated—he once gave a customer a ride in his airplane and flew directly into a thunderstorm until the customer promised to get current on his bill. I didn't want him doing something crazy involving Hillary or Bill, so I went back to the law books. I found a case that I believed upheld the bill's constitutionality and wrote the governor a letter asking him to reconsider. I had it hand-delivered. I still didn't know Bill Clinton as well as I knew his wife, and I felt very uncomfortable doing this. But I wouldn't have presented the letter to him personally in any case. Clinton still vetoed the bill.

And from that day forward, Seth had no use for Bill Clinton. He "didn't trust him." In Arkansas, friendship, family, and loyalty are matters of grave importance—give me a piece of graph paper and I could diagram the intersecting feuds based on personal and family loyalty in Little Rock—and Seth thought Bill had betrayed his friendship with me. Never mind that Bill didn't *have* a friendship with me at the time, and wouldn't have done what he felt was wrong in any case.

Eventually Datsun did set up a competing dealership. Seth blamed Bill for the downward turn of his car business, and for his eventual need to sell it. Never mind that interest rates were shooting through the roof then—that's what really hurt Seth's dealership. But I don't care if my wife owned part of the business, Bill Clinton *should* have rejected that bill. It was anticonsumer. It was bad law. But Seth isn't a man who respects other people's principles, so I could never convince him otherwise.

At about the same time, Seth made a move that on the surface looked wise, magnanimous, and progressive—he persuaded the Airport Commission to name Hillary Rodham as its attorney. I was very pleased when I heard. I wanted to think that Seth was able to rise above his bitterness and see Hillary as a person separate from Bill.

The truth was less pretty. The Airport Commission was being pressured to appoint a female to it. It also needed an attorney. Seth figured that if the commission appointed a female attorney, it could hold off that much longer in naming a woman to its membership.

One reason my father-in-law has never been accepted into old Little Rock society is that he doesn't play by the rules of "polite company." That's a term you hear often in the gracious salons of The Heights: "We don't talk about that in polite company," the perfectly coiffed matron will sweetly say. What she means is that life operates on two parallel planes. On the bottom plane is business, and you can fight your adversaries in court or in the boardrooms all day long, but then you ascend to the polite plane. Business is business, but we're not cannibals. We leave the bloodletting at the office. On weekends, competitors join one another at cocktail parties, fund-raising events, and private dinners. There's another favorite saying in Arkansas: "Never get mad with your money." That's because alliances may last only as long as the present business deal. Then, like square dancers changing partners, you may strike up a fresh new relationship with a former foe. In Arkansas, business is ever-changing but connections are everlasting. How can you afford to get mad with your money at old so-and-so? You're having dinner at his house on Friday night.

I learned a lot about polite company when I was on the Little Rock City Board—especially during the cable TV vote. It was probably the largest financial transaction in the board's history. All the major cable companies linked up with local powers (giving them part ownership) to increase their chances. As one of seven city board members—even one who'd promised to recuse, since the Rose firm was involved in the bidding—I found myself one of the stars of polite company. It felt like being back in the Sugar Bowl. The level of your game defines you—which is another way of saying you're known by the company you keep. During the cable vote, I liked having such high-profile players making presentations to me. I liked being invited to power breakfasts and power lunches. I liked being sought after at cocktail parties and sit-down dinners. I liked seeing in my wife's eyes that she was proud of me. When I walked into the Country Club of Little Rock's polite company, I enjoyed the tacit respect and approval of my peers. Sitting in the club's glass-enclosed dining room, I could look over the bluff at the city lights sparkling far below. *My* city. I was a powerful, successful man. I was a pillar of the community.

But while I was reveling in my high civic profile, my personal financial situation was deteriorating. I wasn't billing much. Inside the Rose firm, in spite of the fact that he hadn't succeeded in getting his way on the firm name ("We answer the phone 'Rose firm' Gaston had said. Let's just call it that. I don't need my name on a piece of stationery"), Joe Giroir continued to be the main agent of growth and change. In acknowledgment of that, he was elected chairman of the firm. In practical terms, that title meant nothing. He might as well have been known as rainmaker in chief. But knowing his own power, he was never shy about pushing the envelope. He persuaded the partners that each of the four sections should be free to handle its billing as it wanted. Joe's Securities group promptly voted not to toss its billings into the firm pot, which meant that Joe and his Securities lawyers, some of whom had been toiling for years in Joe's shadow, were all becoming rich very fast—much faster than anyone else in the firm.

But in polite company, we didn't discuss how angry and jealous such developments made us. In polite company, everyone was expected to pretend that everything was just swell.

*   *   *

In the fall of 1978, my ego sustained a prolonged siege from my fellow city board members. When I had joined the board the summer before, it was a house divided. Three members regularly voted against three other members. I wielded a swing vote from day one. I saw my mission as bringing compromise and consensus to the city's governing body, and I had done that job well.

I won't bore you with the internal politics. I'll simply say that, under the city manager system of government—which Little Rock had then—the mayor is the member of the city board who presides over meetings and cuts ribbons. But a mayor can do good things if he shares the spotlight with his fellow board members and quietly nudges policy in the right direction.

Many people wanted to be mayor at the next election, but most couldn't garner the required four votes. The ones who could were a threat to the ones who couldn't. Several board members came to me with a plan: If I would join them in opposing the incumbent mayor, they would propose that a long-standing board member named Sandy Keith would become mayor *for no longer than six months*. Then he would resign and I would take over.

It was a strange proposal. The thinking behind it seemed to be that even though I had proved my worth as a conciliator, I'd never stood for election, and so they couldn't support me for mayor right off the bat. But they had qualms about Sandy's judgment. Still, he deserved a shot. He had been around a long time. They would caution him to keep his mouth in check and share the ceremonial duties with me. I was flattered, of course. I felt the warming glow of success. I told them they could discuss the plan with Sandy.

Their scheme worked. In January 1979, Little Rock had a new mayor. God love him, he was a disaster.

Very early in Mayor Keith's administration, the police reported an alarming statistic. Little Rock's rape rate was the highest in the United States. At a city board meeting, as the chief of police was explaining to us his thinking on this ominous trend, Sandy piped up and said, "I know why Little Rock has the highest incidence of rape in the country."

I cringed when the chief took the bait. "Why, Mr. Keith?" he asked.

"Because," the mayor said, "we have the prettiest women!"

Happy to be fed something besides dry, city board fare, the press went to town on this story. It was picked up nationwide and a massive demonstration took place in front of City Hall. Sandy loved the publicity. He wallowed in it. He told another assembly that he had figured out that blacks were smarter than whites. When somebody asked why, he said, "Every day I watch the Arkansas River bridge from my window. White people always walk across the bridge. Black people always hitch a ride."

The chamber of commerce held a private meeting and asked me to do something, but all I had to do was wait. When Sandy flipped the bird to an *Arkansas Gazette* reporter during a board meeting, his wife asked him to step down. She spoke for all of Little Rock in saying that she'd had enough.

I wish I could say that I simply sailed into the mayor's job, but it didn't happen that easily. One of the board members who had concocted the Keith/Hubbell plan was Charles Bussey, a black businessman; Lottie Shackleford, a black female board member who wanted to be mayor, attempted to shame him before his constituents for voting for a white male over a black female. On election night she filled the room with people from the black community. Bussey didn't back down.

At age thirty-one, I became mayor of the city of Little Rock. In my acceptance speech, I put on my best conciliator face and stressed the equality of the seven of us. I stressed the need for consensus building. I promised to share the ceremonial duties that came with the mayor's job. I invited everyone over to my house for drinks.

The very next morning, I received my first harsh lesson about life in the spotlight. At the Rose firm, I took a score of congratulatory calls, and then I picked up a pink phone slip asking me to call a reporter named Bill Simmons, from the Associated Press. I assumed he wanted to interview me about my election.

I returned the call and Simmons offered his congratulations.

Then his tone changed. "I hate to do this," he said, "but I have it from an impeccable source that you're having an affair." He named a woman who worked at City Hall. When I picked myself up off the floor, I said, "Who told you that?"

"I can't reveal my source," he said.

"You're kidding."

"Mr. Hubbell," Simmons said, "I wouldn't joke about something like this." He told me the woman in question not only denied the affair, but denied even knowing me. She was married and begged Simmons not to run with the story.

"I take it you're denying it, too," Simmons said.

"Of *course* I'm denying it." When I got off the phone, I almost threw up. All I could think about were Suzy and the kids. Twelve hours on the job and already my career was over.

I walked down the hall to Hillary's office. Pale and shaking, I told her what Simmons had said and that it was untrue. I asked what I should do.

"Bill Simmons is a good reporter," she said. "He wouldn't go with a story unless he had a reliable source. Obviously you've upset somebody's apple cart by being elected mayor and they're out for revenge."

She suggested I get back on the phone with Simmons, emphasize my denial, remind him of the seriousness of the allegations, reiterate that I was happily married with a family, and suggest to him that the source's motive might be suspect. Then I should immediately prepare Suzy and the children. As I left her office, she gave me a wan smile. "Webb," she said, "welcome to politics."

I was waiting on my doorstep the next morning when the paper boy arrived. There was no article. Hillary had been right—Simmons was a good reporter and had gone back to recheck his source. Usually reliable, this time the source turned out to be consumed with anger. This person wanted to hurt me. It was a lesson I didn't have to be taught twice.

Hillary and Bill still had some lessons of their own to learn. I'm sure they thought they knew all about the subject of politics, but they were just beginning their education.

One smart thing Sandy Keith used to say is that in local government the most important things are catching the crooks, putting out the fires, paving the streets, and picking up the garbage. To some extent that's true of government at every level: It's the day-to-day ways in which government intersects with the people that the people most judge government by.

Bill Clinton didn't grasp that at first. He came in talking blue skies and grand visions. He had a million goals. He was so busy looking toward the horizon that he failed to see the people smack in front of him. Those people's horizon was somewhat closer to their noses than that of their governor. Aside from deer and duck hunting, they were concerned with getting up and going to work and raising their kids and making their house payments and keeping their cars running. In Arkansas, to maintain some minimum standard of safety for automobiles traveling the state's roads (not to mention providing revenue for government coffers), car owners must buy a "car tag" every year. In order to do that, they have to show proof of insurance, proof of payment of last year's property taxes, proof of having assessed property taxes for the coming year, and proof of a recent automobile inspection. At the time, this was a cumbersome system at best. People groused about it. You went to the revenue office and took a number and waited through an interminable line—and then the lady told you you were missing one vital piece of proof. She said you'd have to get in your car and drive over to the county clerk's office, where you would wait in another line to get a piece of paper that would entitle you to drive back to the revenue office and take *another* number.

Governor Bill Clinton walked blindly into the middle of this hornet's nest. To help pay for one of his blue-sky programs, he raised the price of car tags.

The people were furious. In truth, I think it wasn't the fact of the car tags so much as what his rate increase symbolized: Bill Clinton wasn't in touch with everyday Arkansans. The people didn't like his staffers. They were too young and too full of themselves. One editorial cartoonist took to depicting Clinton as a curly-haired toddler tooling around on a tricycle.

It was during this period that I first got to know Bill. Hillary tried her hardest to give him a "normal" life, and one weekend when Suzy and the girls were out of town, she invited Walter and me to spend the night at the mansion. I was flattered, but had no idea what to expect. I really hadn't been around Bill much. Walter and I showed up late on a Friday, and I felt like a child whose mother had arranged for me to play with another little boy. Bill was wearing jeans and a plaid shirt, and I had on a golf shirt and khaki pants. I had the feeling we were both a little better dressed than we might have been on a Friday night at home. We had supper in the kitchen, finishing with chocolate-chip cookies from Liza Ashley, the mansion cook. Liza took a special liking to Walter, and Bill was charming with him, too. Then Hillary went to bed. She had to leave on a trip early the next morning. Suddenly Bill, Walter, and I were left with nobody to direct our play time.

Fortunately, a new pinball machine had been installed in the mansion basement, so we took our chocolate-chip cookies and went downstairs. There was also a Ping-Pong table. Bill and I soon drifted to that common denominator of Arkansas topics, the one just past the weather—Razorback sports. He especially liked basketball, so we talked about the coming team's pros and cons. Before the night was over, we had arranged to play golf—all three of us—the next day. He liked to play golf, but hadn't gotten out much since he became governor. Over the next year, I would occasionally hear from his scheduling person asking if I was available "to play golf on Thursday," or whatever time he thought he could get away. Again, I was flattered, and sometimes I made time even when it wasn't convenient. "Sure," I would tell the assistant, and she would pass the word to the governor. Eventually he would call himself. "Can you really play?" he would say. I always felt he was worried about imposing. That fall of 1979, I invited him to go with Vince, William Ketcher, and me to see Arkansas play the undefeated North Carolina team, the one with Michael Jordan on it. We took my van and a state trooper drove. Bill was thrilled—he was getting to do a "guy thing." We were surprised at how wildly he cheered.

Such moments were increasingly precious to him as his political life turned embattled. As if the car tag issue wasn't enough, in the spring of 1980, another issue rose to help seal Bill Clinton's fate. It wasn't his fault, but when you're the governor you take the blame along with the credit. Down in the choppy Atlantic waters between Cuba and Miami, boatloads—*raft*loads—of refugees fleeing Castro's regime were washing up on the shores of the United States. This was the "Freedom Flotilla." Overwhelmed, immigration officials in south Florida began putting these people in fenced camps until some decision about their future could be made. Before long they had filled the south Florida camps, and more boats were arriving daily. President Carter and his staff began looking for other places to hold some of the Cubans. One of those places turned out to be Fort Chaffee, Arkansas, in the western part of the state. Soon thousands of Cubans began arriving for temporary internment at Fort Chaffee. It sounds harsh, but most Arkansans didn't want them here. They blamed Bill Clinton for letting it happen. In the coffee shops and watering holes, "car tags and Cubans" became a galvanizing slur. And then one of the people at the table would inevitably say, "Somebody needs to teach Bill Clinton a lesson."

Inside the Rose firm, Hillary was fighting a new battle of her own. In February 1980, she had given birth to Chelsea. I reiterate—these weren't Stone Age lawyers Hillary was working with. Many were Ivy League educated, Rhodes scholars, members of the Foreign Relations Committee. But in spite of that, they had been brought up in a certain world, and that world was changing. Hillary was the messenger.

They had assumed she would quit "when her husband got a real job." They had assumed she would quit "when Bill became governor." *Surely* she would quit "when she had a baby." One of our male partners could be rumored to have had an affair with a secretary, announce he needed some time off, take nine months—then return and expect not only full pay, but three fourths of a year's worth of allocations earned by his section. Yet when Hillary gave birth to Chelsea, the partners questioned whether she should be paid for the six weeks she took off. They also thought it was shameful for her to leave her new baby and come back to work.

None of this carping was done to her face, you understand. That wasn't the Rose firm way. But in private meetings and over lunch, they would say, "Does she really expect to be *paid* for when she was away?"

They criticized her every chance they got. Not all of the partners, of course—I want to make that clear. Ken Shemin, George Campbell, Jane Dickey (by now we'd hired two more female attorneys), Bill Kennedy, Allen Bird, Brantley Buck, the firm's treasurer—all of them liked Hillary. Joe Giroir saw the business benefit in her association with Rose, so he didn't talk bad about her. But others had it in for her, and for Vince and me for supporting her.

Their double standard was blatant. They asked us to talk to her whenever she wore jeans to the office, even on Saturday—yet we thought nothing of doing our weekend work in golf shirts and shorts. The partners who disliked Hillary seemed to make a point of showing a lack of respect to women. One poor secretary told me she was tired of listening to her male boss belch into his Dictaphone and not bother to erase it—but the last straw was when he called her into his office and asked her to hold out her hand so he could flick his cigarette's ashes into it. He said he didn't have an ashtray. She quit, and I didn't blame her.

Seeing that such partners would never appreciate her skills, Hillary began—subconsciously at first, I think—taking her show on the road. She looked for causes, board memberships, other ways she could expand her career as a lawyer and her persona as an independent person. But she was also feeling the pressure of Bill's problems in the state—especially when it became clear that some of the criticism of him was due to her. You could hardly go anywhere in those days without hearing somebody complaining that if the first lady loved her husband so much, you'd think she would "take his name." I know she heard it, and I know it hurt her. Sometimes in the morning, I could tell she'd started her day with something like that. But Hillary was in a box. If she tried to explain how she felt about the name issue, she risked offending those women who did take their husband's names. And if she didn't say anything, she offended everyone else.

My own political life was consuming most of my days and a good portion of my nights. Judging from the way my home phone rang, you'd think I lived at a sorority house. I had feared that after my brush with the press that first morning, my family's privacy was a thing of the past, but we hadn't had much trouble after that. Probably the worst was that parents who sent their children to the same parochial school we sent ours to began criticizing me for not sending mine to public school. Occasionally Walter and Rebecca would hear something bad about me on the school grounds and would come home in tears. I had to sit them down and explain. Or I had to get up early and grab the newspaper before anyone else could see it—so I would know whether to gather Suzy and the kids and give them *my* side of the story.

Mostly, though, the problems and the criticisms were precisely as Sandy Keith had said—practical, day-to-day considerations. One morning my phone rang about 3 A.M. I groped for the receiver and mumbled hello. "Mayor," a nasally voice said, "I got a dead dog under my house."

"Hmph," I said.

He explained that he'd been calling City Hall for three days trying to get them to come pick up the carcass. "Mayor, that dog stinks."

I told him I surely understood, and that I would get right on it as soon as I got to the office. I would have the city manager talk to—

He was in no mood to discuss the delegation of functions under the city manager form of government. "Mayor, I intend on getting rid of that smelly dog *tonight*."

I told him the city landfill wasn't open at that hour of the morning.

"Mayor," he said, "the dump isn't the direction of town I'm heading. You live at number nine Robinwood, right?"

I asked him to wait a second while I called the night supervisor of sanitation. The dog was picked up immediately. As I hung up, Suzy stirred. "Honey, who's calling at this time of night?"

I said, "Just a man about a dog, darling. Go back to sleep."

Despite being kept awake at night, I was having fun as mayor. I felt like the city board, and the city, were making progress. Striving for more in-house harmony, I aimed for votes of six or seven instead of the just-passing four. We kept discussing issues until we came closer to that. The members began to feel more involved and the city board became more predictable in its actions. We started a Rape Prevention Program. We brought more women and blacks into city government. We put in place the funding for a new convention center, made improvements at the airport, and the sewer and water systems all underwent expansion. We built a new riverfront park.

Of course, I didn't win them all. Trying to honor my father, I proposed that Little Rock impose a twenty-four-hour waiting period for anyone who wanted to buy a handgun. I might as well have suggested banning hunting. Even one of the females on the city board was a card-carrying member of the National Rifle Association. I lost six to one.

I also continued to bump up against my own law firm. When I began a very vocal campaign to beautify the city by banning billboards, the advertising community screamed in unison. That's when I discovered that the local billboard industry was represented by none other than the Rose Law Firm, and the attorney in charge was Vince Foster.

With egg on my face, I made the long walk down to his office. I apologized for shooting off my mouth before gathering all the facts. I believed what I said, of course, but I would simply recuse and that would solve the problem. Vince said that wasn't necessary—Rose had been fired. "How can the Rose firm cotton to that communist Webb Hubbell?" had been the client's parting shot. Vince said he hated to lose the client, but he understood my position and wished me luck. That was the difference between Vince and the rest of the firm—money wasn't everything. Anyone else would have been frantically calling meetings to see if they couldn't salvage a compromise.

As the elections of November 1980 loomed, I had to make a decision. My income was continuing to drop and my partners were continuing to begrudge me the time it cost the firm to get together and discuss my city board conflicts as they arose. As with Hillary, they enjoyed the prestige of having one of their own as mayor, but that was simply image. In practical terms, my holding office hadn't helped feather their nests.

Also, the law firm was taking on a major expense, so my anemic billing stood out all the more. Joe felt that we had to move into a larger space. We had completely filled up our present building, and that meant there was no more room available to accommodate our ongoing expansion. One morning at the members' meeting, Joe recommended that we buy the old red-brick YWCA building at the corner of Fourth and Scott downtown. Over months of discussions, clutches of Rose firm lawyers would troop downtown to inspect the building. It looked like a schoolhouse. It was empty, and it had seen better days. A big old rambling structure built in the 1930s, it even had a swimming pool, now filled with fallen plaster. When Hillary, Vince, and I went down to see the building, I couldn't help thinking of all the hopeful young women who had boarded there while they tried to fit themselves into the harsh men's world of their time. They would take heart at Hillary Rodham making her office within those walls.

Joe proposed that we set up a limited partnership to buy the building, renovate it, and lease it to the firm—pool and all. He painted a glorious picture of a healthy, happy law-firm family taking a dip together after a hard day at the office. One of the older partners was especially concerned with that part of the proposal: "Males and females swimming *at the same time?*" he said.

I liked the building and voted to buy it. Each partner was offered a unit of ownership, which cost $12,000. Then, because we paid less in rent than the debt service cost, each partner would have to come up with an additional $5,500 a year. That was steep—I had to borrow the initial amount. And yet our modern building was tacky. The YWCA building's age, history, and tradition made it a more fitting office for the oldest law firm west of the Mississippi.

Suzy and I had also been gravitating toward older homes. Houses in The Heights might lack the amenities of those in West Little Rock, but they made up in character what they lacked in his-and-her marble baths. The houses of my parents had always been small and not particularly distinctive. These older Heights abodes had decorative molding, carved fireplaces, hardwood floors, rich woods. I felt I belonged in an older house.

For two years Suzy and I had been eyeing a big, brick-and-stone Tudor on a curvy road in a beautiful section of The Heights. The house wasn't just big; it was massive. And it was empty. It had been built in the 1920s. Sometimes on Sunday we would drive by and if nobody was around, we would stop and peer through the big windows in the front of the house. On the first floor we could see a huge step-down living room, which took up most of the front of the house. At the far right was a screened porch set off by an arch of native stone. The stucco second story was white with the cross-hatched dark planks typical of the Tudor style. For me the house represented a place that was big enough to accommodate a troupe of kids and everything that evoked—sleepovers, their friends coming for snacks after school, the happy noises of a contented family. For a man my size, it represented uncrowded comfort, a spacious atmosphere in which I could really enjoy welcoming friends.

It also cost what seemed then like a king's ransom—$210,000. We had no business looking at it, but we couldn't stay away. Our friend William Ketcher, the one who'd driven Suzy and me on our first date, lived on that street, and he kept urging us to take the plunge. After looking through the windows and staring at the red slate roof jutting above the soaring pines, Suzy and I would drive around and talk about it, obsess about it, plot about it, *rationalize* about it: I was the mayor of Little Rock; I was a successful lawyer in a grand old firm. Suzy had assets (and, let's not forget, a wealthy father). We had three children and I wanted more. We had outgrown the house we were living in. If not now, when?

In the autumn of 1980, we moved into the big house on Sherwood Road. I wanted to believe that anyone who could live in so solid a house must be solid himself. But as if to fend off with humor the inevitable troubling questions about such a move, we gave the house a disarming name—Hubbell's Folly. In years to come, that house would live up to all my dreams (and nightmares). On summer evenings, I could sip a drink in my big living room and look out at children—including the Fosters' and the Clintons', when Chelsea got big enough—bouncing happily on a trampoline in the shade of my big oak trees. Such a scene made me feel successful.

The November after we bought the house, my name was again on the ballot for the city board. When I thought about giving up city politics, I couldn't help remembering the rich experiences I had had so far. I had met Rosalynn Carter. I had attended the Kennedy School of Government for a week. I had been invited to the White House to discuss energy and transportation policy. I felt I was doing good work for the city.

We raised nearly $10,000 for the campaign and spent only two thirds of it. After the vote, I sent a portion of the remaining money back to every contributor. That caused the wily old investment banker and political string puller Witt Stephens to summon me to his office. Everybody called him "Mr. Witt." When I was ushered into his office, I found him chewing on his cigar like a poster boy for backroom politics. He stared at me from under his bushy white eyebrows. "I just wanted to meet the fool who would return campaign money," Mr. Witt said.

As Bill Clinton's reelection race went into the final stretch, Hillary was already seeing the wrong colors at the finish line.

Bill's opponent in the general election was a Republican banker named Frank White. He and his campaign strategists had heard all the grumbling about "teaching Bill Clinton a lesson," and they trotted back all of his supposed sins before the eyes of the voters. Their coup de grace was a TV ad labeled "Car Tags and Cubans," and you can imagine the rest of the words. At Clinton headquarters, his team kept pushing their agenda for next time—telling the voters all the good things Governor Clinton was going to do for them next time around.

I didn't see Hillary as much during the campaign, because she was out helping whenever she could be. But she also had Chelsea to take care of, so she was in the office more than we might have expected. She was getting very nervous about Frank White's negative ads. "We've got to hit back!" she said. "We can't let those charges go unchallenged." When no one in her husband's campaign seemed to grasp that, she threw herself into the battle with a ferocious energy. It was too late.

On election night 1980, my family, friends, and supporters—including my sister Terry and the group of fellow nurses called "Hubbell's Honeys" that she had organized to carry signs at polling places—waited for the results at my new house in The Heights. There were multiple TVs and open bars and tables full of food that night. Grown-ups talked and laughed and whooped when some piece of good news flashed across the screen. Kids ran in and out, more taken with the party than the politics. Sitting there in my big easy chair with my supporters around me, I felt like a *statesman*, not just a candidate for the Little Rock City Board. There's nothing more uplifting to a fragile ego than winning an election, and I won big that night—more than 85 percent of the vote.

My election was confirmed at around 10 P.M., and from then on we waited and watched to see Bill Clinton pull it out. He never did. I had hoped it would be a perfect night, but as we gazed at the TV coverage of Clinton's watch party at the Camelot Hotel, the glum faces revealed the shock and disappointment that all of us felt. The room was as silent as the cold Arkansas River coursing along its shadowy banks just outside.

Our complacent little world was jarred that night. President Jimmy Carter gave up the Oval Office to a seventy-year-old actor. And in Democratic Arkansas, Bill Clinton lost to a Republican. It was a stunning defeat. White had no apparent charisma and none of the brilliant political savvy the state had come to look for in its leaders. And yet he obviously had something Bill Clinton did not have—the confidence of the people.

This, I think, was the night Bill Clinton first had a chance to become President of the United States. After that defeat, he and Hillary never made the same mistakes again. From then on, they ran their campaigns themselves, going on their gut instincts. And they never again failed to hit back fast when the situation demanded it.

But that night in 1980, Vince and I couldn't believe what we were seeing. Occasionally we would catch a glimpse of Hillary on television. She had on her brave mask. I think both of us wanted to wrap her in our arms and comfort her.

About midnight, Vince and I drove down to the Camelot to console our friends. When we got to Clinton headquarters, almost everyone was gone except a battery of waiters and busboys taking away the celebratory feast. No one had been very hungry.

As we turned to leave, one of the service people came up to me. "Mr. Hubbell," he said, "tell your friends that they'll be all right. I'm sorry I didn't vote for him. I just wanted to teach him a lesson."

Vince and I drove back to my house and got slowly, positively, drunk.

5

No Pain, No Gain

There are times in this life that cry out for sports analogies. In Washington, the Gipper had just won a big one for himself, but down in Arkansas Bill Clinton's bruised and battered ego had to be hauled from the field on a stretcher.

She asked Vince and me to the Governor's Mansion the day after the election for Bill's concession speech. It was like going to a funeral. Bill's eyes were puffy and his voice was hoarse. Hillary had dark circles under her eyes. Both of them looked more fragile than I'd ever seen them. As they stood on a balcony overlooking the backyard terrace, Bill groped for words. He didn't yet know what had hit him. Though his friends and supporters were vocal in their anger and disbelief, Bill would have none of it. He was gracious, offering the new governor-elect any needed help during the transition. Then he and Hillary came down into the crowd. Vince and I hugged Hillary. She was trembling. "You need to get some rest," Vince told her. Bill was already talking to people about the vote in different counties. I still didn't know him well, but I knew we had at least one thing in common—we both wanted to be loved. The vote was a rejection that he felt as a knife in his heart.

Hillary and I talked several days after the loss, and I tried to summon up all the motivating clichés that coaches had used on me throughout my playing years. *When you get knocked down, you have to pick yourself up. No pain no gain. It takes heart to be a winner.* She listened to me politely, and then she said, "Webb, why don't you tell Bill that."

Afterward I wrote him a letter. I wish I had kept a copy. I'm sure Bill did—he keeps *everything*. Maybe this letter will turn up in his presidential library someday. In it, I talked about things I had learned playing football in Arkansas. Arkansans like underdogs, I said. We like someone who fights back. For years we played Texas in the Southwest Conference, and though we seldom won, we were loved by our state. It was because we never gave up. The people of Arkansas expected Bill Clinton to fight back. The pundits might write him off, I told him, but in spite of what the "experts" were saying, I believed one thing to be absolutely true: If he didn't run again next time, he would never be elected again.

It must have been hard for him to absorb such a thought amid Arkansas's postelection climate. The rats weren't just jumping ship; they were doing swan dives from the main mast. In the Rose firm, the same people who'd complained that Hillary had taken too much time off were now panicking at the thought that she might actually work full-time. As always, the top concern was profits. How would having Hillary on board affect our bottom line *now*? Watt Gregory and others in the Securities Section were the most vocal about Hillary's impact. It was the 1980s, and the state of Arkansas was about to get in the middle of the bond business. Watt was especially concerned about positioning the firm to handle much of the state's business. Why, he asked, would Governor White want to send us any of the state's bond work when doing so would just help Bill Clinton's wife make a living until Clinton could run against White again? The apolitical firm I'd joined seven years earlier was no more. "You need to talk to Hillary, Webb," was the mantra. The message to her boiled down to this: Either leave so the firm can make money, or start billing to make up for the liability you create. Their preference couldn't have been clearer. They wanted Vince and me to talk her into leaving.

"Dammit," I told them all time and again, "she's a helluva good lawyer." Neither Vince nor I ever said a word to her about leaving. Vince was furious, but the way he expressed it was by burying himself in work and closing his office door. He wanted me to take the lead in mediating between Hillary and the firm. "I'm afraid I'll lose my temper," he said. It's clear to me now that Vince Foster had a deep fear of confrontation. I didn't notice it at the time, because Vince was so reticent, anyway. But in hindsight, it appears that whenever a face-off was brewing, Vince ducked. That may sound as though I'm judging him, which I'm not. I'm simply trying to understand him. What makes this observation all the more fascinating is that such a trait seems totally out of character for someone known as a top litigator. But Rose wasn't the typical litigation firm. Ninety-nine percent of our cases were settled out of court. Also, Vince could deal with the courtroom confrontations because court is a venue with the kind of hard rules a man like Vince Foster could cling to. What he dreaded, I think, was the wild, spontaneous eruption—the street fight, the office brawl.

As for Bill Clinton's immediate future, the firm's partners didn't even consider hiring him. But they also didn't want to see him go to work for the competition. Ideally, Bill and Hillary would pack their baby and their belongings and leave the state, never to be heard from again. Short of that, the Rose partners hoped Bill would hang out his shingle as a sole practitioner. Whatever prestige there was to be gained from an association with Bill Clinton, they certainly didn't want the Wright firm to get it.

In spite of the nasty atmosphere, Hillary seemed to bounce back from the loss much faster than Bill did. After a little time off, she came back to work. She, Vince, and I would gather in one of our offices to talk, or go out for one of our Italian lunches, the later the better. Hillary usually picked at her food like a bird, but not when we ate Italian. Over heaping platters of antipasto and garlic bread and pasta, washed down with wine, she told us about the opportunities Bill had inside the state and out. He'd been approached about running for the chairmanship of the Democratic National Committee, and Hillary asked me to write to my mayoral colleagues around the country spelling out Bill's vision of the party and asking them to consider him. He'd also been asked to consider becoming president of the University of Kentucky in Louisville. None of it seemed to satisfy him. Hillary said he was having a very hard time regrouping.

I wondered aloud if he'd like to go out for a round of golf. I had only played with him once, that time a couple of years before when Hillary had invited my son Walter and me to spend the night at the Governor's Mansion. Hillary liked the idea and urged me to call him. "It'll do him good to get out," she said. I phoned him that night and he sounded glad to hear a friendly voice. We made a date to play in a day or so.

When you lose a big public battle, your instinct is to hide. I thought about that as I drove over to pick up Bill. He and I could easily slink off to some out-of-the-way course where we would hardly be noticed, and we would have a nice, quiet round of golf. But the game here wasn't just golf.

The Country Club of Little Rock was established in 1901 in a new area of the city called Pulaski Heights. (Little Rock is in Pulaski County, named after the Revolutionary War hero Count Pulaski.) There was ample space for a golf course, and the view was spectacular. The site of the first clubhouse was on a bluff overlooking the Arkansas River and the burgeoning downtown a mile to the east. When the club was built, the bridge connecting downtown to The Heights hadn't been built yet, so the club was hard to get to. That also may have been part of the point. Suzy and I had forked over the $4,000 for a junior membership to the Country Club in 1975, much to my father-in-law's dismay. But we lived in The Heights, and I played golf and Suzy played tennis. Our friends belonged to the club, and so did my parents. I told Seth it was only natural for us to join the club that was most convenient to get to from where we lived.

I won't pretend to ignore the club's social aspect. Just as it was when it was built, the Country Club of Little Rock when I belonged was the most prestigious social institution in town. It was also the bastion of old-money conservatives, whether they called themselves Democrats or Republicans. Of course, now that the Reagan Revolution had come, people were no longer ashamed to use the R-word. In a culture in which friendships were based on what-can-you-do-for-me, Bill Clinton was a has-been. Bill played golf there thanks to a special privilege extended to the office of governor. But Frank White was part of this culture. It was his country club now, in every way. *He* would preside over the Round Table at the Men's Grill.

That's precisely why Bill Clinton and I had to walk in there and face the astonished stares of the opposition.

We played first, laughing about our bogey putts and slicing drives. We talked about sports, the weather, our golf games. The greens looked vibrant even in November. As I steered the cart past dusty leaves toward a far snapping flag, Bill began talking about needing to find a house. When he was attorney general, they'd rented a small one in the Hillcrest area, a more populist section of the original Pulaski Heights. They liked Hillcrest's old houses, big trees, and front porches. They also liked the idea— though Bill seldom actually had the time—of strolling along the old sidewalks in the evening, saying hello to their neighbors. They were thinking of looking there again. But of course they didn't have much money, and he had no idea what he was going to do to earn a living.

We rode in silence for a few moments, and then he said, "Webb, what do you think happened?"

We selected our clubs as I selected my words. "I don't think people really meant to throw you out," I said. "They all thought the next guy would vote for you—but *they* could vote for Frank and send you a signal. They thought you were taking them for granted."

His eyes moistened. "I never took them for granted. I wanted to do so much for them that I wasn't patient."

As he lined up his putt, I tried to tell him that this was just a temporary setback.

"You don't think my career is dead?" he said.

"Hell no. If the election were today, I think you'd win. Thousands of people are wishing they had their vote back. They didn't mean for this to happen. They just meant to send you a message."

That seemed to comfort him. He looked away for a second as if to find his focus. Then he bent down over his putt and gently hit it in. We celebrated with a high five, and didn't talk about that subject again.

At the eighteenth hole, I could almost see the tongues wagging in the Men's Grill. The drumbeats had been going on all afternoon, and I wondered what kind of reception we were about to receive. I expected whispers, nudges, head-shaking disbelief. And not just because of Bill Clinton's presence here—my showing up *with* him was maybe even harder for them to fathom. As mayor of Little Rock, I was probably putting at risk funding and legislation that would benefit my city. Clinton hadn't run the state that way, but the widespread expectation was that we would now revert to the spoils system of the Orval Faubus days. I was willing to chance it. Even though Joe, Watt, and others at the firm wanted me to do what they were doing— say I'd always had reservations about that liberal Bill Clinton and his Yankee wife—I didn't feel that way and wasn't going to say it just to do business. I was making a statement of my own— Bill Clinton was my *friend*.

Sure enough, Frank White was there. People watched for fireworks, but both Frank and Bill were gracious, according to the rules of polite company. They shook hands, joked a bit. But what surprised both Bill and me was that several people came up to say hello and wish him well. I guess it was like I had told him in the letter—Arkansas likes an underdog. And that's exactly what he had become.

Between November and the turnover of power in January 1981, Bill held several "strategy" meetings. The agenda can best be described as, "I just got beat because of car tags, and what can I do about it?" I was asked to attend those sessions, and I was happy to help in any way I could. The meetings took place in the big living room at the Governor's Mansion. I recognized most of the faces there—people from his administration, political advisers from around the state. I'm sure they wondered why I was there, but I mostly kept my mouth shut and absorbed what I could.

Bill wanted to call a special session of the legislature to repeal his "car tag" bill. He knew Frank White would do it the minute he was governor, and Bill hated letting White make such easy points with the people. But that wasn't Bill's primary motivation. Mainly, he was looking for a way to show that he'd learned his lesson.

This was the first time I'd seen his decision-making process in action. Some will quibble with the term "decision making," since we ended meeting after meeting with nothing decided. But that was part of the process. As former Labor Secretary Robert Reich noted, Clinton used his hundreds of advisers to test his own ideas against. Then he went home and tested what he'd learned against Hillary.

Usually she didn't sit in on the meetings, and if she did, she took a spot in the corner and never said a word. Bill began by arguing a certain position, and he wanted to hear from everybody in the room. He listened as they discussed the pros and cons noncommitally among themselves. Then he started going in some obvious direction, and people started jumping on the bandwagon— "That's right!" "That's right!" As soon as they did, he began arguing the opposite point of view. The staffers then looked chagrined, embarrassed that they'd had the rug publicly pulled from under them.

Many years later, after we all got to Washington, I thought often about those meetings. Not so much for the content, but because of the dynamics of leaders and followers. Such a style can be frustrating to young staffers looking to provide the right answers in order to move up the ladder, or others trying to enhance their own credibility by reporting which way the government is heading. But that's what Washington lives on, and Clinton's style didn't fit the pattern. There was frustration inside and outside the White House, and leakers whispered the word "waffling" to cover their own embarrassing lack of reliable information. To those demanding simple answers—for whatever reason—searching is tantamount to being lost.

Ultimately, Bill decided not to call the special session, but the meetings continued through the winter and spring. When Bill turned over the reins of government, he and Hillary moved to a friendly yellow house in Hillcrest. It had a wonderful front porch, and the meetings, though smaller, continued there. I was flattered to now be considered both Hillary's *and* Bill's confidant.

To be honest, it was easier to think about my friend's problems than my own. I wanted to stay away from Hubbell's Folly as much as possible in those days. Every time I turned the corner going home, I saw a workman's truck in my driveway. Before I even stepped inside the house, I could hear the buzz of saws and the whir of drills. I came to think of it as the sound of money being spent.

Everything about the house was costing more than I had anticipated. First, my banker had said, "Webb, don't lock in on those exorbitant interest rates." The rate when we bought was 9 percent. I took his advice and opted for the fluctuating rate, a mistake that eventually cost us 21 percent a year. But that was just the house payment. Once we got moved in, the house turned into a veritable tar baby. It was 5,600 square feet, and plenty in that sprawling space needed fixing.

The structure was sturdy, but the house hadn't been upgraded over the years. The galvanized steel pipes were so corroded that the water opening was no bigger around than a pencil. We had five bathrooms, but two people couldn't shower at the same time. The kitchen was old and dingy, with metal cabinets. As a housewarming present, Seth offered to take all the cabinets down and have them sanded and repainted in the shop at Ward Datsun. I tried to decline his generosity—the cabinets seemed to be the least of our problems—but I knew from the start it was a losing battle. He had his people come in and rip the cabinets out. While they were gone, Seth said, "If I were you, I'd take advantage of the cabinets being gone and have the walls shectrocked." So off went the plaster—and then the suggestion was, "If I were you, I'd take advantage of the walls being gone to replumb and rewire." The plumbers and electricians said they *could* do just the kitchen, but eventually they were going to have to do the whole house. I tried to buy time. Fifty thousand dollars later, Seth's cabinets went back up, and they looked great. But before long, the plumbers' predictions proved true—leaks began popping out all over the house. For every leak, we ended up replumbing and rewiring, sheetrocking and repainting. We eventually replumbed, rewired, sheetrocked, and repainted the entire house. In the midst of all this, Seth offered to help us buy new windows. I told him we couldn't afford it. He said, "Don't worry." After all, he was in the storm window business. We replaced all the windows in the house, and then Seth called and told me he needed his money. He presented me with a bill for about $5,000. I just shook my head and paid it.

My weight has always been an indicator of my stress level. I used to joke that I can gain and lose a human being every year. In the spring of 1981, I had ballooned to three hundred pounds. I had taken out a home equity loan to pay for the repairs, and hoped to repay that money from increased income at the firm and the cash flow from the warehouse. In hindsight, it's obvious I was kidding myself. I was playing a mental shell game. In January 1981, I was reelected mayor. If three quarters of my time was being spent doing pro bono public service, then how on earth was that going to translate into more income?

That spring I also heard some disturbing news about my warehouse tenant. A new member of the Little Rock City Board, Gale Weeks, asked if I would support the president of Falcon Jet for the Airport Commission. I told him I thought that was a problem for several reasons: First, the board was still seeking minority members; second, Falcon Jet was the airport's biggest tenant, and many people would see that as a conflict of interest; and third, Falcon Jet was the tenant at my warehouse, so in any case I would have to recuse. That's when Gale told me that Falcon Jet was also a client of his security business—and that they were very unhappy about leasing my warehouse. They hadn't needed one away from the airport, Gale said, but they were in negotiations with the Airport Commission about expansion and the major force on the commission suggested they take a lease on his warehouse. Not wanting to disrupt the negotiations, they signed on the dotted line.

Stunned, I went to Falcon Jet. After hearing their side, I reached an agreement with them on terminating their lease. I never told Seth because he would say he hadn't done anything wrong and I was a fool to let them off the hook. Maybe I was, but at that point I still had enough pride to think I couldn't live with myself.

I thought Suzy and I would be okay if I could rent the warehouse soon. It turned out I couldn't. But even though the warehouse cash flow had dried up, I was still obligated to make the monthly payments—$3,375 to the bank and $1,461 to Seth. I went back to the well—the bank—to borrow money for that. We had charge accounts at every store in town by then, and credit cards coming unsolicited in the mail. It was about this time that I also began using credit cards to help keep us afloat from month to month.

When I came home late after a day at the office and an evening of meetings or civic events, I took to fixing myself a nightcap or two, or even three. The silence was frightening. I went to my quiet porch and sat in the dim lamplight. There I flicked on the TV, sipped my drink, and tried to anesthetize myself.

Bill Clinton went to work for the firm of Wright, Lindsey and Jennings, though I guessed he wasn't planning to be a lawyer long. In the summer of 1981, he introduced me to a woman named Betsey Wright (no relation to the law firm), who had just started helping him with his "files." While Bill took a phone call, she showed me what she was doing—taking his handwritten index cards on contributors and supporters, organizing them by county, and computerizing them. It was an amazing arsenal. If I'd seen the one on me, it would have looked something like this:

Hubbell, Webb
BD 1/18/48
Rose Law Firm (Litigation—H's partner)
Played Football at U.A. (Grad 1969)
Drafted Chi Bears '69 (Torn knee ligament—never played)

He had similar summaries of everyone he had ever met. Betsey was clearly there to organize more than his files. She was organizing his political comeback as well.

As for my own political future, I had decided I couldn't afford one. I began talking to my family and friends about resigning from the city board. Suzy, who had never let on that she was lonely, said, "It'll be nice to have my husband back." Hillary was sympathetic, but claimed she wasn't the one to ask. "Webb, I'm the *last* person who can defend your public service." Vince said he would support me whatever I decided, but both he and Hillary knew I was getting close to having to choose one life or the other. I hadn't told anyone about my financial problems, but I'm sure they could guess. In every partners' meeting, somebody said something about my lack of business—or about the work my public service cost the firm. "I talked to so-and-so, Webb. Stephens is hiring Herschel [Friday] for their city board business. They don't want to deal with your recusal."

My mind was made up to quit the board—until I told the board about it. The next thing I knew, my phone was ringing and the voice of a member of the "Good Government Committee" was asking me to meet with that group. This was an old-line organization of businessmen dedicated to watching out for the status quo. They told me there was a bill before the legislature calling for a popular vote for mayor should there be a vacancy on the board. The Good Government Committee was working to kill the bill, but now would be the most inopportune time imaginable for me to step down. It would mean the end of Little Rock government as we knew it. They also said I didn't have to be mayor, as long as I stayed on the board—"for just a little longer." They promised to speak with my partners to smooth it over.

I knew as they were talking that I couldn't say no. I never could. I would give up being mayor but remain on the board. My family and bills would have to wait.

Predictably, my partners were astounded, perplexed, dismayed. It was just one more in a series of incidents that was gradually tearing me from my colleagues. Even some of my supporters in the firm shook their heads. Only Vince and Hillary accepted my decision as the best I could make at the time.

The three of us grew even closer during this period. We weren't simply three people gravitating toward one another because we enjoyed their company; we were three people who realized we depended on one another for something approaching *sanity*. When I think back on our relationship, the two-year period when Bill was out of office seemed to be the time of our greatest intimacy. I use that word deliberately. We all had relationships with our spouses that, for different reasons, prevented totally frank discussions. Hillary knew that Bill was more wrapped up in his own career than in her need for a life of her own. Vince couldn't talk to Lisa because she was so insecure and possessive. I couldn't talk with Suzy about her father and the money pressures until it was too late. So, Vince and I each shared a part of ourselves with Hillary that we shared with no other woman. And she had no men in her immediate life like us—males around whom she could be the person she wanted to be. As greatly as Bill respected her, she was also a wife and mother in his eyes. That brings baggage. With Vince and me, she was a warm friend and a brilliant colleague with no strings attached. She was just Hillary. We enjoyed her, respected her, loved her, accepted her.

She had become a senior partner the month Bill had relinquished power, and she was working nearly full-time. We moved to the new building that summer, and each of us had a big corner office on the third floor. Vince and Hillary were in the back, separated by the library; I was in the front. For the days when she couldn't get someone to watch Chelsea, she had set up a playpen in her office. Vince and I were thrilled to have her back. Though he didn't quite lose his nickname of Silent Sam, he seemed to emerge more from his shell, and she did what she could to draw him out. I confess that I felt jealous that she sometimes seemed closer to him than to me. They discussed things she didn't talk about with me, such as movies they'd seen or books they'd read. They often worked late when I was off doing my civic things.

Vince's reserve seemed to be a challenge to Hillary. Once when we were in the old building, she had sent a belly dancer to perform for him for his birthday. While everyone had laughed, Vince stood by with his trademark smile on his face—though he seemed anxious over the propriety of such an event happening in a law office. At parties—for example, Lisa and Vince's "Mad Hatter parties," to which everyone had to wear a hat (predictably, Vince wore a rakish but dignified Panama)—Hillary quizzed his high school and college friends about him, trying to uncover some story she could tease him about. She didn't find much. Vince had kept his lip buttoned since boyhood, and had done his level best to maintain a spotless dignity. I still remember Vince at that first Mad Hatter party. It had started with daiquiris around the Fosters' pool. As Lisa gave Hillary and me water ballet lessons, Vince stayed in the shade watching his friends get wild.

But in spite of himself, Vince would occasionally hand Hillary a juicy cause for kidding. Once, he hired a secretary who couldn't type. She was beautiful and very shapely, but she acted as though she'd never heard the word typewriter. That would have been a problem for almost any lawyer, but for Vince it was a disaster. His vaunted perfectionism was in jeopardy. Finally, I suggested we find that secretary a different place in the firm to work. On the day the secretary was to be confronted, Vince conveniently came up with an excuse to be out of town. He never could bring himself to fire anybody. Hillary kidded him mercilessly about his timely trip.

The most memorable of our escapes together took place in the early 1980s when the three of us went to New York together. It wasn't just the first time we'd traveled together; it was the first time we'd been on the same case. We were to depose the then-richest man in the world, the shipping magnate Dr. Daniel Ludwig. Acting the Neanderthals Hillary already knew us to be, Vince and I suggested that because Ludwig was old and male, Hillary would have a better chance of drawing him out. She laughed, but agreed.

When we got to his office—which was approximately the size of Madison Square Garden—we were met with a veritable army of attorneys, a doctor, a nurse, and some man who wouldn't identify himself. All of them tried to persuade us that the deposition wasn't necessary. We stuck to our guns. When Ludwig was brought in, there before us stood—just barely—this ninety-year-old man on the arm of a nurse. He immediately lay down on a sofa and started drinking a milkshake through a straw. Vince positioned himself near Ludwig to hear his answers. I positioned myself by the bagels and doughnuts. Hillary began by trying to put the old man at ease, while his strange supporting cast hung on every word. They acted as though any question might provoke a heart attack. Hillary was charming but persistent, but Ludwig had been carefully trained not to remember a thing. Then she asked him if he had ever been sued for breaking a promise or a contract (the basis of our lawsuit). Somehow, that happened to hit the right chord.

The old man stopped sipping his drink and looked at her. "By breach of promise," he said, "do you mean you want to talk about sex?"

Without missing a beat, and in her most charming adopted southern drawl, Hillary said, "Sure. If you want to talk about sex, I'll talk about sex."

Ludwig sat up and leered at her. "What kind of sex can we talk about?" he said. Immediately, his lawyers decided it was time to take a break. When they came back in, they cautioned Hillary "not to excite Dr. Ludwig again."

That afternoon the three of us laughed about it over a long lunch at La Grenouille, a restaurant I had heard about for years. We had no reservations, but when we got there Vince asked Hillary and me to step out while he had a word with the maître d'. In a few minutes we were asked to come back in and were escorted to a quickly made, excellently placed table. We both quizzed Vince, but he clammed up as only he could—eyes twinkling the whole time—and refused to tell us what he had said to the man. I noticed, though, that any time the captain or waiter were near, Vince made a point of referring to me as "Senator." He was very proud of himself, and Hillary and I were duly impressed. Vince chose a bottle of wine. It was a wonderful meal.

Afterward we walked down Madison Avenue arm in arm,

Hillary in the middle, three friends enjoying a magical spring day in the big city together. Hillary needed a hat because she and Bill had been invited to the Kentucky Derby, so we stopped into a millinery shop and Vince and I stood around oohing and aahing on command. Finally, the proprietor, a lady with a heavy Eastern European accent, offered a very expensive hat that Hillary loved. That was when Hillary admitted that she hadn't brought her purse. Vince and I immediately agreed to split the cost of the hat and give it to her as a present. Vince put it on his credit card.

We strolled back to the hotel, all had naps, and then went to see *Evita*. After the show we met Hillary's friend Susan Thomases and her then-boyfriend, now-husband, at a small Italian restaurant that I'm sure I couldn't find again. The meal was amazing, course after cascading course, with numerous bottles of wine and loud opera piped in as accompaniment. By the end of the evening, we were all singing, Vincenzo included, and Hillary was trying to convince us that we should stay up and go to a place she knew where we could dance to Brazilian music. To this day I regret that we didn't do it. Hillary never let either of us forget that we gave out.

The next day we all went our separate ways for separate clients. When I saw Vince again in Little Rock, the first thing he mentioned was the hat we'd bought Hillary. He asked if I would reimburse him for the whole amount so he could tell Lisa the hat was for Suzy. I asked no questions. "Sure," I said, and wrote him a check. Then he gave me back half the amount in cash.

It's no secret that Bill Clinton ran again in 1982 (until 1986, all statewide officials in Arkansas were elected to two-year terms) and retook the governor's office. But one of the major building blocks of that victory was first discussed in a golf cart between the third and seventh holes on the course at the Country Club of Little Rock.

I felt that Bill and I had become friends by then—as much as it's possible to be friends with someone who requires the constant love of an entire state. For two years we had played golf and cards, and had watched ball games together. I had also been his shopping companion on two successive Christmas Eves. As the 1979 holiday season shopping days dwindled, I mentioned to Hillary that I hadn't bought a single thing. She said Bill always waited until the last minute and that we ought to go together. Bill liked the idea—he was on a high then, and he loved being out among the people. He saw it as an adventure. I commandeered my sister Terry as designated driver, just in case we were offered libations along the way. When the governor's security staff cast an uneasy eye at the arrangement, Bill said, "Webb's my bodyguard and Terry's a nurse." Off we went. The next year, a month after he'd lost to Frank White, the security detail didn't seem to care as much. But this time Bill didn't want to go, for the same reason he felt uneasy about showing up at the country club. I told him it would be good for him. We made stops at a half-dozen stores in The Heights, and both of us had fun that afternoon. He found the people kind to him, and he was touched. In the car we laughed and told jokes and gossiped a little and debated about the Razorbacks. We even managed to check off everything on our gift lists. To Bill and me, this last-minute shopping spree was destined to become a tradition as cherished as Christmas trees and midnight church. Only Washington would finally kill it.

But on that hot summer day in 1981 at the country club, Bill and I were playing golf with a couple of other men and Bill and I were sharing a cart. I was behind the wheel, since the course manager had asked me not to let Bill drive. He spent so much time talking and gesturing that more than once he had run the golf cart into a tree. In her autobiography, *Leading with My Heart,* his mother, Virginia, said much the same thing about his proficiency in an automobile.

We had talked that day about his running again, but Hillary's name hadn't come up. Then as the four of us were putting, one of the other men in the foursome said something that brought a chill even to an Arkansas summer day. "Bill," he said, "there are a lot of women out there in the state who love you—but who think Hillary must not because she won't take your name. Hell, it even bothers my wife, and she loves Hillary. You will never be elected again if she doesn't."

I had heard that talk for years, of course, but never had I been with either Bill or Hillary when the subject was brought up. It made me extremely uncomfortable, so I could imagine what Bill was feeling. But he didn't let on. He just went on playing, while those raw words reverberated in the air like an echo.

I've read recently that Hillary says Bill never once brought up the name issue with her. That doesn't surprise me—I know how much he hated the thought of it. A couple of holes after the man expressed his opinion on the subject, Bill and I were riding silently in the cart. Suddenly he said, "You think he's right, don't you? She needs to do this."

I dreaded this conversation. "I don't agree that she *should*," I said, measuring my words. "But I agree that it's an issue that's hurting you politically. In a close election it might cost you."

After a couple more holes, he said, "Webb, you're her friend. Will you talk to her about it?" What, I wondered, had I gotten into.

I tried to enlist Vince in this mission, but he would have nothing to do with it. Not that he disagreed—he had heard the talk. But we both knew our friend well enough to be nervous about raising the subject. It was her *name:* Was this state now going to strip her of the emblem of independence the way it had stripped her of the fact?

"Chicken," I said to Vince. I couldn't read the look in his eyes as he watched me go off to war.

Sitting in Hillary's office, I went through the usual pleasantries—and then bravely blamed her husband. "Bill asked me to talk to you about the name issue," I said. I'm sure I held my breath.

To my immense relief, she smiled—though it made me sad that the smile was so wistful. It was the old demon in a new guise. The world didn't want to let her be herself. "I know I have to do it, Webb," she said. "But you're my friend—tell me why you think it's important." We had a long conversation that day, and

I understood a lot more about her afterward. She told me her friends from the East already thought she had "sold out" by coming to Arkansas with Bill instead of staying in New York or Washington where she could have had a brilliant career of her own. She had hoped that by maintaining a professional name different from her husband's, she could perhaps avoid the problem she felt with jurors. All this uproar over the name hurt her. It hurt her that people would think she didn't love her husband. It hurt her when someone asked what Chelsea's last name would be. It hurt her that people in Arkansas didn't try to understand her as much as they wanted her to understand them. But the name had become an issue, and she was prepared to change it to help her husband. She just wished she would be allowed to exhibit her own talents and skills as well. Instead, her real self was forced to live so far inside her that she sometimes didn't know who she was.

It was clear to me that she was going to do it, but it hurt very deeply for all the reasons she said. I suspect it hurt for some reasons she's never understood herself.

Bill beat Jim Guy Tucker for the Democratic nomination, and went on to take Frank White in November. The powerful Stephens family, who hadn't wanted Bill Clinton back, nevertheless supported him against Jim Guy. It was retaliation against Tucker for defeating Ray Thornton four years earlier. It was a costly race, a big gamble for both Clinton and Tucker. Clinton won and Tucker lost, and the loss was financially devastating to Jim Guy.

It's interesting to me, reading the know-it-all national press about Arkansas. Bill Clinton and Jim Guy Tucker are presented as close friends, so close that in 1985 they might have conspired together to defraud Madison Savings and Loan. Bill and Jim Guy are the last two guys I can imagine as co-conspirators. After that hard-fought 1982 election, the Tucker camp and the Clinton camp were mortal enemies. The wounds didn't even begin to heal for years.

Bill returned to office a different man, and the people around him were different, too. Instead of a blizzard of issues, the governor put forth just a handful—education first among them. Instead of a young and bearded staff of outsiders, he brought in a more mature, more down-to-earth lineup of Arkansans from around the state. And instead of a Yankee mate with her own separate name, he had a wife whose three names now captured the cadence of the old, familiar South. Hillary Rodham Clinton— it felt *comfortable* to the voters.

In August 1984, I took my family to Sea Island, Georgia, for a vacation. We loved Sea Island—the beaches, the golf, the bingo, the tennis. Something for everybody. Walter was eleven, Rebecca was nine, Caroline was seven, and Kelley was three. We played in the surf, took long walks on the beach. In the evenings we dressed for dinner, me in a coat and tie, and we all sat down together the way we did less and less at home. It was a wonderful escape from reality.

Usually I stay in daily touch with the office during vacations, but Suzy had urged me to let it go during the end of our week away. I agreed. I deserved some distance from whatever was happening back in Little Rock. As the week wound down, though, I found myself sleeping less and obsessing more. I lay awake thinking of all that was waiting for me at home.

In Arkansas the entrepreneurial spirit was booming. Just as Joe Giroir had predicted, the securities business was making millionaires by the score. Friends of ours, slightly older friends, were now "Wal-Mart millionaires." They had bought stock in the initial public offering in the early 1970s and had watched it split and split and split again. Similar stories were being acted out in the 1980s, only faster. Dillard, Tyson Foods, Systematics, Alltel— those were just the best known of the hot Arkansas properties that were making smart people rich. Inflation was raging and so were interest rates—which was great if you were on the right side of them, which I wasn't. Our firm's securities and tax lawyers were working sixteen-hour days, seven-day weeks just to keep up with all the limited partnerships being formed. People were buying investments for the losses just to shield other income. Me, I had the losses without the income.

The scent of money had brought forward all sorts of troublingly colorful characters, including one whom the Rose Law Firm had represented in 1981. His name was Jim McDougal and the case involved a bank McDougal bought in the little northwest Arkansas town of Kingston.

Many people have asked, How could the reputable Rose firm get involved with a character like Jim McDougal. The answer is, in 1981, Jim McDougal didn't look like Daddy Warbucks. Back then he was known simply as a former aide to Senator J. William Fulbright in whose employ he had met the younger Bill Clinton, an erstwhile college political science professor, a man who had run for and come reasonably close to winning the congressional seat of John Paul Hammerschmidt. As the world knows now, prior to McDougal's becoming a banker and prior to Bill Clinton's becoming governor, the two men and their wives had bought a parcel of land together with an eye toward developing it and selling off the lots. This was the property now known as Whitewater.

The McDougals and the Clintons bought that land in 1977, when Bill was attorney general. For now, however, that fact is just background. Bear it in mind as you hear the rest of the tale.

In 1981, McDougal and two partners (Steve Smith, a first-term aide to Governor Clinton, and Jim Guy Tucker, soon to be in fierce competition with Clinton for the governorship) bought the little Bank of Kingston from people who also owned a bank in another hamlet—Huntsville—in the same county. Though he had signed an agreement not to install a branch of the Kingston bank in Huntsville, McDougal promptly tried to do exactly that. The Bank of Huntsville sued McDougal and his two partners. Jim Guy wanted the Wright firm to represent them, but Joe Giroir's reputation in banking and finance circles was such that he was seen as the best possibility of winning. In addition, Joe was offering the meticulous and well-regarded Vince Foster to handle the litigation.

Despite all the Rose firm's expertise, we lost the case. And if that wasn't enough of an injury to Vince, McDougal and his wife, Susan, refused to pay the remaining $5,000 of the legal fee. I heard about this mostly from Vince—from whose allocation the unpaid fee was deducted.

By 1984, Vince had become thoroughly disgusted with McDougal. He found him symbolic of how the world had changed. Here you had Vince Foster, who tried to be upstanding in all things, and who spent his personal time working for the Arkansas Bar Association and the Arkansas Repertory Theater; then, increasingly, you had slick operators like Jim McDougal trying to cut corners and line their pockets any way they could— and to hell with the ethics. Vince was appalled at the blatant lust for money reflected inside the firm and out. It bothered him that the new associates coming along didn't seem to care for community work, or even for the grand tradition that the Rose firm once stood for. Following the times, the new associates had become lawyers so they could get rich. I listened to Vince rail, and I understood and agreed with his point. I, too, found the new atmosphere of the Rose firm distasteful. I also wished I could make more money.

My father-in-law was another subject I obsessed about in the wee hours at Sea Island. In 1980 he had sold the Datsun dealership. People often said of Seth that his instinct for when to sell was even more golden than his hunch for when to buy. The man who bought the dealership declared bankruptcy the very next year. In 1981, Seth had bought a company called Park-O-Meter, widely known as POM. As usual, I did the legal work for him. Most people don't know that Arkansas is the world capital for manufacturing parking meters, with POM and Duncan being the two largest. POM was located in Russellville, about ninety miles from Little Rock. Seth thought this would be a good business venture for Skeeter to run. Skeeter, in turn, saw it as a chance to get out from under Seth's thumb. More and more Skeeter stayed in Russellville and discouraged Seth from coming up. The effect on me was that Seth wasn't busy enough, so he called me constantly. He also demanded that I be at his house when Skeeter came to make his weekly reports, which tended to be overwhelmingly positive. "Everything's going great in Russellville; no need to come up," Skeeter said. I had a vague worry that the main thing going great was Seth's absence in Skeeter's daily life. Of course, I supposed that was worth a lie or two.

Such were my thoughts over my last couple of beach days, and they intensified as we zoomed along the interstate getting closer and closer to home. When we walked in the door of Hubbell's Folly, there was a message waiting for me labeled "urgent." It said to call the Governor's Mansion immediately.

I did and Hillary answered. "Where have you *been*?" she said. I started to explain but she cut me off. She said that State Supreme Court Justice Bob Dudley—the judge from Pocahontas who brought inns of court to Little Rock, and who was by now a good friend of mine—had called the governor and reported that the chief justice was planning to step down before the next session, which began in two weeks. Many times I had mentioned to both Hillary and Bill that I thought a judge's bench would be the perfect spot for my temperament. They agreed, and that's why Bill was looking for me. He wanted me to serve out the remaining four months of the chief justice's term. "If you want it, you better call Bill fast," Hillary said.

I got off the phone and told Suzy. So many decisions would have to be made—I would have to resign from the firm. I would have to resign from the city board. I would have to cloister myself in my chambers and read and write all day. The court was in disarray, the justices fighting among themselves. I would have to bring all my skills of conciliation to bear.

"Take it," Suzy said. "You've always wanted to be a judge."

I called the governor's office and was put through to him right away. He said the same thing Hillary did. "Where've you been, Hub?" After I explained what had happened, he asked if I wanted the position. I told him I did, and he said there were a few hoops he had to go through to get me ready for nomination—mainly, he needed to have me "rated" by the Arkansas Bar Association so this wouldn't come up in the fall campaign looking like he'd simply named an unqualified crony to the state's top bench. The rating was finished by the weekend, and I was set to go.

My parents were thrilled when I called and told them the news. *Chief justice of the Arkansas Supreme Court—at age thirty-six.* My father finally thought I might have done the right thing to leave the phone company.

The response from my partners was predictably mixed—from the total support of Gaston Williamson all the way across the spectrum. "Congratulations, Webb," Gaston said. "You'll do a great job."

"Well, we finally got you off the city board," said another colleague. "I hope this'll get politics out of your system for good."

"When are you going to settle down and be a real lawyer?" another asked.

And then came the one that stung the most. "I'm pleased for you, Webb. But can you afford it?"

I couldn't afford *not* to do it. The sense of freedom I suddenly felt made me giddy. As for my clients, all but one were generous in their praise and well-wishing. Seth Ward said, "Who's going to take care of my work while you're gone?"

My daughter Caroline wrote me a letter after my life came unraveled. She told me that I was at my best during the brief period when I was a judge. "And our family was at its best, too."

I dearly loved those four too-short months. My life changed overnight. From the constant jangle of telephones and the endless round of business breakfasts, power lunches, cocktail receptions, and city meetings, I had retired to a monastery. My phone didn't ring for the first week. I walked across the street to a hospital cafeteria for lunch. Then I came back and spent the afternoon as I had spent the morning—reading and writing and thinking. I presided over a couple of meetings a week—one on Monday and one on Friday. The rest of the time I was alone with my thoughts. Finally, I had found the Law that I had hoped for in school.

I could write any number of pages describing those four months—such was my love for what I was doing. Never before or since was I happier personally or professionally. I felt smart, successful, and pure. I helped bring a discordant court together again. When I got there, the justices were hardly speaking to one another. I instituted weekly lunches, and gradually the walls came down. There's nothing like good barbecue to heal wounds.

My days were busy, but I still had time to know myself. I didn't have to fall back on simple advocacy the way I did at the Rose firm. I wrote opinions on such vital issues as capital punishment and its constitutionality, which I upheld. (Unlike my friends Bill and Hillary, I was personally against it.) I also had to prepare the budget for the next two years, and since I wouldn't benefit from it, I could be aggressive in trying to bring Arkansas judicial salaries in line with those in our neighboring states. At night I got to spend time with my family. I sang my children to sleep. I became reacquainted with my wife. I didn't drink as much. In essence, what I had was a much-needed sabbatical.

But as fall gave way to winter, I began to feel the old worries. Suzy and I talked about my not going back to the firm, but I didn't know what else to do. My finances were such that I couldn't afford to go out on my own. Maybe later, I thought. Maybe now that I'm out of public office, I can make enough money to leave. It was a comforting thought.

Once I was back at Rose, though, I had a hard time retaining the hope. I missed my quiet, dignified days on the court. My old college friend and early-morning walking companion William Ketcher says he has one overriding memory of me during that reentry period. On a crisp winter morning as the sun rose over the Country Club of Little Rock, I told him I was desperate to escape to a different life. But I didn't know how.

6

The Mouse
That Roared

If I had to choose one perfect image of Arkansas in the mid-1980s, I would choose the bridge crane. Those are the huge L-shaped machines that you see on the tops of buildings-in-progress in booming cities. The cranes came in flocks back then. They loomed over the Little Rock skyline like giant waterbirds in a marsh. In fact, they built up that skyline the way birds build nests—hoisting up a sprig of steel, tucking in a ton of stone. To those of us on the ground, their precarious high perch came to seem almost natural.

In the 1970s, the three major Little Rock banks—Worthen, Union, and First Commercial—had raced to erect signature skyscrapers. But by the 1980s, the banks' asset bases had been overtaken by the growth of the major savings and loans. First Federal, Savers Federal, and First South enjoyed tremendous competitive advantage over their banking cousins. By law, S and Ls could have branches in every city, while a bank could only have branches in the city of its main bank. Also, in most cases the thrifts weren't subject to Arkansas's onerous usury lending cap, which restricted lending at any interest rate over 10 percent. When interest rates soared, as they did back then, banks were all but taken out of the lending game. In order to lend money, banks have to attract deposits. But depositors shunned Arkansas banks because they couldn't make money on their money. S and Ls could make loans at the prevailing rates, so depositors flocked to them. Probably most important, the regulatory oversight was limited. If anything, the regulators were encouraging S and Ls in Arkansas and other states to grow, grow, grow. The major thrifts would each brag of asset bases surpassing one billion dollars. So this time when the bridge cranes came, they perched upon the rising profiles of the savings and loans.

Wherever I traveled in those years, lawyer friends would pass on the good wishes of someone from one of my state's major thrifts. "They're lending thirty million for a development in . . ." Take your pick: New Orleans, Dallas, Houston, Los Angeles. Arkansas S and Ls were players in what we called the boom-boom days, financing real estate growth to "shelter" income against taxes. The term *tax shelter*—more often reduced to just *shelter*—took on a life of its own. Real estate agents suddenly sold each and every project as a *shelter*. At cocktail parties, doctors and lawyers and bankers mouthed the word *shelter* between sips of Scotch.

These murmurings weren't lost on old Jim McDougal, still up in northwest Arkansas trying to make a go in the banking business. He must have felt out of the game up there. Little Rock was where the action was. So McDougal bought a little S and L in the rural northwest Arkansas county of Madison, and, taking advantage of the favorable S and L laws, proceeded to move to Little Rock where he would open a *branch* of the little Madison S and L. The branch is now known to all as Madison Guaranty Savings and Loan.

In light of the notoriety that Madison Guaranty has attained in recent years, it's difficult for me to place that little thrift in the proper perspective of the time. I'm reminded of that wonderful Peter Sellers movie *The Mouse That Roared,* about a tiny principality that declared war on the United States in hopes of being defeated and thus enjoying the benefits of reparation. While the major S and Ls operated from their towers in the downtown business district, Jim McDougal's Madison Guaranty was established in a former laundry on Main Street, but fifteen blocks south, over the expressway—out, literally, of the loop. It was in an area called the Quapaw Quarter, where the sprawling (and decaying) Victorian mansions of the city's first leaders were now being brought back to life by young couples looking for space and character without high prices. Madison lent money for renovations on these historic houses, and in so doing derived a reputation for community service. Otherwise, it was known as an aggressive but specialized savings and loan, focusing on the low end of the lending market—mobile home lots, small tract housing, small office buildings, and so on.

It was also known for Susan McDougal's television commercials. Madison had backed a housing development called Maple Creek Farms, whose TV ads featured Susan, in tight jeans and a plaid shirt that highlighted her ample bosom, riding up on a horse. It was one of those local television ads that every market airs—one everybody knows and chuckles at for one reason or another. Either because it's especially corny, or funny, or, in this case, because Susan cut a pretty arresting figure atop that horse. I doubt these ads did much to enhance Madison's reputation as a serious business. Madison was just not thought of as a big deal.

While I was serving on the Arkansas Supreme Court in the fall of 1984, McDougal finally paid the $5,000 he owed the Rose firm. He then retained Rose at $2,000 a month to help with his development work. We weren't a retainer firm, and maybe this was an arrangement worked out because of his problem with the previous fee. Rick Massey, a Rose associate, had been lobbying within the firm for us to do business with Madison. But as an associate Rick wasn't eligible to be the account's billing partner. The billing partner is the one who determines how the fee is allocated within the firm. To my knowledge, nobody at the firm knew then that Hillary was in any personal deal with Jim McDougal. She just seemed to know him, apparently through Bill. That's my guess as to how she got involved: Rick wanted to bring in Madison work, and he couldn't be the billing partner; Hillary knew McDougal so the business went in her name.

Many years later, sitting in prison watching Rick Massey telling a television interviewer that he didn't know how the Madison business came to the firm, I was really amazed at his memory loss. Especially since Rick had explained it all to Vince and me in 1993, when Jeff Gerth of *The New York Times* first started questioning us about Rose, Madison, and Hillary.

In hindsight, it was a bad idea to get involved with McDougal again. We already had had one bad experience with him. People have asked me, Who was watching the shop? I can tell you that by then, the Rose firm was mainly watching dollars. Our older partners had retired or slowed down, and we now had a stable of young partners and associates hungry to get in on the boom. I call it the "bridge-crane mentality." It was rampant at Rose in the mid-1980s.

My personal experience with the McDougals was very limited. Once, Susan made a run for one of the seven city board seats, and I endured a lot of kidding from my friends about maybe sitting next to the woman in the tight jeans and plaid shirt. Suzy wasn't amused, and was happy when Susan lost in the election. My other McDougal experience occurred when I attended a cocktail party at the Country Club of Little Rock hosted by Jim McDougal, Sheffield Nelson, and Jerry Jones, the current owner of the Dallas Cowboys. The purpose of the party was to convince the city's swells that the greatest investment opportunity in America was this trio's development of Campobello Island, the former vacation retreat of Franklin Delano Roosevelt. The hors d'oeuvres were good and the drinks were plentiful, and McDougal was all he had been warranted to be—slick, flamboyant, and entertaining. But there emanated from him the cheap scent of hucksterism. I didn't buy a Campobello lot. For the life of me, I couldn't figure out how I could justify a weekend home in Maine.

My partners and friends, however, were snapping up such deals—if not in Maine, then closer to Arkansas. It was a time when debt was said to be smart. You could make payments on the interest and deduct it from your taxes. Plus, you could write off the depreciation of whatever it was you had bought. At every party Suzy and I went to, people were telling about their new homes, second homes, new additions, new cars, elaborate vacations. Somebody somewhere had turned a spigot, and money was flowing like champagne. At the Rose Law Firm, one of the major beneficiaries of this financial frenzy, securities and tax lawyers worked literally around the clock to put together the latest deals.

Joe Giroir was even buying banks. While the thrifts thrived, Arkansas banks were just trying to keep up. But many fine legal minds were focused on ways of getting around the banking regulations and the usury law. For example, an Arkansas banker and borrower might fly with their attorney to Dallas for a closing—that way, they could get around the Arkansas 10 percent lending restriction. Another ingenious trick was the bank holding company. A single bank couldn't own branches in other towns. But with the flick of a fountain pen, attorneys could form a holding company. The holding company could own banks in many different places.

Within the Rose firm, it was assumed that Joe had some kind of deal with Worthen—he would buy up individual banks, and eventually Worthen would buy them from him. He borrowed from his profit sharing fund to buy his first bank, in Conway, thirty miles from Little Rock. Then he bought a bank in Harrison, in the northernmost part of the state. After that came the National Bank of Commerce in Pine Bluff, an hour south of Little Rock. Finally, he again looked north to acquire the First National Bank of Fayetteville.

All of this was very impressive, even for someone known as a risk taker. Joe seemed to have some internal map to the pot of gold. Naturally, that made some people jealous. Behind closed doors you heard murmurings about Joe's bank buying. There was some speculation that he was getting in over his head, or that he was becoming a banker instead of an attorney. But nobody ever approached Joe and said, "Hey, how are you paying for this?" One reason is that Joe's bank purchases brought business to the firm. Our bank lawyers did the paperwork. "I guess Joe knows what he's doing," everybody said.

Meanwhile, the firm didn't exactly know what *it* was doing. We now had more than thirty partners and associates, and we were beginning to step on one another's toes. The morning meetings were now weekly, and we no longer had the time to go around the table probing for conflicts. Instead, we circulated a daily newsletter reporting the new business for every day. Partners were supposed to scan the newsletter for possible conflicts. But now we were often discovering them after the fact. More than once, one Rose lawyer turned out to be suing another Rose lawyer's client.

Obviously, we had problems in the short term—but we were extending them into the future as well. We were taking on more associates, but there was no formal training for them. They were just given a desk and a chair and put to work. Vince, especially, thought that was dangerous. For one thing, he had had Phil Carroll as a mentor, just as he had been Hillary's mentor. Vince felt it was important for older hands to pass along their wisdom. Also, he thought it crucial that Rose's rich history be taught to the new recruits. He seemed to have a sense that the firm's soul was seeping away.

Our "management structure" was largely nonexistent. For the past seven years, Joe Giroir had held on to the title of chairman, but that was essentially an honorific. The day-to-day business was supposedly handled by a seven-member "Executive Committee," which met to deal with such administrative questions as which copy machine we would buy. Even that committee had no real power, though, since the firm's deep-rooted sense of democracy made each partner bristle at the thought of being told what to do. Democracy was anarchy at Rose.

When I came back after my supreme court stint, I was appointed to the Executive Committee. I also assumed responsibility for dealing with our firm's malpractice insurance carriers. So far, there had been no malpractice to speak of at the prestigious and upstanding Rose Law Firm. I thought of this post as a kind of purgatory, symbolic in some way of my life as a whole. I was miserable—bored, tired, scared, confused. I was thirty-seven years old and drifting. Occasionally, Hillary caught me with my mask down, and she'd say, "Are you okay?" I would smile and say, "Fine." Of course, she knew my father-in-law well by this point, having served as attorney for the Airport Commission for five years. Sometimes I mentioned that Seth and Skeeter were driving me crazy. I was being asked on a daily basis to "stop by for a drink" and listen to my father-in-law and brother-in-law talk about POM. Seth wanted to hear good news, and Skeeter wasn't about to disappoint him.

Seth and Skeeter were an acceptable part of my problems to discuss. But I never mentioned my financial worries to Hillary or Vince.

While the firm was trying to find structure and stability, Joe Giroir set in motion a chain of events that would soon test both of those qualities to the absolute limit. After Joe bought the Fayetteville bank, he announced at one of our meetings that the firm was about to receive a big piece of new business. Joe and some partners planned to take over—hostilely, if need be—one of the major Little Rock banks. They weren't sure which one. We all listened in awe as Joe informed us that his partners were the Stephens investment group, and some friends of Stephens who were even richer than Stephens—the Lippo Group from Indonesia, headed by a man named Mochtar Riady and his young son, James. The Riadys had brought in another Indonesian, a Mr. Salim. I never heard him referred to as anything but "Mr. Lim."

The foursome's first target turned out to be Commercial Bank, a locally owned institution headed by a steely ex-military pilot named Bill Bowen. Joe's group entered into discussions with Bowen, who wasn't at all happy about having his bank taken over. Joe and his team were coldly persistent. They gave Bowen a deadline. But at the last minute, Bowen outfoxed them. In the middle of the night, he engineered a merger with First National Bank, creating a new and stronger entity called First Commercial Bank. Joe and his partners had to look elsewhere.

They didn't look far. A major block of Worthen Bank, one of Joe's prime clients, had been owned by a Texan who had intended to hold on to his stock. Then the oil and gas business in Texas went bad, and the man needed cash. He sold his Worthen shares to Joe's group. Joe traded his own banks for Worthen stock. Suddenly our partner Joe Giroir was a major stockholder in the city's major bank. He took a place on the board of directors, along with a Stephens representative. Incurring the wrath of the old Little Rock establishment, the board promptly named as one of the bank's two presidents the twenty-nine-year-old James Riady.

As one of Worthen's lawyers, I first met James when I was in the bank's executive offices. From time to time I would run into him there or stop in and say hello. He seemed like a nice young man. On occasion, I would hear grumbling that his father had put him in the position of bank president for "face"—the Oriental concern with status.

The summer of my discontent was 1985—the year I decided to run for the U.S. Senate. As a Republican.

In hindsight, I can see that this was evidence of a psyche in an advanced state of disrepair. My opponent was to be none other than Senator Dale Bumpers, one of the state's most loved officials. I knew Dale Bumpers personally. Not only did I admire his politics, I admired him as a man. But again my ego, combined with my desperation, conspired to get the best of me.

It started when a couple of old friends invited me to lunch. One of them was Charlie Owen, my former Rose law partner and by then CEO of the Arkansas Rockefeller family businesses. The other was William Ketcher, my college teammate and early-morning walking companion. Ronald Reagan had just been re-elected, and some people believed that it was the Republicans' time. William and Charlie had gone so far as to attend a seminar about running a successful campaign. As I write this, it sounds very nearly like a bunch of bored kids saying, "Hey, let's put on a play!"

But they were serious. Over lunch they reminded me that I'd been extraordinarily successful as mayor and as chief justice, and they knew I was looking for another opportunity. Some people— *many* people, they said—believed Senator Bumpers was vulnerable. And those same people thought I would be just the man to take up the mantle.

I loved this conversation, of course. After months of feeling hopeless, here were the strokes I needed. I told them I was flattered, and that I would certainly consider it. They promptly lined me up for a campaign seminar in Atlanta, for conversations with former Governor Frank White, and for meetings with other state GOP bigwigs such as Asa Hutchinson.

Then the press got wind of the story. My phone rang and it was Hillary. "What are you *doing*?" she practically screamed. She had no problem with my running for the Senate, she explained, "but don't do it as a Republican." She told me Bill was going to call to invite me for golf. "Listen to him," she said.

As we teed up, he got right to the point. "How did this happen?" he asked. I explained how much I had enjoyed my public service, and how—even though my head might be getting a size too big—I was nevertheless seriously thinking about running. Over the next few holes, he gave me a lesson in national politics.

"The days of Win Rockefeller and Jacob Javits are dying in the Republican party," he said, watching his ball bounce in the distance. "Politics is going to get uglier and uglier. And when Reagan is gone, the Republicans will be pushed further and further to the right." I drove the cart, as usual. He talked as we rode, and on this day he didn't seem to care how well he swung the clubs. He had a bigger game in mind. His friend had strayed deep into the rough, and Bill Clinton's job was to help land him back on the fairway.

He explained how important it was for fiscally conservative but socially progressive people to stick with the Democrats. Never once did he say, "Don't do it." But he told me he planned to run for President of the United States someday. If I were a Republican, he said wistfully, I couldn't help him pull that off.

By the eighteenth hole, I told him I'd made a decision—I wasn't going to run. He was relieved, I could tell. As we tallied our scores, it turned out I'd had a much better round than he had. "Hubbell," he said—beginning a joke that would go on for many, many years—"you're already playing golf like a Republican."

I had cast my lot with Bill Clinton. But many years later, after we came to Washington, this episode surfaced once again. During my confirmation hearings for associate attorney general, Senator Strom Thurmond cleared his throat and said, "Mr. Hubbell, I understand you once considered running for the Senate as a Republican."

"Yes, Senator," I replied, "it was my one moment of insanity." The entire committee room broke into laughter.

Less amusing was my experience with Seth that very same summer. The heat must have gotten to him, because he went into business with Jim McDougal.

Seth had gotten bored with POM. He needed something else to fill his time. As it turned out, an old friend of his, Don Denton, was now the senior loan officer at Madison Guaranty Savings and Loan. Occasionally they would get together for drinks after work, and I'm sure Seth told Don that he was looking for new business ventures. An item of interest to Don was that Seth—and also Skeeter—had gotten real estate licenses between the time Seth sold Ward Datsun and his purchase of POM. Everybody else was making a fortune in real estate, so Seth and Skeeter thought they could, too.

I would hear all of this only through Seth. One night as we were sitting on his back porch overlooking the beautiful Arkansas River, he told me he'd been offered a great new opportunity. Don Denton had introduced him to Madison's Jim McDougal as "a responsible businessman with a nose for good deals." Seth was very pleased with the description.

Seth and McDougal were like googly-eyed contestants on *The Dating Game*. As different as they were—Seth the ex-Marine, Republican businessman, and Bill-Clinton-hater, and Jim the former Senator J. William Fulbright aide who was still a friend of Clinton—they each immediately saw something seductive in the other. Jim offered Seth a nominal salary to "locate and help bring to Madison various real estate deals." The salary—$35,000—Seth described as "a little gin rummy money." Before long, Seth had set up an office in Madison's ex-laundry building on South Main Street. He even bought a foreclosed red Mercedes coupe from Madison, and made sure he had a letter from McDougal saying that "because of your position with Madison, you should be driving a luxury automobile." Seth figured this would allow him to write off the car.

Before long, Seth brought a parcel of land to Jim McDougal. Without venturing too deeply into Little Rock's ancient past, I have to ask you to flash back for a moment to the 1960s. A couple of local businessmen had convinced several banks to advance them the money for a parcel of land in far southwest Little Rock. They told the banks that they wanted to develop the property and bring industry into the state. For twenty years they paid on the interest but not the principal. I knew about the parcel because the Levi Strauss factory had taken part of it. When I was mayor, this site was shown to every prospective commercial developer.

By the mid-1980s, however, the banks were tired of carrying the note. One bank—Worthen—had talked with one of my Rose colleagues about starting foreclosure proceedings. Seth, who had contacts at another of the lenders, Union Bank, had no doubt heard the same rumblings. The piece of land was known as the Industrial Development Company property, or IDC. Seth called it to Jim McDougal's attention. He thought it would be a perfect property to parcel out for sale.

The owners of the property valued it at $3 million. That was too expensive for McDougal. His S and L didn't have enough assets to take that kind of chance. Seth received that news like a bird dog on point. He was determined to wear down the own-ers—to track them and stalk them and hound them into submission. When he had gotten the purchase price down to $1.75 million, he carried the deal back to McDougal. I don't know how they decided to go to the Rose firm to do the contracts, but I can imagine that McDougal said, I'm paying the Rose firm a $2,000 retainer, and they aren't doing much for me. Let's use them.

What I remember most vividly about all that was something Seth's wife, Vonnie, said one night in their kitchen as we were all getting ready to eat dinner. Vonnie didn't like what she knew of Jim McDougal. She was bothered by Susan's sexy TV ads. She tried to tell Seth that he really shouldn't get involved with a man like McDougal. "Remember, Seth," she said, "if you lie down with dogs, you get up with fleas."

*   *   *

Actually, the Rose firm *was* busy on Madison's behalf that summer. Madison had informed the firm that it was considering two new developments—a public offering to raise capital, and establishment of a broker-dealer operation within the thrift. Each required the approval of the Arkansas Securities Commission.

Rick Massey, the associate who had sought the Madison business, wrote several letters to Securities Commissioner Beverly Bassett, submitting Madison's requests for approval of their proposals. Curiously, Bassett answered Massey's request by writing directly to Hillary. Bassett eventually approved Massey's requests, even though people were beginning to question the financial soundness of Madison.

No one involved could have predicted that a decade later analysis of this detail would launch a multimillion-dollar industry. The investigation began in 1993 after Jeff Gerth implied early in the campaign that Bassett wrote to Hillary because Hillary was putting pressure on her husband's appointee—Bassett. Beverly Bassett has denied this repeatedly. She denied it in a twenty-page letter to Gerth. It didn't sway him, because he went ahead and wrote his article.

While that was going on, Seth and Jim McDougal made a change in their IDC land deal. Like everyone else who has tried to figure out why Whitewater and Madison are such a big deal, I've read numerous books and regulatory reports on the subject. So it's difficult to give you my perspective at the time without its being tempered by everyone else's recitation of the facts and the conclusions that they draw. But as I recall, Madison was initially to buy the whole parcel. Then Seth and Madison became partners in the deal. Madison came up with $900,000 of the purchase price in its name. Seth took out a loan—from Madison—for $850,000. Seth then had a letter of agreement with McDougal, whereby he would receive a commission of 10 percent on his sales of tracts from the entire property.

Ten years later, Congress questioned whether Seth was a straw man—a stand-in for Madison—because his loan was a nonrecourse loan and his deal provided that he receive commissions on the sale of parcels that both Seth and Madison owned. The Rose firm's commercial banking lawyers closed the transaction for both Seth and Madison. So, at the time, I thought they were in good hands with our commercial banking team.

In 1995, Congress also questioned me about why, when the deal came to the firm in August 1985, the file was opened with my name as billing partner and then later was changed to Hillary's. How, the congressmen asked, did this happen? I don't know. The first I heard of it was in 1995. I can only imagine that it happened this way: As part of our new record-keeping efforts, we now had a "client matter form," one of which was filled out for every piece of new business. A secretary saw Seth Ward's name and assumed his son-in-law would handle the work. When it was clear that this was Madison business, the form was changed to reflect Hillary as the billing partner.

By that winter, Madison had made a couple of major sales from the IDC property. One of the tracts had been bought by Senator J. William Fulbright. The other, a parcel that included an independent sewer and water company, was sold to Jim Guy Tucker. This tract would become known as Castle Grande. Both deals were financed by Madison.

By the spring of 1986, Seth had commission sheets showing that McDougal owed him $300,000. He was beside himself. After I'd heard about his financial brilliance for weeks on end, one night over drinks I asked him a simple question: "Have you gotten your commission yet?"

The days were getting longer, and there was still a mottling of pink and blue in the sky. I could see Seth's face. "Soon," he said. But I thought I detected a hint of uncertainty in his eyes.

The firm still hadn't found its footing, and so in early 1986 we came up with a new plan—we would fire our professional manager and make one partner the chief operating officer. It would be a salaried position, and the partner wouldn't be expected to bill very much. I seemed to fit the job description perfectly. I had run the Little Rock City Board and the Arkansas Supreme Court, and my billing was still dismal as a result. I welcomed the $60,000 guaranteed salary to go with my $60,000 bonus at the end of the year. I hoped I could improve on that with a few new clients.

One Monday morning in April 1986, I was called out of a meeting and summoned to the conference room "to answer a quick question." When I got there, I found Joe Giroir and other partners looking ashen, as though they had just been told of a death in the family. They quickly filled me in. Our major client, Worthen Bank, had been investing its own and a customer's funds in short-term debt instruments called "repos." Properly collateralized, these are a very safe way of earning interest on your money. Worthen's customer in this case was the state of Arkansas. For several months, the bank's securities department had been investing the state's money with a New Jersey brokerage house called Bevill, Bresler and Schulman (BBS). Over the weekend, BBS had filed for bankruptcy protection. In limbo was $52 million that Worthen had invested on behalf of the state.

Some parts of the situation were immediately clear. First, if Worthen were to go under because of this, it would affect the Rose firm tremendously (not to mention the city itself). Second, Joe Giroir was the palest person in the room for a very good reason—he was one of the bank's major stockholders. Joe told me one of our attorneys, Allen Bird, was on his way to New Jersey to find out what he could. The question I had been called in to answer involved a unique insurance policy the bank maintained that was a potential source of recovery of $20 million of the invested funds. I was asked to evaluate the policy and advise whether I thought we could recover on it. As we discussed this, I began to feel a hysteria building in the room.

That Monday morning interruption introduced a full week of round-the-clock meetings and conference calls. I won't take you through it blow by blow, because that really isn't important to this story. Later that first afternoon, I was able to advise that I thought we could collect the $20 million. The Stephens group agreed to advance the bank $32 million, against a rights offering of new stock. That meant that for every share of Worthen you owned, you could buy another share at a lower rate. The Stephens family, the Riadys, and Joe Giroir agreed to fund any shortfall in the offering by buying any unexercised rights. Thus the bank was made whole, the state of Arkansas didn't lose its money, and a major financial disaster was averted. Some bank executives (not James Riady) were blamed and were asked to leave. Stephens then placed one of its own, Curt Bradbury, in the bank to watch over its interests. Bradbury ultimately became president and chairman.

But the importance of the BBS disaster was that it was a wake-up call—to a lot of people. Bradbury, for one, soon found that the problem at Worthen wasn't the investment in BBS's repos (though the person in charge should have made sure they were secured repos; they were not). The more insidious problem at Worthen was that it was engaging in some of the lending practices that were beginning to be exposed throughout the Southwest. As oil prices plummeted, interest rates and inflation were easing, and the 1986 Tax Reform Act (disallowing the deductions that had made "shelters" and "debt" such watchwords) took hold, it was clear that Worthen had a long road to recovery. The bank's stock fell from the 40s to around 4.

In Little Rock, that April morning was pretty much the beginning of the end of the 1980s. The most jarring wake-up call had to be to Joe Giroir. I'm sure the Stephenses and the Riadys hated losing so much money, but they had plenty of other resources. For Joe, his Worthen stock represented his only major asset. Joe didn't let on what pressure he was under, and the firm went on to have a tremendously profitable year. For me—since I spent much of the next six months working with the insurance carrier, with whom I'd negotiated rights to a percentage of the money recovered from the BBS bankruptcy—it was my best year yet. I couldn't *wait* until the January distribution. Finally, I thought, my finances might be turning around. For once in a long while, I was glad to have my money problems and not Joe Giroir's.

In the spring of 1986, the Federal Savings and Loan Insurance Corporation (FSLIC) was taking over more thrifts and needed lawyers. They called Vince. Thanks to him, we had a good relationship with FSLIC, based on his work in their takeover of Guaranty Savings and Loan of Harrison, Arkansas, the first major thrift to fall to the regulators. The one condition of this new and potentially lucrative work for FSLIC was that we couldn't represent any savings and loans. We were given a potential list of conflicts, which we thought we could work through. In staff meetings, we spent many hours trying to decide who would handle the work. Vince wanted Hillary on the team, but Madison presented a clear conflict. Hillary felt she couldn't prevent Vince from taking on such lucrative business just so she could keep our tiny involvement with Madison. The monthly retainers were just building up in our client trust fund. Hillary wrote Madison a note ending Rose's representation of the thrift and sent along a firm check for the unused $14,000 balance of the retainer.

In the Whitewater saga, that episode plays differently. Here's the Whitewater version: Within the same week, Beverly Bassett was in a meeting with Madison and heard the thrift was going into receivership. She called the governor's office and told someone that since Bill knew McDougal, she thought he might want to know about this development with Madison. Then, in the tortured logic of the conspiracy theorists, Bill told Hillary and she immediately sent back the retainer. This is seen as Bill Clinton taking care of his buddy Jim McDougal.

As we surveyed our possible FSLIC conflicts, Joe disclosed that he had a loan at First South in connection with his ownership of Worthen. Since Joe's First South loan didn't show up on the "troubled loan" sheet that FSLIC sent out to prospective law firms, we felt that wasn't a problem. At the Rose firm we made it a point not to press our partners too hard on their personal finances, so we didn't press Joe on his First South loan. In fact, he was being promised that whatever "his deal" was, it would be worked out prior to any takeover. No other partners spoke up about conflicts. Vince's only potential problem was that his brother-in-law, Lee Bowman, was president of a First South subsidiary. But Lee was taking steps to rid himself of that conflict. We felt we were a shoo-in for this business.

Near the end of the year, though, the Rose firm was passed over. Vince guessed it was because of his brother-in-law's position, which he fully understood. He assured us that other FSLIC work was waiting in the wings.

*   *   *

That Christmas, our traditions seemed all the sweeter to me. Vince and I ambled over to the courthouse for cheer with the clerks, secretaries, and other lawyers. The governor and I confirmed that we were on again for our last-minute gift-buying spree. At Hubbell's Folly, we bought an especially huge tree, one that reached almost to the ceiling. The blinking lights made magic in our room. I remember sitting alone by the tree late one night before Christmas, basking in the love I felt for my family. I hadn't been fair to them, I felt. I'd been gone too much. I'd spent too much time with city business, law firm business, community business. But I would make it up to them on Christmas morning, I told myself. I toasted that thought with another glass of wine.

We had long settled into a strict holiday routine. On Christmas Eve, we went to my parents' house. It was a small house, and in some ways I felt too big for it. But the children loved my mother and father. My dad pulled up in our driveway every Saturday morning of the year and honked his car horn, and if any of the kids came out he would take them to breakfast. If they didn't show, he went by himself. He was never offended. He just wanted them to go if they wanted to.

My mother made the children laugh. Hiding the remote control gun under her hand, she convinced Kelley that Kelley had special powers. Kelley would touch the TV screen and the TV would turn on. She would touch it again and the TV would go off. All of us tried hard not to let Kelley see us stifling our laughter with pillows.

But my parents didn't give the children many material things. Each child got one gift at Christmas. Being children, they expected more. To them, my parents paled next to the Wards' lavish giving. And I guess they paled in my mind, too. We would open our own gifts at home first thing Christmas morning. I always saved Suzy's special gift until last. Usually about the time she was opening that, the phone would ring and Vonnie would be on the line. "Seth wants to know where you are," she would say. We would then all rush to get over there, where Skeeter, Sally, and their families would already be waiting. Seth would be gruff with impatience. He could hardly wait for us to see what he had done for us this time.

The Wards' house looked like FAO Schwarz on Christmas morning. Anything anybody wanted, they got. It was overwhelming, but fun. We would have champagne and then a big breakfast. Later that evening, we would have a big turkey dinner. My children loved Seth's generosity, but winced on occasion at his idea of humor. "Better get to the buffet fast," he would announce to everyone. "Webb's coming." My beautiful Rebecca still remembers Seth's sting. "Rebecca," he said while the whole room listened, "everybody thinks you're an ugly duckling, but I always think of you as a swan." I don't think Seth knew that his humor also hurt.

At the firm, the Litigation Section also had a Christmas tradition. It had started the year Hillary joined. Back then there were only five of us, and since Rose had no general Christmas party, Vince and I decided we ought to have our own. We mentioned it to Phil, and he thought it was a good idea. On the Thursday before Christmas, I brought a nice bottle of brandy. At about 4 P.M., the Litigation Section repaired to the library.

As senior member, Phil consecrated the brandy by making hash marks on the side of the bottle, portioning it out according to seniority. An inch or so down from the top he marked a line for Hillary. An inch and a half below that, he marked one for Bill Kennedy. Then he marked off my portion, Vince's slightly larger portion, and then his own—the entire bottom third of the bottle. This was all in fun, of course. We filled our glasses and toasted one another. Then each of us was asked to tell one war story from the year just past.

We all loved this tradition, which became known as Brandyfest. We loved the camaraderie and loved the sharing of the stories. Litigators are good storytellers, and we each tried to regale the others with the funniest, most ironic, most absurd story we could come up with. Hillary, that first year, probably told the Barefoot Joe Giroir Interview story. When I was mayor, I told my Dead Dog Story. Over time, these stories became more than anecdotes.

It was as though we were a tribe reaffirming who we were by recounting our common myths.

Nineteen eighty-seven was the year most of us expected Bill Clinton to begin running for President. He had successfully reinvented himself as Boy Wonder, and in November 1986 he again beat Frank White to win the state's first four-year term as governor. In his inaugural speech, he presented a comprehensive set of initiatives for "Making Arkansas Work—Good Beginnings, Good Schools, and Good Jobs." Hard economic times and slumping tax revenues might once have suggested cutting back on education and human development spending, he said. "But that will not work today. In our highly integrated, highly competitive world economy, either we press ahead or we are pushed back. There is no status quo." It was a brilliant speech, delivered well. Time and again he was interrupted by applause.

With a four-year term, the pressure of getting reelected to the job of governor was lessened for a while. Now he could focus on the presidency. I felt that the next year might well be the most exciting of my life. Little did I know that the excitement would have nothing to do with Bill Clinton.

That same month I was in New York when I received a call from Vince. FSLIC wanted to talk to us immediately, he said, "about our firm's opinion."

"What opinion?" I said.

"I don't know. It has something to do with Joe's loans with First South." Vince told me I should come home right away. I caught the next plane out of La Guardia.

When I got home, Vince was livid. It turned out that Joe had a major loan with First South, as well as with a Dallas bank. For the regulators, the important issue was that our firm had acted as counsel to both Joe and First South and had rendered unqualified opinions on the transaction. In layman's terms, that means that Joe had our banking lawyers do the paperwork for his loan with First South. But for the entire month that Vince was holding meetings about getting the FSLIC work, not one of those attorneys had so much as mentioned their conflicting work on Joe's behalf.

Even worse were the opinions. The attorneys for this transaction were required to submit to the lender an opinion letter once a year, attesting that the situation hasn't changed and that they still believe the transaction to be acceptable. The Rose firm, despite representing the borrower and the lender, had been signing these ongoing opinion letters.

Vince and I were summoned to Washington to be lectured by FSLIC officials. On the plane, Vince was even less talkative than usual. We both felt angry, embarrassed, betrayed. The night before we met with the regulators, we had dinner with his sister and brother-in-law, Sheila and Congressman Beryl Anthony. Vince and Sheila had the kind of special brother-sister relationship that I have with my sister Terry. Sheila always brought a light to Vince's eyes.

The next morning we screwed up our courage and went to meet with the FSLIC. The people there said they had great respect for Vince, and because of that they'd asked us to come and hear what they had to say in person. They then outlined what they termed "a most serious claim" against our firm. Vince and I listened with our mouths open while they explained what our partners had done. Vince, after circulating a conflicts memo, had certified to FSLIC that the Rose firm had never represented First South. Now we learned we had. And the representation was on a major deal involving one of our partners.

When Joe bought the First National Bank of Fayetteville, he pledged money to the bank's stockholders. He secured that pledge with a letter of credit for $10 million from M Bank in Dallas. M Bank had been pledged assets from First South. Joe had paid First South a fee for use of collateral and pledged his Worthen stock to First South. When Worthen's value plummeted and First South went under, the whole house of cards came tumbling down.

Now FSLIC was at risk for the $10 million. The Rose firm had represented both Joe and First South, and had rendered follow-up opinions. Out of respect for Vince, the regulators were allowing us to notify our insurance carriers and quickly resolve this matter. It was unlikely that we were going to get any more FSLIC business, they said, and they were appalled at our bidding for the

First South business in light of this situation. But they accepted Vince's explanation (lame as it seemed) that none of our partners had told us about the conflicts.

Finally, they made it absolutely clear that if they had to sue us, they would.

Over the next few weeks, the Rose firm became a kind of hell. Vince, I finally figured out, was angry at himself for not having ferreted out the conflict from Joe's simple admission of a loan at First South. I think he felt like the scapegoat, the buffoon—like some kind of cosmic trick had been played on him. On the way home he told me he wanted to stay out of the firm's investigation of the facts. He still hoped to do more work for FSLIC, and if he got involved in negotiating a settlement, he might become more tainted than he already was.

Vince and I reported to the partners, and as chief operating officer I was given the task of hiring attorneys and notifying our carriers. Joe didn't make my job any easier. He maintained that he had done nothing wrong, and he seemed to feel personally under siege. We still weren't fully aware of the financial pressures on him, but every day more bad news leaked out from Worthen. The bank was beginning to seem like a big, old beached whale that was trying to get back in the water before it died.

As in a divorce, sides began forming. Some partners supported Joe. Others said they did to his face, but then criticized him behind his back. True to the rich history of the Rose Law Firm, very few were openly critical of him. Instead, the office became a hissing place of whispers. More than once I turned a corner to find two or three partners standing there awkwardly as though they hadn't been talking before I appeared. My role in this internal investigation made me the lightning rod for all of the anger, on every side.

Perhaps that was expressed most clearly in our annual allocation meeting that January, the meeting I'd been looking forward to because of all the fees I had collected for the firm from Worthen regarding my work on the Worthen insurance matter. My partners didn't want to pay me for those fees—they argued that since

I was collecting the COO salary, I wasn't *supposed* to be billing. It was a statement I never thought I would hear at the greed-fueled Rose firm. But they wanted all that money split among themselves. We finally negotiated a bonus, but I didn't get what I thought I was due.

Now I was seething, too. I had done everything I could to save the Worthen situation, and had been very successful at it. Nobody appreciated that. Maybe this was the cumulative effect of all my years of public service. I had long felt like an outcast at the Rose firm, but never like this.

Hillary, Vince, and I began meeting in her office almost daily. Hillary was angry, too. She had participated in several of Vince's phone calls to the FSLIC assuring them that we had no conflict. She felt betrayed. She also worried that a $10 million claim would finally put the oldest law firm west of the Mississippi out of business. Years later, she would tell me that the years 1987–88 were the two hardest years of her life—and that included the nasty year of the presidential campaign.

During those days I often thought about a Rose firm retreat that we'd had years before. We invited a psychologist to speak to the partners and their spouses. She gave us a questionnaire that ascribed points to certain life events, such as divorce, death in the family, change in income, financial pressures. I still had my chart from her visit, and now my score put me squarely in the category of "health risk." Anybody who understood my relationship to food and alcohol could have told that simply by looking at me. Empty inside, I was trying to fill myself. I weighed 295 pounds. *I* felt like the beached whale.

At the office I spent my days trying to get the lawyers on board and trying to get FSLIC's claim analyzed, in order to see if we could avoid a lawsuit. At every turn, it seemed, I ran afoul of one of the new factions that had been taking shape within the firm. To everybody, I was the messenger they wanted to kill. Vince and the commercial lawyers who had brought in more than a million dollars in fees from FSLIC were trying to salvage that relationship. Joe wanted to sue FSLIC. I remember one meeting at which one of the younger partners, Jerry Jones (not the Cowboys' owner), spoke up in Joe's defense. "I don't like the FSLIC; I don't like the FDIC. Why don't we stop representing the regulators altogether." At the time, it seemed like a stupid statement. In hindsight, it was one of the smartest things anybody said during the whole mess.

Eventually we and our insurance carriers settled with the FSLIC—for $3 million, $500,000 of which came out of the partners' pockets to pay the deductible on our insurance. Few people were happy. Joe didn't want to settle—he felt it made him look bad. Others thought we ought to get a better deal. I tried to explain that we risked a much greater amount by going to court— not to mention possibly having a jury declare our representation "fraudulent."

As word of this settlement trickled out into the community, other clients and business leaders began buttonholing various partners and asking how we could afford to keep Joe in the firm. Every news article about him identified him as "chairman of the Rose Law Firm." They said he was taking the firm's reputation down with him.

Though he tried to slip out of it, Vince was given the job of negotiating with Joe about relinquishing the chairman's title. That decision was made in one of our closed-door meetings in Hillary's office. Vince wanted, as always, to avoid the confrontation, but even Hillary was against him on this. "Vince, you have *got* to get involved," she said. We had surveyed the possible bearers of bad tidings, and there weren't all that many candidates. Hillary wasn't right, for so many reasons—the partners would have turned on her had she dared deliver the ultimatum. I had spearheaded the settlement of the claim. The job fell, by default, to Vince.

He went to Joe's office and they sat behind closed doors for hours. Joe wanted his protégé, Bill Kennedy, in attendance, so Vince agreed to that. Finally, Vince called me in. Joe was resisting giving up the chairman's title, he told me, unless I gave up the title of chief operating officer and Bill be named to the position of managing partner. I suppose Joe felt it wouldn't look like such a demotion if one of his own ascended as he stepped down. By this time Bill Kennedy had the respect of both the senior partners, like myself and older, and the burgeoning force of junior partners that had poured into the firm over the past five years. Although it wasn't spoken to my face, I was beginning to sense that the younger partners resented both Hillary and me as "not real lawyers" because of our outside work.

"What do you think?" Vince whispered as we conferred in the corner. I could tell from his eyes that this was the best he could do. I didn't really care about the title—at the Rose firm, we made up titles whenever the situation called for one. And I didn't mind giving up the headaches of managing the firm. According to this deal, I would still continue to handle malpractice matters.

"Okay," I said.

And with that a new regime took over the Rose Law Firm. Joe had engineered this turnover thinking he could trust Bill and his faction. But the scent of blood was too rich in the water.

My after-work musings with Seth continued, at his insistence. I had learned not to mention the commissions anymore. Through 1986, he still worked at Madison and had taken out a substantial loan there during that time. Then he quit. Vonnie was glad to see him stop working with Jim McDougal, and so was I. The only one who probably hated it was Skeeter, who could foresee Seth's renewed interest in POM.

By 1987, Seth was talking about suing Madison for his $300,000 commission and asked if I would take the case. I was relieved to have an out that even Seth Ward could understand— "Madison used to be our client," I said. "I just can't do it." He turned then to one of his gin rummy partners, Alston Jennings, who agreed to file the lawsuit.

For many reasons, I was relieved not to have to involve myself in Seth's battles. I tried to hear as little about them as humanly possible, but that was difficult since they were the topic of every night's conversation. However, I was usually preoccupied. That summer of 1987, Bill Clinton asked me to work almost full-time on a commission that would rewrite the state's lobbying laws. After his January speech announcing his new education programs, he had been stymied in the regular legislative session. The education package was going to cost some $200 million in new taxes, and the state legislators bowed to the pressures of affected interest groups. Eventually, in a special session, Clinton got enough funds to at least get his program under way. But he was angry at the legislators, and he resolved to do something about the cozy relationship between legislators and lobbyists that always seemed to keep Arkansas from moving forward. The relationship was less regulated in Arkansas than in almost any other state.

In June 1987, Bill called on Chris Piazza, the Pulaski County prosecuting attorney, to head a special Code of Ethics Commission. The commission's mandate was to develop a strong, comprehensive state code of ethics. Chris said he would take on the job on one condition—if his old high school football teammate Webb Hubbell would also be on the commission.

That fall I spent most of my time working with Chris. It was fun, like old times. He and I had been pals at Hall High, and he had spent many an hour sitting around my kitchen helping me clean out the refrigerator after football practice. But aside from giving me a reason to spend time with Chris, I felt that this commission was doing something good for the state. I also confess that sitting in my office, behind closed doors, writing a new state law felt comfortingly similar to my days on the Arkansas Supreme Court.

The Rose firm was roiling with predators that fall. More than once I glanced down at the old YWCA swimming pool and imagined I saw a dark fin slicing the water. Joe was busy trying to disentangle himself from the situation he had created. Meanwhile, Bill Kennedy and the younger attorneys were involved in an elaborate ballet of sincerity and deception. They genuinely liked Joe. But as Joe had become busy with his banking work, he had relinquished billing status of his lucrative clients to other attorneys. As billing partner on the Beverly Nursing Homes accounts and for many Stephens matters, Bill Kennedy, for example, was now responsible for a tenth of the firm's business. And other attorneys had taken over the billing of Joe's other accounts.

The whispering was deafening. Hillary had been out of the office a good bit that year, obviously working with Bill on what everyone expected would be an imminent announcement of a presidential run. Yet she still had a corner office and a secretary.

The younger attorneys resented that. She didn't *bill,* and yet she had all the trappings. And Webb—he was now spending all his time working for Clinton. Not only that, but this *ethics* thing— what in the world was that about? There were already rumblings from various Rose clients about changes in the lobbying laws. Whose side was Webb on, anyway? They didn't seem to resent Vince, because everyone knew he was "a real lawyer." But he was wounded somewhat by his association with us. I had no idea at the time, but most of the other attorneys in the office thought that Hillary, Vince, and I had been plotting an overthrow of the firm behind closed doors that spring. They assumed we litigators were jealous that Joe had made so much money, and we wanted to oust him because of that. It never occurred to them that we might simply have the good of the firm in mind.

In September 1987, Bill Clinton declined to run for the presi- dency. He said it was because of Chelsea—that she was too young to be left behind while her parents went off to face the all- consuming rigors of a major campaign.

But in the coffee shops and watering holes, the talk was of some- thing less noble. Senator Gary Hart had seen his political career de- railed when he was caught in an affair with a young woman. The rumors about Bill had been rampant for years—he was a man with an appetite, people said. He couldn't pass up a pretty face. I had other friends like the Bill Clinton of those rumors—except their lives weren't lived under a microscope. Those friends were boyish in their impetuousness. They never set out to hurt the one they loved, but sometimes opportunities came along and they went with them. It meant nothing, and so they never considered that they might lose the one they were married to. They came home like puppy dogs with their tails between their legs—and once they were forgiven, they were right back in the street again. For many rea- sons, I wasn't like that. I never forgot how much I loved Suzy. But I didn't judge my friends for their impetuousness.

I never asked Bill *or* Hillary about the truth of those rumors about Bill. I knew both of them too well to ask. Bill and I never once talked about the rumors until much later, after he was elected President. And Hillary never came to me and said, "Bill and I are having trouble." But I could often tell from Bill when they were having tense times. On the golf course he might say something oblique about Hillary being angry at him.

The night after Bill's announcement, he and Hillary and about twenty of their friends—many, like Mickey Kantor, who had come great distances expecting a different outcome—had dinner in a private room at the Capital Hotel. I didn't get a chance to talk much with Hillary that night, but several days later she came to the office. "Are you disappointed?" I asked. "Do you agree with his decision?"

She said she did—that she and Bill had talked long and hard, and they felt it wasn't the time to leave Chelsea for that long.

What I think was happening was that Bill and Hillary had decided that before a presidential run, they had to get their house in order—in whatever ways it needed ordering. Something she said later also seemed to shed light on Bill's decision not to run. A few months had passed, and one day Vince and I overheard Hillary say to one of our banking lawyers, Allen Bird, "We've got to straighten up Whitewater."

Vince and I didn't have any idea what she was talking about.

On the surface, Bill Kennedy was seen as trying to hold the firm together—by keeping Joe on, tempering the hotheaded younger attorneys, and maintaining a semblance of camaraderie. But he was quietly creating undercurrents. He had doubts that the firm could survive if Joe stayed. Some of the attorneys to whom Joe had handed clients were now making more money than Joe was. They liked Joe, but by now they had created lifestyles appropriate to their earnings. They *couldn't* let Joe take his business back.

The initial skirmish came in January 1988. Joe had had a bad year. He approached Bill and said, basically, "Don't you think I deserve some of the credit for the billings I sent your way?"

And Bill said, "No, Joe. I did the work. I don't think you should get any of the credit."

Joe countered by doing exactly what the young attorneys feared most—he took back his business. Soon, we received letters from

Stephens, Tyson, Beverly, and maybe others, saying, "For coordination purposes, all billing to us should henceforth be through Joe Giroir."

I handed the young Rose lawyers the excuse they were looking for. One day our malpractice insurance carrier was visiting, and he said his company was concerned about Joe still being in the firm. "You have a maverick partner on your hands," he said. The unspoken threat was that they might take away our malpractice insurance if we didn't do something about him. That, of course, would mean the dissolution of the firm.

I've thought about this episode for years, and I feel bad about it to this day. In hindsight, I wish we had gone to Joe a year and a half earlier and asked him to take a leave of absence. I wish I had sat down with him and listened to his problems more. I wish I had been a better friend. In light of my own situation, I now think I could have handled Joe's situation better. Maybe then the waters could have had time to calm.

But as I took the malpractice carrier's unsaid message to the partners, the firm was in open warfare and had been for months. Vince was convinced the firm would break apart soon—and if that happened, he wanted to take the name Rose Law Firm with him, instead of letting it go to the younger lawyers who had no respect for our rich tradition. My work on the Ethics Commission had also become a subject of open conflict. Some of our clients had approached Joe and asked that I stop working for the governor. And several of my partners were actively plotting with clients to analyze proposed legislation and devise strategies to defeat the proposals of the commission. For a year my own litigation partner, Jerry Jones, and I didn't speak to each other. We shared a secretary, and we communicated through memos dictated to her.

In January 1988 we had the bitterest partners meeting I had ever attended. Heightened by anger over my commission work, my role in handling the malpractice claim, and the perception (I know now) that I was trying to take over the firm with Vince and Hillary, words were spoken that can never be taken back. Hillary wasn't there. She wouldn't go to firm meetings about my work on her husband's Ethics Commission. I told my attackers that I was not going to give up the commission work. I felt I was doing something beneficial for Arkansas, and I was deeply invested in this process. "I'll quit the firm before I quit the commission," I said. Those were precisely the words some of my partners wanted to hear. In a long afternoon's meeting, Vince and Hillary persuaded me to stay. They said that if I left, the "bad guys" would win.

In March, prompted by Joe's letter taking back his clients, Vince and Bill Kennedy met with a firm breakup specialist—a kind of marriage counselor for law firms on the rocks. He recommended keeping everyone on board no matter what the short-term cost. A larger group of partners then met on a Sunday afternoon at a restaurant Bill owned in Hillcrest. Vince and Bill told everyone what the breakup specialist had said—that we had to keep everybody together. Then they left the restaurant and fanned out to visit with all the partners, asking them to please stay put.

We all went to work the next day not knowing whether the firm would survive until quitting time. We had a meeting, and Joe was told that either he had to leave or the firm was dissolving. There was no other way. When he agreed, everyone was so relieved that we gave him what we thought was a generous severance package. I doubt he thought it was so munificent. Today, Joe Giroir is better known for being a part of the saving of Worthen bank than for being a Rose firm partner. All of us, at times in our lives, put too much emphasis on that. He now has a very successful and lucrative law practice in Little Rock, and I'm sure he's a much happier man. Out of crisis, good things can happen.

Joe's leaving did help bring at least a semblance of peace within the office. Within a week, of course, we received letters from some clients saying, "Send all the files to Joe." But with him out, Vince could go back to the FSLIC and see if they would reconsider. In time, they said, in time.

One month after Joe left, my father died. It was Good Friday, 1988. That winter my dad had been diagnosed as having brain cancer. For six weeks, throughout the time of the final meetings with Joe, I would go every evening to Saint Vincent's Hospital to sit at his bedside. At first he knew me, but gradually he slipped into some netherworld of consciousness. I talked to him anyway, hoping that he could hear me. I told him I loved him. I told him what a wonderful father he had been. I said I felt that I had disappointed him. I had become something that he didn't respect. My father and Seth Ward had always been opposites. One day in November, in fact, I got a call from the manager of a local sporting goods store. "You better get over here, Webb," he said. "Your dad and Seth Ward are about to have a fight."

The conflict was diffused before I got to the store. My dad and Seth had run into each other shopping for a present for Walter's sixteenth birthday and Seth had said, "Hey, Webster, I'm about to buy our grandson a shotgun for duck hunting."

My father's old fury got the best of him. "Over my dead body," he said.

"You can't do a thing about it," Seth said.

"Oh yeah?" my dad said.

Seth did buy the shotgun. Later I visited each of them at home to help smooth over the hard feelings, but I don't think they ever really went away. I guess it was a confrontation that had been building for sixteen years. Suzy's and my parents were polar opposites. My parents never entertained. Seth and Vonnie threw lavish parties, taking over a wing of the Arts Center. My father drove a stripped-down brown Ford; one of Seth's cars was a flashy red Mercedes. For most of his life, my father didn't drink, but the Wards poured liquor like there was no tomorrow. Seth and Vonnie gave their grandchildren gifts. My parents gave them only time.

Hillary stopped by my office a few days after my dad's funeral. She shut the door and asked how I was doing. Something about the tone of her voice caused me to break down and begin to cry. I hadn't done it all week long. She put her arm around my shoulder and told me to go ahead and let it all out. If only I had.

After Dad was dead and buried, I met with Mother to see if she was okay financially. What I found made me relieved, but also a little sick. She was fine. She still lived in the house they had bought twenty-five years before. They had taken out a mortgage, long since paid off, of 4 percent. There was insurance money, a savings account, not an iota of debt. I envied my mother her financial situation, and I was ashamed at how far I had strayed.

7

Hubbell's Folly

My friend Marsha Scott remembers getting desperate phone calls from me during this period. She lived in California then. Marsha had grown up in Little Rock in the kind of life that I had aspired to. Her father, Clyde Scott, had been an Olympic silver medalist in high hurdles and a football legend. He was also a successful businessman. Her mother, Leslie, was a former Miss Arkansas. Marsha was a beautiful girl, a cheerleader at Hall. My father always thought Marsha and I should have gotten married. Together Marsha and I could have produced a team of fullbacks, he said.

Marsha walked away from the life I was looking for. Somewhere along the way, she came to despise the Country Club of Little Rock and all that it stood for. Her parents were members of the Pleasant Valley Country Club, but she didn't care about any of that. That life seemed empty to her. To this day, she's a good enough friend to tell me exactly what I don't want to hear.

To Marsha, I was always a "poet in a football player body." But by the late 1980s, I was neither a poet nor did I have the body of a football player anymore. She remembers me telling her about the stresses put on me by the Wards, the problems at the office, the expense of keeping up this elaborate life. I yearned for no pressure. I yearned for peace and quiet. "I want to go to a monastery," I said.

Instead, I began the behavior that triggered my downfall.

I always paid my bills at the office. Once a month, I would pack them in a briefcase and drive over to the firm on a Saturday or Sunday afternoon, when no one was around. It was quiet and I could concentrate. I had also begun drinking while I paid my bills. In the office was a refrigerator where I kept a carton of orange juice. In my drawer was a bottle of vodka.

My bills took all afternoon. The monthly stack must have been six inches high. We had every credit card known to man, and more arrived in the mail each day. I was considered a "good credit risk." I had been mayor and chief justice. I was a prominent lawyer, Seth Ward's son-in-law, the governor's friend. If Suzy was traveling around the state and wanted to buy something, the shopkeeper would say, "Let me open you an account." Nobody wanted our check or cash—our credit was fine.

To pay for all my renovations at Hubbell's Folly, I had taken second and third mortgages—and then rolled them over into a new single mortgage. By the late 1980s, my house payment alone was $5,000 a month. I paid the utilities and the monthly household expenses with a personal line of credit. On the credit card bills, I made sure I paid at least the minimum amount requested—sometimes taking advances from one to pay another. I always tried to keep a couple of them paid down enough so that we still had credit. "Use the Optima Card this month, Suzy," I would say.

There was no master plan. There simply came a day when all the elements were in place, and an opportunity presented itself. I don't recall which bill started it all. Maybe it was the American Express bill after Suzy and I took a trip to St. Lucia. I know now that some of my closest friends were wondering, How can they afford that? We just did it. And then it was up to me to figure out how to pay for it.

So on a fateful Saturday or Sunday afternoon, as the sun sank behind neighboring buildings, I sat at my shadowed desk staring at, say, a $3,000 American Express bill and wondering how I was going to juggle the money this time. Two thousand dollars of this was for legitimate business, but $1,000 was for personal charges Suzy and I had incurred that month. The answer I came to was a shocking one, and I probably had a hundred rationalizations for my conduct over the years—though no real excuses. I want that understood now: There *is* no excuse for what I did. I committed a crime, and no one made me do it. Not Seth, not Suzy, not my children, not my partners. I did it myself, out of my own weakness, and I accept the punishment that continues to this day.

I was angry at my partners, and felt unappreciated by my partners *and* the firm's clients. Maybe all that figured into this in some way. Maybe this was what the shrinks call passive-aggressive behavior. But I didn't really set out to steal from my partners and my clients. I intended only to borrow.

Essentially, the conduct went like this. I would get a bill—that American Express bill for $3,000, say. In Rose's democratic system, any member of the firm could write what is called a client-advance check for that bill. That means you're assigning that expense to a client. When it came time to actually bill that client for that money that had now been charged to them by the firm, there were two ways I could deal with it. I could put on the bill "travel expenses," so that if this was a client I was traveling a lot for, they wouldn't question the bill. Or, I could bill a client, say, $10,000 for a fee and then tell the internal bookkeeping system, "Only credit me seven thousand dollars toward the fee. That extra three thousand, credit it to pay that cost. I just don't want to tell the client that I'm charging for travel expenses." As long as the client paid the bill, there was no problem.

The first way, billing the client for the travel expense, is defraud of a client. The firm isn't actually out any money. The second way, the firm is out the money. That's stealing from your partners. As I say, there were always rationalizations—"I'm only borrowing my own money," and so on. And my goal, from the very beginning, was to pay it back. If not next month, then in January when the annual allocations were made. Somehow, though, there was always another need for that money.

On that first day I did it, I probably stared at the client check on my desk, wondering if this was something I would regret. I probably sat back, maybe made myself another drink, and tried to think through all the steps, as in a game of chess. When I figured I could get away with it, I finished up my bills and packed my briefcase and headed home to supper with Suzy and the kids. On the way, maybe I dropped by the post office and turned into the drive-through, where I took the huge stack of stamped envelopes and held them over the open maw of the mailbox. I probably pulled my hand back once and thumbed through the bills one last time. Then I dropped them into the box, and the die was cast.

Bill Clinton's summer of discontent came in 1988, at the Democratic National Convention in Atlanta. Positioning himself for next time, he landed the job of introducing the Democratic candidate for President, Michael Dukakis.

It was a wonderful opportunity, and his friends gathered around their television sets to watch him dazzle a national audience. What we saw was the potential derailment of a brilliant career. A speech that was supposed to last fifteen minutes droned on for thirty-two minutes. Bill Clinton was finally booed off the stage.

When Hillary and Bill got home to Little Rock, Vince and I took her to lunch. She was livid, so we didn't even have to ask what had happened. She felt the Dukakis staff had "set Bill up." First, before the speech, Bill had shown a copy to Dukakis. It was too long, Bill told him, but Dukakis insisted that he leave it all in. Second, the normal dimming of lights to warn the audience that someone was about to speak didn't occur. Hillary had stood offstage trying to find someone to dim the lights. As she was telling us this, it was clear to Vince and me that Hillary was too upset about this for either of us to ask her why Bill hadn't started to ad-lib and bring it to a halt. I later heard from someone who was there that Dukakis's staff was worried about the nominee being overshadowed by Clinton. They had already been upstaged by Jesse Jackson, so they encouraged the length of the speech and the failure to dim the lights. I have no idea whether or not that's true.

Fortunately, Bill had media-savvy friends in California who came to his rescue. Lawyer Mickey Kantor and his wife, the L.A. television anchor Heidi Schulman, and producer-writers Harry and Linda Bloodworth-Thomason all advised him to head off the crisis by poking fun at himself in a very public venue. Johnny Carson's *Tonight Show* was about as high-profile as you could get, and the Thomasons arranged an appearance. Bill was wonderful—funny, self-effacing, human. I've thought many times how difficult that was for Bill to do. In real life, he has a very hard time laughing at himself. Hillary can do it in private, but unfortunately that doesn't come across in public. For Bill, I suppose this is a result of the urgency he feels to succeed—life *is* serious, moments *are* critical. "Laughing it off" is an admission that, hey, it's only life. But for Bill, it's not "only life." It's a mission. That Carson show probably saved his political career. The White House—in fact, all of Washington—would be a saner place if people there could laugh at themselves a little more.

At the end of the year, I sensed that resentment of me had built to crescendo level. I had spent two years working to clean up the mess created by my partners' work during the boom-boom era. But in the only measure that counted—how much you were billing—I was low man on the totem pole.

In January 1989, my partners told me they wanted me out of firm management altogether. I thought about quitting, but once again I couldn't do it. Instead, I took their rejection as a challenge. They wanted me to be like them? Fine, that's what they would get. I resolved to build up my practice, increase my billings. I began lawyering with a vengeance.

Since Joe's departure, many of our commercial attorneys had been lobbying Vince to see if we couldn't now get FSLIC and FDIC business again. Vince made subtle inquiries and was reminded of our firm's continued unprofessional behavior—one partner had shown up at a closing in tennis shorts, and another had referred to a senior counsel at FSLIC as "honey." But Vince was also encouraged to write a letter trying to get back on the approved list. In late 1988, he was asked to "bid" on the business of several institutions that were about to be closed. One of them was Madison Guaranty Savings and Loan, for whom we had not done any work since Hillary returned the retainer in 1986.

We held a firm meeting and argued again about whether we wanted to be in business with the regulators. The commercial lawyers, the ones who would benefit most from this work, won out. Now I wish the vote had gone the other way. Vince and I discussed Seth's lawsuit against Madison and then we made bids on several institutions, including Madison. Not long afterward, Vince told me that the FDIC had responded by saying we were eligible to work on all the thrift closings except Madison's—we had too many conflicts there. I naturally assumed that the conflicts involved the Rose firm's past work for Madison and Seth's lawsuit against Madison. It never occurred to me that the conflicts had anything to do with Bill and Hillary Clinton's deal with McDougal involving the Whitewater property. I had heard about Whitewater in passing, but it wasn't on my radar screen. Hard as it is to believe considering Hillary's notoriety today, I never probed her personal business, nor did she probe me about mine.

In March 1989, one of our associates, Rick Donovan, told me that the professional liability counsel for the FDIC, April Breslaw, had been assigned to the Madison closing. There was a case pending against the institution's accountants, the Little Rock firm of Frost and Company, and she was going to fire the law firm that was representing Madison. She asked Rick if we could take on the case. I called April—wrongfully assuming she knew Rose had been excluded from representing Madison. So I saw no reason for us not to handle this particular case. She said, "Run a conflicts check and get back to me."

This case is now a case study in law school courses on ethics and conflicts of interest. It may not have been a conflict technically, but with hindsight I recognize I exercised very poor judgment in taking on the representation. Considering Madison's reputation today, it's probably hard to understand why I wouldn't have tried to stay as far away from that work as possible—even though I was technically working for the FDIC. But I was in the process of trying to dramatically increase my billings at the firm. In retrospect, my judgment was clouded. As the knight in *Indiana Jones: The Last Crusade* said, "I chose poorly."

My tax partners objected to my taking on this case—not because it was Madison, but because Frost and Company did accounting work for several of our clients. I wish I had listened to them, but I was angry because even though they wanted me to start billing, every time I came up with a case they found reasons for me not to do it—reasons that were for their benefit, not mine. So I wasn't in an accommodating mood. I took on *Madison v. Frost*.

Then a strange thing happened. I received a call from a man named David Hale, a local municipal judge. He said he had heard from the Memphis lawyers who had filed the original case against Frost that I had taken over the case. He said that he had made a $300,000 loan to Susan McDougal's interior decorating firm. The loan was secured by the McDougals' Madison stock. Hale had relied on the financial statements prepared by Frost in evaluating the collateral. He wanted to join in the lawsuit against Frost and have our firm represent him as well. By then I knew that Frost had only a $3 million malpractice insurance policy, and that the FDIC's claim was for much more than that. I doubted if the FDIC would want to share its counsel and its proceeds with Hale, but I told him I would at least look over his materials. He sent me a stack of documents. I discussed this development with Rick Donovan and we both agreed that we shouldn't take on Hale's claim. So I declined the representation and sent the documents back.

This loan to Susan McDougal is the one that David Hale now claims Bill Clinton pressured him to make. In 1989, Hale was claiming that he wouldn't have made this loan except for having good collateral and that he was relying on Frost's audit when he made the loan.

In 1994, when I was being interviewed by the FDIC, I didn't even remember this episode. They showed me a phone bill indicating that David Hale had called me, and I didn't remember what it was about. When Bill Kennedy had called me in August 1993 and asked if I knew of any connection between David Hale and Madison, I mistakenly told him, "No, I know of no connection." At the time, I was up to my ears in Justice Department business in Washington, and Vince had just died. I didn't remember the Hale phone call, the documents, my review, or my declining the case until I met with the Independent Counsel's staff—after I pled guilty to stealing from my partners and clients.

Shortly after I told April Breslaw that we would take the case, she called and said that some Madison employees felt we had a conflict because of Seth and his lawsuit against Madison. We had several discussions about that. I offered for the firm to give up the case, or for me to step aside in favor of another attorney. April said that wasn't necessary—all she needed was a letter from me promising not to represent Seth or his son, Skeeter, in Seth's disputes with Madison. I was more than happy to oblige.

Unfortunately, the conflicts didn't go away. I discovered that the Rose firm had another conflict. One of our attorneys was representing in litigation a company whose president had worked at Frost and was an auditor on the Madison case—in other words, he was the defendant in my case. I was furious. Why they didn't raise this on the front end, I will never know. But after I examined the matter, I decided that withdrawing from the case would do more harm than good to my client. There would be more conflicts before this case was over, but the FDIC ultimately concluded that none of them affected the outcome of the litigation—our recovery by settlement of over $1 million from Frost. Even after the federal government had indicted and tried Jim McDougal, saying he was the cause of the losses at his savings and loan, we were able to get a million-dollar settlement from the thrift's accounting firm.

If you're overwhelmed with this story of *Madison v. Frost*, I can only say, I'm sorry. I wish I didn't have to go into it in such detail, but it's become part of the industry known as Whitewater. I've read where people say I took on the *Madison v. Frost* case to keep the light of day away from Seth and Jim McDougal's IDC deal, or Hillary's prior representation of Madison. Each day there's a new twist and turn—some even speculating that this had something to do with Vince's suicide. The way all of this keeps evolving, I expect *Madison v. Frost* to eventually be linked with Lee Harvey Oswald and Deep Throat.

My sister Terry says she knew I was in trouble the day she was at my house and heard me yelling at my children. I'm glad my dad was dead by then. He would have been horrified.

Not that he was right. It's not right to teach people to keep their feelings bottled up inside them. I had done that all my life. I had listened to everyone else's problems, but had never told mine to anyone. I felt like a latent volcano, churning and fuming deep down, but unable to let the top blow. Sometimes, I guess, I came close. My daughter Caroline remembers a time when she and Rebecca were fighting, and I flew into a rage. They were shocked, because they had never seen me that way. I yelled at them, *screamed* at them. And what I screamed was this: "Don't be mad! *Don't be mad!*"

I continued to steal from my partners and clients. Usually just once a month, on the day I paid the bills. The system was easy, but it took a toll on me. I kept telling myself I would quit, that this was the very last time. Late at night, after everyone was asleep, I would open a bottle of wine and slice a block of cheese and sit in my dim den drinking and eating and telling myself I had to find a way. Then, finally, the wine took hold, and the urgency passed.

The years 1989 to 1991 were largely filled with work. I accomplished what I set out to do—I became a Rose firm lawyer. Nineteen ninety-one was my best year ever. I billed more than $750,000 for the firm, which netted me $150,000. But my expenses continued to outrun my earnings. And my stress level was, if anything, higher than ever.

The Wards also consumed an even greater amount of my time in those years. The pivotal moment arrived one day in 1989 when a friend and I were at the country club preparing to tee off for eighteen holes of golf. I was called to the telephone. The excited voice of our housekeeper, Elizabeth Fitzgerald, came through the line. By that time, Elizabeth had replaced Fanny Taylor in my life. She had a distinctive way of speaking. For example, she always called Suzy "SuzyHubbell," as though it were a single word. On this particular Saturday, I heard Elizabeth say, "WebbHubbell, all hell's done broke loose! Your father-in-law done fell out of the upstairs window!"

I told my golf partner to wait, that I would surely be back soon. I was wrong. Seth had broken his back. Every time Seth came over to our house, he pointed to something I ought to be taking care of but wasn't. To Seth's mind, one of my major failings was our gutter system. It didn't drain right. I suppose it had finally become a principle with him, because while I was off playing golf, he dropped by and decided to fix the system himself. When a drainpipe came loose from the gutter, Seth went upstairs and leaned out the window to reconnect it. Our windows were sixty-five-year-old casement windows. He cranked them open and sat down on the windowsill with his back to the sky. He couldn't quite reach the gutter from that position, so he grabbed onto the vertical bar that ran between the windows and leaned farther out. The bar wasn't made for rock climbing, and it promptly gave way. Seth fell two stories, barely missing being impaled on a rusted, two-foot-high sprinkler head.

He had just recovered from two strokes and kidney failure. Now he would be lucky ever to walk again. It was an excruciating injury. He lives in a great deal of pain to this day. But if I had thought he was difficult before, I hadn't seen anything. He was in the hospital for weeks, and we all had to visit him daily. He was in a foul mood. He felt sorry for himself, and it was clear that he partially blamed me for his fall. If I'd done my man-of-the-house duty and gotten the drainage system fixed, he wouldn't be in a back brace now.

While he was in the hospital, Skeeter and I met with him frequently for Skeeter's progress reports on POM. Skeeter painted a flowery picture, but I knew in my heart of hearts that I was hearing only half the story. Skeeter was having terrible problems. He had refinanced and refinanced again, trying to gear up to produce a solar-powered electronic parking meter that would allow him

Memphis, Tennessee, 1958. Boy Scout Troop 55, Gator Patrol. In 1958 all of my friends were Boy Scouts. My parents were proud to see me in the uniform, but it never quite fit and it was kind of stiff. I was proud that I became an Eagle Scout when I was twelve years old—one of the youngest in the nation.

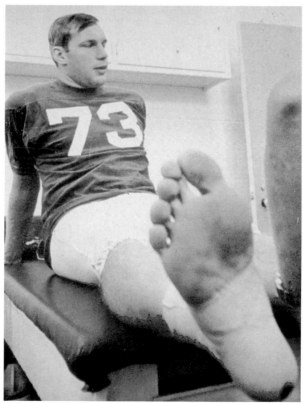

Webb, 1968. After my injury, my knee was drained of fluid every week and injected with cortisone so I could keep playing football. I still get faint at the sight of needles.
Arkansas Democrat-Gazette

Fayetteville, Arkansas, August 1968. Number 73, starting tackle for the Arkansas Razorbacks, Sugar Bowl champions. Being a former Razorback opened many doors in Arkansas; still does. But I've always wondered where I would be today if I had played pro ball with the Chicago Bears instead of going to law school.

Trinity Episcopal Cathedral, Little Rock, July 24, 1971. Suzy and I dated for three weeks and got married about two months later. At the time we had hippie dreams of a wedding with beer, hot dogs, and pets in the Fayetteville City Park, but a good Episcopal wedding has served us well—we're still in love after twenty-six years.

AND NOW—
FROM THE SAME
PEOPLE WHO
GAVE YOU
SANDY KEITH...

From the People
Why Not a Faubus Farkleoreum?

July 1979 political cartoon, from the day after I was elected by the city board to be mayor. This was the first cartoon directed toward me, and certainly not the most favorable. I was viewed with skepticism for a long time because of my predecessor, Sandy Keith, who had once publicly pronounced that Little Rock's rape rate was high because we had prettier girls than other cities. I instituted a rape prevention program almost immediately.
Arkansas Democrat-Gazette

WEBB HUBBELL
MAYOR

Little Rock, 1980. Chairing a city board meeting. Probably the greatest accomplishment of my city board days was to take a warring seven-person board and make it a working, energetic, and respected governing body. *Arkansas Democrat-Gazette*

Little Rock, 1980. As mayor, I am presenting a proclamation to Pat Wyatt, president of the Little Rock Road Runners' Club. I was the youngest mayor; Bill Clinton, the youngest governor; and Paul Riviere *(center)*, the youngest secretary of state in the country at the time. We also had the youngest state attorney general, Steve Clark.
Courtesy of Paul Riviere

Governor's Mansion, Little Rock, 1980. When First Lady Rosalynn Carter *(center)* came to Little Rock, Bill Clinton welcomed her and I, as mayor, gave her a key to the city. Later in the year, her husband's decision to send Cubans—part of the Freedom Flotilla—to Fort Chaffee in Arkansas played a major role in Bill's gubernatorial defeat.
Donald Broyles, Office of Governor Bill Clinton

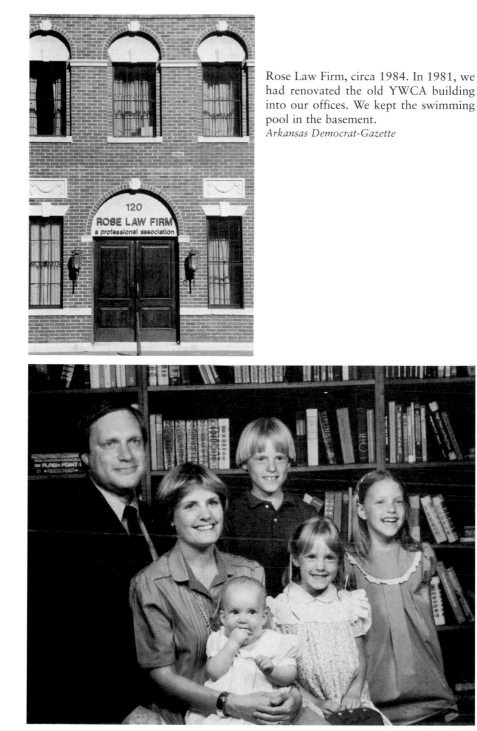

Rose Law Firm, circa 1984. In 1981, we had renovated the old YWCA building into our offices. We kept the swimming pool in the basement.
Arkansas Democrat-Gazette

Early 1982. This picture of me, Suzy, and our children was taken for the directory of the church where I was a member of the vestry. Walter was nine, Rebecca six, Caroline four, and Kelley about seven months. Fifteen years later our children are almost grown up—they're good, strong adults and we are stronger as a family.

Early 1980s. Suzy's sister, Sally, and her husband, Finus Shellnut. They divorced about eight years later. It's a small world: When Gennifer Flowers claimed to have had an affair with Bill Clinton, she was living with Finus. They are now married and live in Dallas.

Little Rock, September 1984. The Arkansas Supreme Court and its new chief justice. How I loved this job and those men. When I started they were all feuding, but over the next four months we really came together. Being chief justice was the best work I ever had. My family remembers those days as the best as well.

Little Rock, November 1991. Walter and Kelley Hubbell, and Seth Ward: On Rebecca's sixteenth birthday, we all met as a family at the Wards' to present Rebecca with a convertible hidden in their garage. Seth is sporting a cane because of a broken back he suffered after falling out of a second-story window at my house.

★ CLINTON

For President

WEBB HUBBELL

ARKANSAS AMBASSADOR

1992
Democratic Convention
July 13 - 16
Madison Square Garden
New York, New York

VIP

Make it Happen!

July 13, 1992. Hillary had asked Vince Foster and me to come to the Democratic National Convention in New York. This is one of the badges. She had been on the road for months, during which we had not seen her. Despite an unbelievably hectic schedule she took time to visit with us, and we began to reminisce about the last time we had all been in New York together, almost ten years earlier. I returned to Little Rock and told Suzy that Bill Clinton would be President. I finally believed.

November 6, 1992. The First Lady—elect grants her first interview to the media after the election: She was interviewed by my daughter Rebecca for her high school (Mount St. Mary's) newspaper. My children had grown up with Bill and Hillary as friends, not as governor, President, or First Lady. Chelsea would jump on the trampoline in our side yard with her across-the-street best friend, Elizabeth Fleming.

Spring 1993. Golf with the President and Vernon Jordan at Robert Trent Jones Golf Club in Manassas, Virginia. Just three guys having fun; but reporters and White House staffers went crazy asking me, "You were alone with the President for four hours. What did he talk about?" "Golf" was always my answer. *The White House*

HOLE	1	2	3	4	5	6	7	8	9	OU
GOLD	544	421	429	197	441	203	464	348	538	358
BLUE	506	384	403	172	409	186	445	325	512	334
WHITE	495	355	369	134	389	176	415	307	491	313
HANDICAP	7	11	9	13	3	17	1	15	5	
W ™	6	5	5	5	6	4	5	5	4	
B ™	6	4	5	6	6	4	5	4	5	4
PAR	5	4	4	3	4	3	4	4	5	36
RED	467	318	318	133	358	151	389	266	423	282
HANDICAP	5	11	9	15	3	17	1	13	7	

11/07/92

SCORER   DATE

"Golf is a game for Ladies and Gentlemen, Ladies and Gentlemen

Spring 1993. With Hillary outside the Rose Garden after a White House announcement. Since I worked at Justice, I had hardly seen her since we had moved to Washington. *The White House*

November 7, 1992. The President and I played golf at Chenal Country Club in Little Rock the Saturday after he was elected; his note to me reads, "Webb—Thanks for all the rounds but especially this one." On the same day twenty years earlier, my son, Walter, had been born and Richard Nixon reelected President.

10	11	12	13	14	15	16	17	18	IN	TOTAL	HCP	NET
410	170	513	380	444	435	541	200	471	3564	7149		
387	154	478	311	415	414	516	169	445	3289	6631		
366	125	451	270	384	378	485	145	414	3018	6149		
10	18	12	14	2	6	8	16	4				
5	5	5	5	4	6	5	4	5	44	89		
5	4	6	3	5	5	5	4	5	42	87		
4	3	5	4	4	4	5	3	4	36	72		
		Well —			*Thanks for*							
all the		*rounds*		*but especially*								
this one		—		*Bill*	*11-7-92*							
312	98	423	245	356	344	413	110	360	2661	5484		
12	18	8	14	2	6	10	16	4				

PRODUCED BY GOLFOTO, INC. DESIGN GROUP

TEE	COURSE RATING	SLOPE RATING
GOLD	75.1	144
BLUE	72.6	136
WHITE	70.2	128
RED	72.4	125

EST

require rules.''

March 1993. The basketball Razorbacks were on TV, and we were all invited to root them on to victory in the theater at the White House.

March 1993. Kelley is thrilled at the opportunity to meet Barbra Streisand after the Razorback game, as Vernon Jordan and Patricia Duff look on. My family finally saw some benefit of having Daddy move to Washington. *The White House*

East Wing of the White House, May 1993. After my confirmation hearing as associate attorney general, Suzy and I attended a reception at the White House for all federal judges. *The White House*

June 1993. My swearing-in at Justice. Janet Reno and I had already been working together for three months, had endured Waco, and were now ready to strike out for justice in America. *Department of Justice*

June 1993. Bernie and Toby Nussbaum and Janet Reno at a party for me at Michael and Harolyn Cardozo's house, celebrating my confirmation. Rumors that Bernie and Janet were feuding over travel office firings could have been dispelled by this picture.

The players at work, 1993. Every morning at 8:00 A.M., Deputy Attorney General Phil Heymann (second from right), Solicitor General Drew Days, and I would meet with Janet to get our marching orders, to discuss the issues of the day, and to report on the previous day's work. Janet was definitely a hands-on micromanager. Her style worked well with me, but later caused a disagreement between her and Phil that resulted in his resignation. *David Burnett/Contact*

June 1993. Vince Foster strikes a typical pose with a twinkle in his eye and the promise that he will never tell what he's thinking. Kaki Mehlburger and Helen Dickey stand by, entranced.

Eastern Shore, Maryland, July 1993. We spent the weekend with the Cardozos and the Fosters. Nick Bollettieri, the famous tennis coach, who was also visiting, gave Lisa Foster and Suzy instructions.

MR. W. HUBBELL

WELCOME ABOARD

On July 22, 1993, I took Vince's body home aboard Air Force One to be buried. This is the seating card. I was too distraught to appreciate the accommodations.

December 1993. A Christmas photograph at the White House. *From left to right:* Our good friend Marsha Scott, Caroline, Kelley, the Clintons, Suzy, and me. The Rose firm chartered a plane to attend this event. *The White House*

December 27, 1993. Rebecca and the President at Jim and Diane Blair's house in Fayetteville after a Razorback basketball game. That morning I had met with a Rose firm partner and had been told that the firm thought I had stolen money. I went to the game with my stomach churning. *The White House*

Camp David, July 1994. Beryl Anthony, a former congressman from Arkansas; his wife, Sheila, Vince's sister; and Lisa, Vince's wife. This was the first time Lisa had been in Washington since Vince's death.

Summer 1995. Brother Skeeter, Sally, and Suzy together when Sally married for the second time. Everyone had great hopes that this marriage would work out for Sally, but she divorced in 1996.

August 1995. I was constantly being called before Congress even after I went to prison. Fortunately I was not required to appear in a prison jump suit or to be photographed with the handcuffs and leg irons used whenever I was transported.
Copyright © Brad Markel/Gamma Liaison

an edge over his major competitor, Duncan. Duncan was well capitalized, and seemed to enjoy doing anything possible to cost POM business. I had privately advised Skeeter to sell, but he wouldn't hear of it. I guess he didn't want to admit he couldn't pull this off. He couldn't bear to disappoint his father.

But things weren't good at POM, and the only person in the family who didn't know that was Seth. When we were all at the Wards' in the evenings, Skeeter's wife, Anne, would pull Suzy aside to talk about it; then Suzy and her mother would disappear for a conversation in the kitchen, while Skeeter and I would drink on the porch and talk about how precarious it all was.

The whole family was turning to me to find a solution that would make things go back to normal. Intellectually, I knew I wasn't responsible for Seth's physical problems, but it *was* my window. This was my wife's family, and if I could in some way rescue them maybe I could rescue myself. So I plunged in and tried to learn as much as I could about POM and why it was going downhill. The more Seth talked about solving POM's financial problems, the more his mind stayed off his own physical ones.

Short of selling the business—something the Wards weren't prepared to do—the solution became apparent. We had to confront Duncan, POM's only major competitor. Soon Skeeter and Seth decided to sue Duncan. Skeeter believed that Duncan had engaged in some outrageous conduct, but the legal issue involved was violation of the federal antitrust law. There was another wrinkle as well. Skeeter had finally gotten his patent on the solar-powered electronic parking meter—but Duncan had one, too. Skeeter's patent counsel told him that Duncan's new electronic parking meter violated his patent. After researching the antitrust issues and consulting with other attorneys on the merits of the case, we made the decision to file suit against Duncan.

Skeeter and I entered into a contingent fee arrangement by which I would recover 20 percent of any judgment or settlement. Skeeter would pay all expenses as they were incurred. We filed suit in the spring of 1989—about the same time Seth's lawsuit against Madison was due to be briefed before the Arkansas Court of Appeals. He had won in the lower court—Alston Jennings had gotten him an award of approximately $350,000 from Madison. But since Madison had been taken over by the FDIC, they wanted to stay the appeal while they changed lawyers and moved to federal court for the fight with Seth. Seth, too, had to change lawyers. Alston and I put him in touch with Tom Ray, the best lawyer we knew. For a year and a half, I spent practically every evening at Seth's, while Suzy and the children waited at home. First, I would hear about his Madison lawsuit, and then I would take him through POM-Duncan.

The Rose firm was in another crisis. By the time Joe left, we had outgrown the old YWCA building. We had close to fifty lawyers, and we needed a plan for the next decade. For years the older partners like Vince and Hillary and myself had made up the difference between the office rent and the mortgage shortfall. Now we were about to reach the point where the amount owed was less than the rent. We were on the downhill side and were looking forward to years of positive cash flow. The younger partners didn't own shares in the building. At first we had tried to give shares when an associate made partner, but after a while that was no longer feasible. We were just hiring too fast. So when it became obvious that we had to add on or move on, the younger partners felt the older ones were trying to take advantage of them—trying to get them to help pay for *our* building.

When Joe left the firm, I became general partner of the building partnership, a position I came to regret. Once again, it put me squarely in the middle, drawing the anger of all sides. Although we ultimately compromised, resentments lingered. My thoughts turned again to leaving. But I couldn't.

In 1990, Bill Clinton was up for reelection for the fifth time, but he had no "fire in the belly," he said. Inside the Rose firm, my partners were trying to convince me to dissuade him from running for governor again. "Our clients are tired of him," they said. "The Stephenses don't want him. Talk to him, Webb." There was even musing within the smoke-filled rooms of the Stephens company that Hillary ought to run in Bill's place. Old Witt

Stephens was the one who floated that idea, and to this day I'm not convinced he was serious. Daily, Witt and Jack had good old country lunches served in their fancy private dining room, and they invited people in to "talk." Judges, lawyers, politicians, businesspeople—all of them were there at one time or another. The okra and greens and tomatoes and corn were all served on exquisite porcelain china, and the *pièce de résistance* was their inimitable corn bread. It oozed butter the way Witt oozed power. At one of those lunches, Witt is said to have lit his cigar and looked up from under his bushy brows and said, "I think Hil'ry'd make a better gov'nor than Bill. What you think about that, Henry?" And then he sat back and smiled while the debate raged on.

I was at some of those lunches. What I never told anyone was that Hillary had actually floated her candidacy past Vince and me, in the event that Bill didn't run. She asked what we thought. We questioned whether if the reason Bill wasn't running was because he had been in office too long, voters would think they were just getting the same thing. Tommy Robinson, her most likely opponent, was known as a firebrand campaigner. Was she prepared to withstand anything he might throw out? Frankly, knowing Hillary, I wasn't worried about that. I knew she could dish it out with the best of them. She also talked about how it might energize a new generation of females in the state, and when she said that I knew she was really thinking about it. But she always closed by saying that Bill had to decide what he was going to do first. His advisers told him that if he ever wanted to successfully mount a presidential campaign, he needed to be in public office when he ran. He needed to have a platform.

Tommy Robinson was an outrageous former sheriff and former U.S. congressman who had once been a Democrat, but he had seen the way the wind was blowing. Backed by Stephens money, Tommy looked formidable. Vying with Tommy for the Republican nomination was Sheffield Nelson, the Stephenses' archenemy. He had once been Mr. Witt's protégé in an oil and gas business, but had had the audacity to want to run things his way. One of the smartest things Bill Clinton ever did was not to get too close to the Stephenses. Some of their detractors called Jack and Witt Stephens by the acronym JAWS, but they never got their grip on Bill.

In the primary, Sheffield Nelson beat Tommy Robinson. That might have been the moment Bill Clinton got his chance to be President. Because suddenly the Stephenses were calling to see how they could help Bill. Did the campaign need money? Did I think Bill could pay a visit to Jack? The Rose firm and its clients made an abrupt about-face, too. Now that the Stephenses backed Bill, everybody backed Bill. All of a sudden the partners were "pleased and honored" to have Hillary in the firm. And people accuse Bill Clinton of flip-flopping. If she needed time off to campaign against Sheffield, that was perfectly fine. Bill beat Sheffield Nelson, and many people say Sheffield has seethed with resentment ever since. Once Bill became President, national Republicans swirled around Sheffield, hoping to find dirt to use against the Clintons.

But Bill wasn't sure he could even run for President. Arkansans are touchy about being used, and everybody knew Bill really wanted to be President. To head off such speculation, he foolishly promised during the gubernatorial campaign that if they elected him governor, he would serve out his four-year term. It was the classic catch-22: He had to be governor to run for President, but he couldn't be governor unless he promised *not* to run for President. He was torn as only he can be. Around this time I was part of a series of strategy meetings being held at the Governor's Mansion, where most of the discussion centered around what had become known as the Pledge—his promise not to run for President if elected governor. I didn't even think he should run in 1992, but my reasons weren't so much about the pledge as George Bush's perceived invulnerability. He asked me once, and I advised him against it. I thought Bush was too formidable. But that's why Bill Clinton was the politician in *our* golf cart.

The moment I knew he was going to run was during a trip the two of us made to Vince's father's funeral. It was the summer of 1991. Bill and I flew to Hope together in a small plane, just the two of us and the pilot. All the way down, we talked about how

to get out of his promise, *if* he should get out of his promise.
During the funeral service, we were seated on the same pew as
Senator David Pryor. Hillary, who had been driven down, was
sitting between Pryor and Bill, and I was on Bill's other side.
Sometime during the service, I saw Pryor lean over and hand Bill
a folded piece of paper. Bill unfolded it and read the message.
Then he handed the paper to me. Pryor, the most revered politi-
cian in Arkansas, had scribbled a single word: "RUN."

On the way home, Bill was upbeat, excited, energized. Pryor's
advice carried a lot of weight. They had talked following the service, and the senator had told Bill, "The ones who love you will
be with you, anyway. The ones who are against you won't change
their minds. Bush is vulnerable. This is the time."

In October 1991, Bill announced his candidacy for the presidency
of the United States. I was happy for Bill, though less so for Hillary. It's what she had signed on for, of course, but it also meant
the end of her last vestige of self. Bill drew energy from being in
the spotlight, walking among the people. When he was down, he
looked for a public appearance. Hillary was much more private.
She liked to kick off her shoes, read a book, go to a movie. I
would miss seeing her old, blue Oldsmobile in the office parking
lot. Hillary had long resisted the accompaniment of the governor's
security staff. She was determined to live as much of a real life as
possible. She drove herself, kept her own hours. After work, she
often stopped by the video store. Many times she convinced Vince
and me to knock off at four-thirty and go catch a five o'clock
movie. Her life, and ours, was about to change.

I missed Hillary once Bill announced his candidacy for President. Until then, I at least had a sounding board. I told her about
how the Wards were draining me. I wish I had told her my whole
story, but I couldn't. I don't know what she would have said, but
I know I would have been better off. She listened to my Ward
woes and sympathized, often making me laugh when it was the
last thing I felt like doing.

As they hit the campaign trail, I was consumed by POM. Trial
was scheduled to begin on November 4. I had crisscrossed the

country deposing witnesses and lining up experts. We hired a patent attorney and an economist. It was going to be all-out war in the courtroom. I had to prepare Skeeter to testify, not the easiest job in the world. We booked a suite at the Legacy Hotel, across the street from the federal courthouse. It was a place to work during lunch recess, and a convenient place to give last-minute coaching to witnesses before they headed to court. My secretary, an associate, and a paralegal manned the suite twenty-four hours a day. I had told the Wards we had a fifty-fifty chance to win.

My friend was running for President of the United States, I was starting the trial of my life to save my family's business, but my thoughts constantly drifted to the hospital room where my mother lay. She'd had a bout with cancer in the early 1980s; the doctors had urged her to quit smoking, and she had—cold turkey. That bought her another decade, but cancer finally returned to her spine. She entered the hospital again as I went into court to do battle for POM. I visited her every morning and evening, but soon it was obvious she would never leave the hospital. She died right in the middle of the case. I felt terribly guilty—why hadn't I spent more time with her? The day she died I asked the judge for a one-day continuance to attend to the funeral arrangements, but the judge wouldn't hear of it. He would either declare a mistrial, causing us to have to start all over, or court would proceed. An associate handled the case that one day I was gone. At the end of the month, we gave closing arguments and rested our case. After a day and a half of deliberation, the jury rendered a verdict. POM lost.

It was devastating to me, to Skeeter, to Seth, to Suzy, to the entire family. I felt that I had let them all down.

One day Hillary took a break from the campaign and stopped at the office to check her mail. She invited me to sit with her as she went through her messages and cleaned off her desk. She apologized for not having been able to get back for Mom's funeral, and inquired how I was holding up. She had heard about the POM verdict and surmised how devastating it had been. She imagined I was going through a pretty tough time. This time, rather than breaking down, I simply said that I was okay and turned the conversation to what was going on with the campaign. I was beyond emotion.

Hillary visted the office very seldom during that period, though the campaign hadn't really geared up yet. Once she called from the road and got both Vince and me on the phone. She told us that there would be press inquiries about her work with the Rose firm, and she wanted to be sure there was a system for dealing with that. She wanted to make sure the calls were handled responsibly, with sound judgment. Vince and I persuaded the firm that all press inquiries about Hillary would go through either Vince or me.

Sure enough, we started fielding calls immediately. People wanted to know if she was a "real lawyer." People had heard that she, Vince, and I had tried to take over the firm. Then, just before the New Hampshire primary, in one day the stories took on a nasty tone. A lounge singer named Gennifer Flowers was about to go public with a claim that she'd had a long-term affair with Bill Clinton. The phones really started ringing once that story had been leaked. Suddenly I received an urgent call from Vince, asking me to come to his office right away. I practically ran down the hall and knocked on his door. When I saw his face, I closed the door behind me. He was pale, shaking. He could hardly talk. No wonder he had called me to come to him—he probably couldn't have even walked to my office.

"What is it?" I said.

He finally managed to tell me. He had just received a tip from the Clinton campaign that not only were the tabloids going with the Gennifer story, but there was a possibility they were going to also run with a story about Hillary's having an affair, too. He and I were the likely ones to be named.

I remembered a similar day thirteen years before, after I'd been elected mayor. Hillary had given me good advice then. "You've got to prepare your family," I told Vince. The campaign painted a pretty bleak picture of the story that might run—lots of innuendo, very few details. We talked about how to react in case a horde of reporters showed up on his doorstep. He panicked at the very thought. He was worried about Lisa and his children. What would they think? How would they take such a thing?

By coincidence, Vince's sister Sheila was visiting from Washington that day, and she later stopped by the office to say hello. She could certainly tell that Vince wasn't himself. I saw him hug her in the hall and then take her into his office and close the door. She was probably the one person in the world that he would bare his soul to. I've often wondered what he said to her that day.

After Sheila left, Vince asked if I would mind staying at the office while he went home to talk with his family. I told him fine, I would hold down the fort. I would call him if I heard anything. And if nothing had happened by the time my kids got home from school, I would go home to prepare my family.

My children were much older than they'd been when I was mayor. They asked many questions:

"They wouldn't come to the house, would they?"

"Well, baby, they might."

"How can they publish such a thing if it's not true?"

"Well, honey . . ."

"Is Momma okay?"

The story never ran. The next day at work, Vince came into my office. He was like a man who had seen the fabled white light and then received a reprieve. "Hub," he said, "I just can't *deal* with the press. I'll do all the background work, the legwork, all the research—but, please, *you* take all the press calls."

I told him not to worry, that would be fine.

I was a little surprised—Vince Foster could handle anything. But in the midst of life you sometimes fail to see the patterns.

The Gennifer Flowers story did run, of course, in all its tawdry detail. Vince and I talked about how Hillary must be feeling. We wished we could tell her we knew exactly what she was going through. Not that we did. This was a particular burden that Hillary had learned, through unenviable experience, to bear with a remarkable level of dignity. I'm sure it required even more retrenching behind the mask. I didn't hear from Hillary while any of this was going on, and I never talked to her about the Gennifer story.

Within a few days, I found myself watching my two friends being questioned about their marriage on *60 Minutes*. My heart reached out to them, having to justify their marriage on national television. Suzy commented, "Doesn't anybody ever get any credit for keeping their marriage together?"

While the Gennifer story was in the news, Suzy got a call from her mother. "Tell Webb to call Sally," she said. "She knows something about Gennifer." I called my sister-in-law and she told me that her former husband, Finus, was Gennifer Flowers's boyfriend. Oh, the old Arkansas interconnectedness! Finus and Sally and gotten married in 1977 but had divorced in the late 1980s. I had always liked Finus, and we'd stayed in touch after the divorce. I called him. "Finus, tell me this is all some cruel joke." He stood by Gennifer's story, and I wished him well. The Finus angle helped my family put these kinds of stories in perspective. Uncle Finus had always made everybody laugh. Even his name was his mother's attempt at humor—he was the last kid she was going to have. Once he was involved here, the story somehow didn't seem to have such bite. My kids began to take tabloid journalism with a grain of salt.

As the campaign heated up (and everyone, including my Rose firm partners, began to count Bill Clinton out), Vince and I worked with Betsey Wright, the governor's right hand, to try to prepare for any eventuality. Betsey worked downtown in what we called the Bunker, an old block building filled with metal desks and rickety chairs and young people we didn't know. Nothing would be sacred, Betsey predicted. She suggested we try to think of all the issues that might be sensitive, or embarrassing. She wanted us to go through Hillary's files to see if she'd written any controversial opinions. Betsey had me cross-reference and check firm clients against Bill's contributors. I asked a Washington law firm to give us an opinion on whether the way we compensated Hillary had violated any federal election laws. Two lawyers from the campaign, Jim Lyons and Kevin O'Keefe, came and interviewed Vince and me for hours, asking every conceivable question about Hillary and her work. Afterward, on the way back to the office, Vince turned to me and said, "Webb, I know Hillary said to talk to those two, but"—and here he paused to deliver, with a wry smile, one of his favorite movie lines—"who *are* those guys?" We were Butch and Sundance, trying to find footing in a dangerous world. I called Betsey, just to make sure Jim and Kevin were okay. She assured me they were.

Every morning my phone rang with calls from more reporters wanting answers to questions about Hillary and the firm. At first the lines of communication between us and the campaign were indirect. More than once, Vince and I picked up the newspaper to see some staff person we had never met being quoted about Rose firm business. Where did they get *that*? we wondered. I attribute the confusion over the initial inquiry about Madison to just such a communication gap. The initial questions were fired at us so rapidly, we hardly had time to answer, let alone to elaborate or explain anything. Had we ever represented McDougal? they all wanted to know. Vince and I started to assemble all the files, and then a call came from the campaign: "We have to say in one hour that you never represented Madison Savings and Loan."

"You can't say that," I told them.

"Why not?"

"Because it's not true."

"Well, what do we tell them?"

"What is the *question*?"

Occasionally I would get a call from Susan Thomases, Hillary's good friend, and I knew I could unload a bit on her. "Susan, we've got attorney-client issues here; we have old records we can't locate; we have other partners involved who aren't sympathetic to this race." I knew she would understand—especially about the firm's dynamics. There were all these young campaign people who didn't know Vince and me, and we didn't know them. We weren't sure whom we could trust with our answers.

The next firestorm involved Hillary's representation of Madison. I was talking to Susan. She told me the focus of the inquiry was, "Did Hillary, through Bill, use her influence with Beverly

Bassett to take some particular action on Madison's behalf?" Normally, this would be just one of a hundred such inquiries, and we would tell the campaign "no" and they would tell the press "no" and that would be the end of it. But because of Jerry Brown's attacks on Hillary, a simple no was not sufficient. Susan explained that Jeff Gerth of *The New York Times* had an excellent reputation, and thus we—meaning the campaign and the Rose firm—had to try to honor his very specific requests. (I have my own opinion of his reputation now.) Vince interviewed Rick Massey, now a partner, and verified that Hillary's involvement in this part of Madison's business was "minimal" and that Rick was responsible for bringing the business to the firm. His story on the latter point would eventually change. Vince was skittish about Rick, because he had never been one of Hillary's fans. Also, Rick seemed reluctant to let Vince look through the files. Instead, he kept them in his office and made copies for Vince.

During the campaign, Hillary would sometimes call and say, "I'm landing at five o'clock." Vince and I would stay late and wait for her. She loved shortbread, and usually brought some for us to snack on. We would fix drinks in the office—in the old days she had liked Crown Royal, or, if it had been an especially tough day, vodka on the rocks. But now she would drink only tea. We would spend a couple of hours catching up on one another's worlds. The next morning she would fly away again.

I saw Bill more than I did Hillary during this time. He would come home for a day or two to rest his voice and take a look at his desk (after all, he was the governor), and his assistant would call and ask if I could get him out for a round of golf. I always made time. He loved playing at the Country Club of Little Rock. It was close to his office, it had a high, beautiful view, and there usually were no crowds so he could play fast. We played with Hillary's two brothers on one of these campaign breaks. Hugh and Tony Rodham were great fun to be around, and they enjoyed kidding their brother-in-law. Bill told them about my playing golf like a Republican. After our round, the Rodhams and I went to the Men's Grill for a drink, while Bill greeted all the people who wanted to talk with him. Hillary had sent me about six messages telling me not to let Bill smoke, because of his voice, but I didn't even try to keep him from his usual Diet Coke and cigars. I watched him absorb energy from the scores of outstretched palms he shook that day. Everything had already changed.

I thought about the time, years before, when he'd called and said he wanted to meet in the middle of the day "for just nine holes," because he had to get back to an important meeting. I had the cart ready when his car pulled up. We went out alone, and he was playing very well. After nine holes, he said, "I just can't quit. Let's play ten, eleven, and twelve." He parred the tenth hole. On eleven, he came within an inch of a hole in one. Then he bogeyed twelve. "Let's play thirteen," he said.

It was a par four, and he hit it in for an eagle. It was an amazing moment. We played all eighteen holes, and he dashed off—an hour late—for his meeting. We were two bad boys who had played hooky, and because of that he never could brag to anyone except me about that great shot he had made.

I remember thinking, We'll never be able to sneak away again.

As the Democratic Convention approached, I got a call from Marsha Scott, who had been working on the campaign in California. "When are you getting to New York?" she said.

I told her I wasn't. I hadn't been traveling with the campaign, and I was too good a friend just to show up for the party.

"You're nuts," Marsha said. "Bill and Hillary will be hurt if you don't go."

Wondering if maybe I was skewed in my thinking, I wandered down the hall to Vince's office. "You going to the convention?" I said. He wasn't—for almost the same reasons I gave Marsha.

A few days later, I got a call from Nancy Hernreich. "When are you and Vince coming to New York?" she said. I started to give her the answer I gave Marsha, but she cut me off. "We only have a few rooms for family, and Hillary has put you and Vince on the list. The hotel needs to know when you're arriving." Suddenly we couldn't say no.

We got to the InterContinental Hotel to find the place a madhouse. The lobby was full of media, sightseers, and the occasional

Razorback fan in red and white. Every time someone walked through the lobby, you could hear the onlookers whisper, *"Is that anybody?"* Vince and I were surprised to find that our rooms were on the same floor as Bill and Hillary's—a great luxury, except for the Secret Service bringing bomb-sniffing dogs through your room bright and early every morning. But we didn't know that yet.

Sometime that first afternoon, while Vince was off sightseeing with his son, I met up with Mickey Kantor for a drink. He started telling me about this wonderful "event" that Harry and Linda Bloodworth-Thomason had conceived for the next night. Linda had found a remarkable piece of footage showing a young Bill Clinton shaking hands with President John F. Kennedy. They were going to show that tomorrow night—and at that moment, Bill and Hillary were going to enter the arena. They would make this televised "walk" from the hotel to the convention hall. No nominee since JFK had entered the hall prior to his formal nomination. Bill and Hillary would arrive just as the crowd was whipped to a crescendo. Harry saw history in the making. I listened, nodding. I was beginning to feel I was caught up in a surrealist movie.

Hillary had said to come by at three in the afternoon. At the appointed hour, Vince and I ambled down the hall to see if we could find her. The Secret Service detail blocked all access. As we were walking away, Nancy came out of the suite. She told us Hillary wasn't there, that she was late for a meeting. We probably wouldn't be able to see her, she said.

Disappointed, we headed for the elevator. When the door opened, there was Hillary—along with a dozen other people carrying notebooks and cell phones and walkie-talkies. "Hub! Foster!" She threw her arms around us and said we just *had* to come back to the suite. "Now, Hillary," someone said. "You need to get some rest."

"I need some time with my *friends,*" she said.

We had a wonderful, warm visit—though it was not long enough. We reminisced about the last time the three of us were in New York together—the day of the Daniel Ludwig deposition, the night of the wild Italian opera dinner. Her eyes moistened with the memory. It was a long time ago. I mentioned the "walk" lined up for the convention tomorrow night.

"Oh, I don't know," said Hillary. "I'm not sure it's a good idea. We may not do it." All around the suite were blowups of the *People* magazine pictures of a made-over Hillary. I remember meeting Vince's eye as we admired the photographs. They were stunning. Her hair was blonder, her lips were redder, her eyes were prettier, and her clothes were fancier. The person in the photographs was someone we recognized, but didn't really know. She had become a cover girl.

A campaign person came and told her she had to be somewhere in a few minutes, so we got up to leave. She hugged us good-bye. "If you guys don't want to fight the convention floor madness," she said, "come watch it on TV with Bill and me." Then she was whisked off into some inner room.

Vince and I were flattered to get the invitation to watch the convention with our friends. That evening we hooked up for dinner with Marsha Scott, Mickey Kantor, and his wife, Heidi Schulman. I happened to mention to Mickey that Hillary wasn't sure they were going to do "the walk."

Mickey was beside himself. "What?" he said. "They've got to. If they don't, all the planning we've done for this week will be for nothing."

Then he said, "Webb, you've got a job to do. Make them take this walk."

I told Vince he would have to help me. "No way," he said.

That night when we got to the Clinton suite, I had no idea how I was going to convince Hillary and Bill to do this thing they didn't believe in. *I* was no media adviser. What credentials did I bring to this task? But that soon became the least of my problems. Once we were ushered through the crowd and past the grim men guarding the door, then through a phalanx of buzzing aides and advisers, I suddenly heard a loud and disturbingly jolly voice calling through the din. "Hub! Vincenzo! Come on! We're celebrating!" Vince and I looked at Hillary and then at each other. We were both thinking the very same thing: Oh my God, she's . . . tipsy.

Hillary and Bill were dressed casually, relaxing on the couch. A half-empty bottle of champagne sat on the table in front of them. There was an empty chair next to Hillary. "You take it," Vince said. "You're the one who has to talk to her."

I confess I fixed myself a strong drink first. "Hillary," I began, summoning up my best negotiating manner. "Mickey was telling me how important this 'walk' is tonight. A lot of people have gone to a lot of trouble to make this happen." I caught her catching me glance at her glass.

Her eyes twinkled, and she acted the slightest bit woozy. Then she said, "I know—we're going to do it!" I then found out she was still nursing her first glass of wine. Bill was drinking Diet Coke. She fell out laughing at how relieved I looked.

The next thing I knew, she was asking us to go with them over to the convention hall. I could hardly believe it. She was asking us about a minute and a half before it was time to go. "You're going with us, aren't you?" she said. Vince and I looked at each other with faces that said, "Yeah!"

On the way down in the elevator, Bruce Lindsey gave us instructions: "As soon as the governor breaks through the crowd and enters the limousine, we have to sprint to the car immediately behind the limo. They get him in the car and they go."

So, as soon as Bill broke through the crowd, I heard Bruce yell, "Run!" I was the first to arrive at the Suburban immediately behind the limousine—I can still move pretty quickly when I want to. I yanked open the door and staring me in the face was a high-powered weapon held by a surprised Secret Service agent. I heard Bruce yell again, "Hubbell, you're gonna get your ass shot! Get in the van behind the Suburban."

I ended the evening standing with a group of proud Arkansans watching our governor walk into the convention hall while silver confetti rained down on all of our heads. I flew home and told Suzy, "Bill Clinton is going to be our next President."

Bill was elected President twenty years after Richard Nixon was reelected to that office. One of the most sought-after interviews was Hillary's first postelection interview, and that honor went to my daughter Rebecca for her high school newspaper. I still cherish a picture of Hillary and Rebecca in the kitchen of the Governor's Mansion. Hillary has dark circles and bags under her eyes. It had been a long, hard journey.

I actually missed election night in Little Rock. The oral argument for the POM appeal was scheduled for the Wednesday morning after the election in Washington, D.C. No matter how much I pleaded, the clerk didn't seem moved by my story that my friend was about to be elected President of the United States and that I wanted to be in Arkansas with him. So I flew east on Tuesday as all the rest of the world was descending on Little Rock. I watched the election returns on TV at the home of Strobe Talbott and Brooke Shearer.

A few days later, I got a call informing me that Bill wanted to play golf. This time we had to go to the new Robert Trent Jones course out in far west Little Rock—at a development called Chenal Valley. The Country Club of Little Rock had become off limits during the campaign when the media reported that the club had no black members. I had been trying to get minority members into the club for years. "Work on that membership," Bill told me, "so we can play again at the country club."

I asked him if he wanted anyone else to play with us, but he said no. He wanted to relax—but I think he also had an ulterior motive that day. Our old friend Mickey Kantor had done brilliant work as chairman of the campaign, and prior to the election Mickey had been named acting head of the transition team. It was a tough and thankless job. Nobody wanted to plan *too* much, because we were afraid we would jinx the election. It's all part of the old Arkansas inferiority complex. We can't actually believe something good's going to happen to us. It made me think of all the years nobody in Arkansas would ever admit to thinking the Razorbacks might actually beat Texas.

Then immediately after the election, all sorts of stories started appearing in the press criticizing Mickey, his law firm, and his management style. He was devastated. He felt betrayed, he said. He felt that these stories had been planted by people in the campaign who didn't want Mickey to be named head of the transition team, which everyone believed would naturally lead to his being named chief of staff. He suspected that George Stephanopoulos and his staff were behind it. I was appalled when Mickey told me that. "Can't we just enjoy the victory for a few days," I said, "before the jockeying for position begins?" I was hopelessly naive.

Mickey was talking about going back to California. There was to be a party for the campaign staff, and Mickey told me he and Heidi had decided not to go. I said that was crazy, that this was *his* party and he ought to enjoy it. They finally relented, and I drove them to the party in my car. I doubt Mickey enjoyed himself that night—I'm sure he didn't. I was amazed at the whispers when we walked in. Everywhere you looked, eyes were slanted and tongues were wagging. Some people actually came up to Mickey and told him how brave it was of him to show. Wasn't this a *victory* party? I wondered. Yes, but it was also something else, though I didn't recognize it at the time. We were in Little Rock, but this was my first real taste of Washington.

The next morning Mickey met with the President-elect. He was told that he was not going to be the head of the transition team (that job would eventually go to Warren Christopher). That afternoon I drove Mickey to the airport and he headed home to Los Angeles. I was probably the only one who knew he would be back. Mickey had sustained tremendous personal loss in his life (he lost his first wife and one son in tragic accidents), and while this loss wasn't in that category, it had to hurt tremendously. Since 1987, he had worked diligently to get Bill Clinton elected President. Now, the day after Mickey achieved that goal, he was forced out in a palace coup.

On the Saturday that Bill and I were to play golf, I drove to the Governor's Mansion so we could ride out to the course. The Secret Service, Arkansas State Police, and Little Rock policemen were blocking all the streets in and out of the mansion. They looked at me like I was crazy when I said, "I'm Webb Hubbell. I'm here to play golf with the President-elect." With a great deal of skepticism, they radioed the guardhouse and the mansion. You could see the surprise in their eyes when they were told, "Let him through." When I was finally able to pull into the parking lot and get my clubs out of my car, I approached the Secret Service detail there and asked them where I was to put my clubs. They first opened the trunk of the President-elect's limo but there was no room for the clubs because the trunk was full of weaponry. I ultimately put them in one of the many vehicles that seemed to escort the President-elect wherever he went.

It was a twenty-minute drive to the course. When we were under way, I turned to Bill and said, "Congratulations, Mr. President." He looked at me and slapped my knee, and we both laughed like little boys. When we got to Chenal, the pro had already set out the cart. Nobody was on the course because it was November and bitterly cold. The press was gathered back near the clubhouse, but then they began following us to the first tee. Bill was furious. He started yelling at the aide who had let them on the course. As the media moved back, the mood they'd created lingered. Neither of us hit very well off the tee. But once we got in the cart and out away from the crowds, we settled down and enjoyed ourselves.

People have asked me time and again what kinds of weighty subjects we discussed on the golf course. It might start with him saying, "What do you think I did wrong on that shot?" That was usually the level of our conversation—which was probably why I was invited. He needed somebody to relax with, and I was that person. I could make him laugh—on that same day, I said something to him about being in the way when I was putting, and he said, "You can't talk that way to your President!" But he also knew that if he had something he wanted to discuss, I was a pretty good sounding board.

After our round he talked with the mob who by now had heard we were there, and he had the car stop once so he could shake hands with people along the way. Then on the way home he asked, "How's Mickey?"

I told him Mickey was hurt, but that he had shown great courage going to that staff party—and that his going also demonstrated a loyalty to something greater than himself. The President-elect watched me closely while I talked. I told him he needed to find a way to get Mickey back to Little Rock. I knew that Mickey was first and foremost loyal to him and Hillary, and from what I had seen the first week of transition, they were going to need a few loyal friends.

Afterward, we went back to the mansion and into the kitchen, where we raided the refrigerator just like in old times.

Hillary hadn't been back to the Rose firm since the election, and Vince told her she really needed to come and say good-bye. He volunteered to organize a reception.

It was, I admit, a delicious moment, and he had a perversely fine time putting it all together. In the office, Vince and I were suddenly greeted with more smiles than ever before. Partners stopped to ask if they could help. On the day of the event, there was a palpable buzz in the office. Spouses began showing up. People were dressed a tad nicer than the day before. Refreshments were set up on the huge marble table in the conference room. The partners and associates and secretaries milled around nervously, waiting for their old law partner, the First Lady-elect of the United States.

Vince and I had given her names to reflect her changing status over the years. Sometimes we called her "Hillary Sue," after the flap over her maiden name. An irascible lawyer from another firm, Bill Wilson, told her that if the people wanted a good old Arkansas name, she ought to go whole hog. "Is this Hillary Sue Clinton?" he would say when she picked up her phone. "Why, Billy Roy Wilson, I do declare!" she would say, and they both would die laughing. She had also been FLA, for First Lady of Arkansas. Now, we decided, she was FLEA—First Lady-elect of America. Soon she would be FLOTUS—First Lady of the United States. I have a picture of her in my study autographed, "To Webb, From FLA, FLEA, FLOTUS."

The secretaries all asked for her autograph during the reception, and the partners and their spouses acted as though she was their long-lost best friend. Everyone wanted to tell her how proud they were of her. Then they squeezed in close while the flash bulbs popped. Vince and I stood on the sidelines and laughed.

The transition energized Vince. Instead of being his reserved and private old self, he was upbeat and outgoing. He was in and out of the office a lot, and I learned that he was working at the transition headquarters every night until after midnight. When I asked what he was doing, he wouldn't tell me. "I can't talk about it," he would say. He did mention that Lisa was furious because he was never home. I figured it was because she knew something I only guessed at—he was going to Washington.

He and I had talked about it one day back in the early fall, when we first started to absorb the outrageous idea that our friend Bill might actually become President. And Hillary would be First Lady! As I say, we didn't like to mention it for fear of jinxing something, but Vince brought up the subject at a party. "If they ask, will you go?" he said. I said, "Only if you go. What about you?" "Only if you go," he said. We shook on it—if our friends became President and First Lady, and if we were asked, we would all go to Washington together.

I too was helping the transition team. Warren Christopher had called and asked me to lunch to pick my brain about how to work with Bill and Hillary. I was receiving a dozen calls a day from people asking if I could get them jobs in the administration. Vince and I were at the Governor's Mansion a lot during those weeks. We had to meet with Hillary on a myriad of issues, including her resignation from the firm. It was hard to get anything finished because so many people were coming and going. One day Hillary told me there was somebody downstairs that she wanted me to meet. From the staircase I saw an attractive woman about my age. I went over and introduced myself. "Zoe Baird," she said. I liked her immediately. At that point, she had not been nominated for attorney general. Daily, people were coming in and out of the mansion, meeting with the President-elect as he was putting together his Cabinet.

After that first golf game, Mickey was appointed to the transition board and returned to Little Rock to organize the President-elect's economic summit. He moved into Walter's bedroom in Hubbell's Folly and soon he became such a part of our family that Elizabeth Fitzgerald started calling him "MickeyKantor." One morning he came downstairs carrying some dirty shirts. He asked Suzy where a cleaners was. Elizabeth overheard and was incensed. "MickeyKantor," she said, "in this house, *I* do the shirts." He tried to protest, but eventually gave in just as the rest of us did.

The economic summit was a huge success and the campaign wounds were quickly healing. Before returning to L.A., Mickey met with the President-elect to discuss his future. Mickey told me as I drove him to the airport that he was interested in becoming United States trade representative. Several days later on the fourteenth tee, the President-elect asked, "What do you think I should do about Mickey?"

I told him I knew that one of the positions Mickey was interested in was U.S. trade representative. Mickey was a hell of a negotiator, I said—I reminded him that Mickey had negotiated with Bush's campaign officials over the terms of the presidential debates, and it was a widely held belief that the debate formats Mickey negotiated were extremely favorable to Clinton. The President-elect listened intently and agreed about Mickey's negotiating talents.

A few days before Christmas, Warren Christopher tracked me down at a friend's Christmas party. The President-elect had asked him to call and tell me he was nominating Mickey to be U.S. trade representative. "Can you get hold of Mickey?" Christopher said. "He needs to get here immediately. We want to announce his nomination the morning of the twenty-fourth." I got on the phone and found Mickey. I told him the great news and to call the mansion.

On Christmas Eve, Mickey, Zoe, and the balance of the Cabinet were introduced by the President-elect. As the congratulatory crowd surrounded Mickey, Bill pulled me aside. He said, "We're going, aren't we?" I wasn't sure what he was talking about. He could tell. "Shopping," he said.

"Are you kidding?"

He laughed. "Meet me at the mansion in an hour. I've got a ton of stuff to buy."

One thing Mickey Kantor had told me was, "Once Bill Clinton is elected President, your life will never be the same." I won't even attempt to plumb all the irony in that line. But the truth of it was abundantly clear when I arrived at the mansion to meet the President-elect for Christmas Eve shopping, 1992. Instead of one or two cars, this time we had a full-fledged motorcade. Chelsea went with us, and we all had fun creating traffic jams throughout The Heights. This wasn't a shopping trip—it was a parade. Bill enjoyed himself so much he decided we should go to Park Plaza Mall. Everybody wanted his picture, and he always obliged. The Secret Service detail looked like they were going to have mass heart attacks.

On the way home, he said, "Hub, are you going to Washington with us?"

I hadn't given a single thought to what I might do about my job, my family, my house, my responsibilities, my financial problems—none of it. But I wanted desperately to go. You know you're in a sick world when you think you're escaping *to* Washington.

I responded with characteristic eloquence. "Sure," I said.

And that was that. I had no idea what I would be doing, but it didn't matter. Bill turned to Chelsea. "Hub's going to Washington with us," he said. "Isn't that great?"

Part II

THE
FALL

8

The Three-Headed Monster

The Department of Justice building looks solid from the outside, as though some god had chiseled it into an Olympian block of granite. But it is not solid. Like many of the capital's buildings, it is really shaped like a fortress. In the center is a courtyard. Ordinary people gather there on nice days, to eat their sandwiches, to read their newspapers, to smoke their cigarettes.

I first set foot in that imposing building on the morning of January 21, 1993. The afternoon before, I had seen Bill sworn in as the forty-second President of the United States. For the few days preceding that, the Hubbells, the Fosters, and Kaki and Max Mehlburger celebrated at any number of dances and cocktail parties throughout the city. Kaki, the interior decorator at the White House, is professionally known as Kaki Hockersmith. Max, a lawyer in Little Rock, is best known on the East Coast as captain of the *Pirate*—winner of the Marin-to-Bermuda sailboat race.

The Rose firm threw a big Washington party of its own that week. Vince checked out the legalities of our (we were now government employees) going to a party being given by a law firm we were no longer members of. We had already learned that we had to think about things like that. Luckily, it was okay. The partners were very excited about everything that was happening and were even talking about opening a D.C. office. The only cloud was a lingering resentment that one of the firm's clients, Aromatique—a nationally known potpourri and soap maker—hadn't been awarded the contract for the inaugural fragrances, which was called Scent of Hope. Since Hillary had been their attorney and was good friends with the owners, the firm asked me to "talk to Hillary." I wrote her a memo, which began with the words, "This is not a *Saturday Night Live* skit." I ended it with a question: "Do you think Boris Yeltsin ever worries about the 'Scent of Siberia'?"

On January 18, my forty-fifth birthday, we had a wonderful dinner at Tiberio's with Mickey and Heidi, Vince and Lisa, Kaki and Max Mehlburger, and friends from California. That week, I saw Bill and Hillary only from afar. At the big gala just before the swearing-in, Suzy and I did manage to sit close enough to them to say hello. This was also where Nancy Hernreich told me to have my golf clubs sent to Washington, which prompted me to have them shipped by FedEx. I was too tired and tense to attend any of the inaugural balls. I was also nervous, thinking about the enormity of what I was facing. So as Washington celebrated on a night of unparalleled glitter, Suzy and I went to bed at 10:00 P.M.—anticipating the cold and very early light of dawn.

While he was still President-elect, Bill told Zoe Baird, his nominee for attorney general, that he hoped she and I would get together and talk. He thought I could be of help to her at Justice. In December, she called me in Little Rock and asked me to fly to Washington to meet with her just after the New Year. Over a long lunch at the Jefferson Hotel, she asked about my background—and why I was willing to give up my law practice to come work with her in a capacity neither of us could be sure of at that point. "Because the President asked me to come to Washington with him," I said. "When the President asks, you say yes." She was particularly curious about Bill Clinton—how he made decisions, who his key advisers would be. I discussed with her how he uses everyone to test his own ideas, and told her that he would listen to everyone on an issue, both in and out of the White House. She was curious about what kind of access she would have to the President, and I told her that more than likely she'd be getting midnight calls from him herself. When Bill was wrestling with an issue as governor, he was famous for calling his friends and advisers in the middle of the night. Suzy would often roll over and ask who on earth had been on the phone at *midnight*. "It was just the governor," I'd tell her. "He wanted to talk." She would cover her head and go back to sleep.

Zoe also wanted to know all about Hillary and Mac McLarty. I assured her that Hillary was not going to interfere with her job, but suggested that she remember that first and foremost, Hillary was a lawyer and that Zoe could count on her to be an ally. I advised her to keep Hillary informed. I also told her that there would be no one easier to work with than Mac. At the end of our lunch, she said, "How soon can you join me at Justice?" The day after the inauguration was about as quickly as either of us could make it.

My family was heading home that day as well. We'd decided that Suzy and the children—except for Walter, who was a sophomore at Sewanee—would stay in Little Rock until June. Rebecca wanted to finish her senior year in her old school, and we still had to sell Hubbell's Folly. I'd made arrangements to stay with my cousin Ruth in Chevy Chase until I found a place of my own. During a brunch at her house, she said she had a basement bedroom I could use. Little did she know that I would be there for two whole months. I was the Man Who Came to Brunch.

Vince had actually started as deputy White House counsel at the moment the President took the oath of office. He had been the Clintons' official representative to open the White House. At the swearing-in ceremony, Vince showed me his White House pass. "This is the most valuable possession in Washington," he said. He had to leave prior to Bill's taking the oath so that he could be at the White House door the very moment the Clinton administration was official. Before Lisa moved to Washington, he was living with his sister Sheila and her husband, Congressman Beryl Anthony. While I was commuting via the Metro, Vince was driving an old white van that Beryl had used for campaigning. It had red shag carpeting on the floor and walls, and Marsha quickly nicknamed it the Pimpmobile. Vince thought it was great fun to pull up to the gate of the White House in a vehicle like that. It gave the West Wing lot the aura of a tailgate party at a Razorbacks game.

The twenty-first of January was just the first official day of work. We had been going nonstop for two months, of course. Zoe had sent me home after that lunch with a massive stack of briefing books and files, and I'd been in lengthy conversations with Bernie Nussbaum, the White House counsel. I liked Bernie, a small man with electric energy, and yet I'd been slightly surprised when Hillary told me Vince was to be deputy counsel instead of the top man. "Three boys from Hope running the White House would just be too much," she'd said. Mac, Vince, and Bill had all played together when they were kids. "Vince will be fine," Hillary said.

During the transition, Warren Christopher had given me several potential nominees and staffers to vet (not that "vetting"—a term that originates from veterinarians checking out horses before they're bought—was something I was familiar with), including Housing Secretary Henry Cisneros and Communications Director George Stephanopoulos. I flew to Texas to see Cisneros, and found him to be extremely candid about a very sensitive subject. He had been involved in an affair, which had been made public more than five years earlier.

As for Stephanopoulos, his background was as clean as a whistle. During the campaign, my contacts in the inner circle had been limited to Mickey and Betsey and her staff. I really didn't know George. But because of Mickey's experience, I was very guarded when I began working with him. That came following the election, when we worked together on the transition team's ethics rules and the President-elect's promise that his high-ranking appointments would be prohibited from lobbying their agencies for five years after leaving office. I found George damned smart, but he was a bit cocky for my southern sensibilities.

Vince and I had split the work of helping Hillary leave Little Rock. She still had to resign from the Rose firm, negotiate a settlement, and get out of the building partnership. Her case files needed to be turned over to other lawyers, and there were other considerations as well. One item on Vince's checklist of things that needed to be taken care of before they went to Washington was "get out of Whitewater." At that moment, Bill and Hillary were still 50 percent owners of the Whitewater Corporation with Jim and Susan McDougal. When we got to that item on the list, Vince said he would discuss it with Jim Blair, corporate counsel for Tyson Foods and a close friend of both Clintons. I later learned that Blair contacted Jim McDougal and arranged to have McDougal buy the Clintons out of Whitewater for a nominal amount.

Not surprisingly, the President-elect had his own massive task of packing up and moving on after a dozen years in office. I played a crucial role in that, a role that has been misunderstood for the last four years. Betsey Wright, who had been Bill's devoted chief of staff for almost ten years, was not going to Washington as part of the administration. Betsey's strength—her ferociousness in protecting her boss—had also become her major liability. She alienated too many people—especially the young East Coast know-it-alls who had jumped on the Clinton bandwagon once he got the nomination. It was time for Bill and Betsey to go their separate ways. It was a painful moment for all involved, and the pain contributed to a situation in which I was asked to intercede. During the campaign, Betsey had been the keeper of the candidate's files on sensitive issues, such as the draft and his early years. Nobody wanted to talk to Betsey about turning over the files. They just didn't have the nerve. Finally, during the week before everyone headed to Washington, Mac McLarty asked me to call her.

"Betsey," I said, "this is Webb. We need to talk about the files." I knew she was hurt and I sympathized. "I'm not going to keep these files," she said, much to my relief. "I just wanted somebody to talk to me about them." I explained that the files had to be in the possession of an attorney, so they could be protected by attorney-client privilege. She was more than willing to have them delivered to my office at the Rose firm. The index she had done of the files piqued my curiosity, but I didn't have time to look at them. These ten file boxes became known as the "Betsey files." I believe it was Vince who also brought three other small file folders to me for safekeeping. Rick Massey had been "squirrelly"—Vince's word—about turning over the Madison files until he made his own copy. The files showed that Rick had done the work before the Arkansas securities commissioner. Vince and I never said the words, but we both understood that we didn't want those files to turn up missing because who had done this work had already been an issue during the campaign. After we left for Washington, Walter moved the files to a small office off our bedroom at Hubbell's Folly. They would be safe there until we figured out what to do with them.

While preparing to take on our daunting new jobs, Vince and I had also had to deal with the prosaic details of extricating ourselves from our old lives. Vince's mentor, Phil Carroll, was furious when Vince told him he was leaving. "I wish Bill Clinton had never been elected!" Phil screamed, loud enough for everyone in the building to hear. He later apologized to Vince. It was just that he had brought Vince along all those years and now that Phil was ready to slow down, Vince wasn't going to be there. Vince also encountered reluctance from Lisa. She was having second thoughts about moving to Washington. So Vince went alone.

My clients were happy for me, even though I couldn't tell them exactly what I might be doing. The very fact that I was going at all had to be kept secret. My partners were generous in their congratulations. They sent me off with a letter of praise and good wishes, telling how much I would be missed. I appreciated that more than they knew. Yet I was glad to be leaving them for many reasons. For one, the firm just wouldn't be the same without Hillary and Vince. But I was also glad to be leaving behind the person I had become there. I saw my moving as a chance to begin anew. Lingering in the background, however, was a warning Bill Kennedy gave me as I left, "Washington is the meanest place I have ever been. It will chew you up and spit you out in a heartbeat." He was referring to his year working for Senator Keneaster Hodges. But in the same breath, Bill said, "If you have some position that you're having trouble filling, I might come." Two months later, he joined Vince working in the White House counsel's office.

Suzy and I still had to tell the Wards, and I asked Skeeter and Anne to meet us at Seth and Vonnie's house. Skeeter congratulated me, but Seth, predictably, couldn't understand why I would go off to work for Bill Clinton. "You know, Webb," he said, "you're going to get in trouble up there, and he's gonna drop you like a hot potato." Then there was his life's refrain: "What's going to happen to me?" He asked if I was taking Suzy and the children. "Dad," Suzy said, "we're a family. It'll be exciting for us. And this is a great honor for Webb—aren't you going to say congratulations?"

Seth just looked at Suzy and we left.

I hadn't really talked to Zoe while she was preparing for her confirmation hearing, but I had been talking frequently with Michael Cardozo, a friend of Zoe's from the days when both worked in the Jimmy Carter White House. Michael didn't want a job in the administration, so Zoe thought he would be perfect to help her get the department set up and herself ready for the hearing. I met Michael when I came out to have lunch with Zoe, and I liked him immensely. He was a sophisticated, dapper man with an easy manner and an unerring instinct for doing exactly the right thing at the right moment. We would become good friends during the next, very difficult year.

So on that cold morning after the inauguration, Michael met me at the entrance to the Department of Justice. By noon, he showed me to my new office, a room as expansive and as dignified as the dreams of a young law student from long ago. I didn't know it at the time, but he had instructed the people at Justice to address me as "Judge Hubbell."

In America we like to think the government goes on, no matter what external changes occur. But as Hemingway once said: "Isn't it pretty to think so." In fact, partisanship is the order of the day. Washington is a top-down town, and when there's a new person at the top, that affects everything below. At Justice we were basically starting from scratch on that morning. The same thing was happening in every other agency in town—even in the White House. Marsha Scott, initially head of White House correspondence, told me that the minute George Bush was out and Bill Clinton was in, a crew of staffers poured into the West Wing to try to get set up. The place had been cleaned out. Some desks didn't even have chairs. Not every office had a telephone. Computers were a rarity, and the few remaining had been cleaned of information. In hindsight, it's easy for me to say the transition period should be longer. But in reality, considering partisan politics (even within the same party), I'm not sure that would help.

Zoe was expected to be confirmed by noon on the twenty-first, and Mike Cardozo was staying only until Zoe was officially in office. Mike's final duty had been to inform all the Bush appointees that their services were no longer required. By law the government is required to have an attorney general at all times, so Zoe had asked Stuart Gerson, the assistant attorney general for the civil division, to stay on as acting attorney general until she was sworn in. As the new administration set up shop that day, I was the only permanent political appointee in the Justice Department. As Zoe's representative, Michael gave me the vague title of assistant to the attorney general.

I was then taken across the street for a drug test. At first I panicked. "What about that bottle of wine I drank to celebrate my friend's inauguration?" I asked the nurse.

"We're *not* looking for alcohol," she said, brusquely. The samples were sent by FedEx to a lab in San Francisco. I made a note to find out how much the government was wasting to send piss across the country.

Afterward, I called Vince to tell him I was safely ensconced in the hallowed halls once inhabited by Robert F. Kennedy and Griffin Bell. We shared stories from the day before; then Vince got serious. "Learn all you can, Webb," he said. "Zoe's nomination may be in trouble."

With that ominous thought echoing in my head, I went with Mike to meet Stuart Gerson. At the employee cafeteria in the basement of the Justice Building, I was introduced to a tall, formal man who made Vince seem loose and easygoing. But though Gerson was a die-hard Republican, he obviously had great respect for the institution he was temporarily heading. He had been following the hearings and said he felt the senators were going to beat up Zoe a bit on the "nanny issue," but then approve her.

That afternoon while I worked, I kept one eye on C-Span. Suddenly, I heard someone say, "Judge Hubbell, can we have a few minutes, sir?" I looked up and a band of press people were standing at my open door. *Now* I knew why everybody kept their doors shut at Justice—there was a press room right in the building, and the media was free to roam the halls.

Mike's office was next to mine, and he came to my rescue. We politely told the press we really didn't have any comment until the attorney general was confirmed. The media people backed off, but I could tell they weren't satisfied. And that, I think, was my first mistake at Justice. Partly, it was prompted by events—there wasn't an attorney general, and until we had one there was no way of knowing what my position would be in the Department of Justice. What none of us knew was that Zoe would withdraw her name from nomination that very evening, and Mike, Stuart, and I would continue to run this ad hoc Justice Department for nearly three long and rocky months. One newspaper called us "Justice's three-headed monster."

In hindsight, I wish I had talked with the media that day. At that point, my role was easily explainable—I was there to be a friendly hand during the transition. Unfortunately, the transition dragged on, and the longer it did, the more my silence created a negative aura about me. Instead of a friendly hand, I became a shadow figure, the Bill Clinton operative, the hulking mystery man doing who-knew-what at Justice. Maybe I was naive, but in Arkansas you wouldn't think twice about a friend helping a friend. I was learning that in Washington, every move is thought to have a motive and is therefore suspect.

Vince and Bernie promised to do their best to come up with another AG candidate quickly. In the meantime, the Department of Justice had to continue running. My greatest fear was that Mike Cardozo was going to leave, but he promised to stay as long as I needed him. Mike knew all the career people at Justice, and he was really the glue that held us together in those early days. He gave up his lucrative merchant banking practice for three months so that he could work twelve- to fourteen-hour days helping us. I don't think he's ever received the recognition he deserves.

The day after Zoe's withdrawal, Stuart called a meeting of all the department heads. He outlined the issues facing us, and then we plunged in. It was a little strange at first—Stuart, the Republican, was in charge, but I was clearly the person representing the new administration. I made a little speech emphasizing that we all had the same goal—to keep the department running until a successor could be named. Meanwhile, I said, we had a fine, hardworking acting attorney general in Stuart Gerson, and we should respect him and give him our support. I also said that a lot of people would be watching us to see how we handled ourselves during this difficult time.

Mike began wrestling with the problem of HIV-infected Haitians at the Guantanamo base in Cuba, coordinating policy making and legal positions with the National Security Council, the State Department, the Solicitor General's Office, and Defense. This was one policy issue Stuart was more than happy to leave to a new administration. As for me, until I arrived at Justice, I don't think I was even aware that the issue existed. I certainly had no idea of its ramifications on our policy regarding Cuba, or on our overall immigration policy. Soon, Mike was bringing to me the recommendations from the various agencies within the administration for my final decision.

There were many other front-burner questions as well. Potentially one of the most explosive was the problem with FBI Director William Sessions. I had read during the transition that he was under fire for his management of the agency. There were also accusations of his having used FBI resources to fix up his house and property. Director Sessions called me shortly after I got there and told me there were issues within the FBI that required my immediate attention. He mentioned several things and also worked in a personal plea: A lot of people were trying to destroy his reputation, he said, and he hoped I would keep an open mind about his side of the story. I assured him I would. Just as we hung up, someone handed me the Office of Professional Responsibility's report on Director Sessions. Things were moving fast. I gave it to Mike to read first. In a while, he came back and said, "Read this carefully. It will show you what can happen to you when you move to Washington."

The White House wasn't as accepting of Stuart Gerson as were Mike Cardozo and I. At first, George Stephanopoulos called me several times a day to make sure the administration's positions weren't being undermined. Bernie asked whether I thought the President should make an interim appointment, which I didn't. I thought Stuart was doing a good job in a difficult situation. When the President invited his Cabinet officers to Camp David the first weekend, Justice wasn't represented. Stuart wasn't invited to the State of the Union Address—until I pointed out that if some catastrophe occurred and everyone there was wiped out, Stuart would become President. Another higher-ranking Cabinet officer was then asked to stay home. The effect of this situation was twofold. The administration couldn't get its programs under way because it still had a Republican attorney general. And the media began focusing on what they called a leadership vacuum at Justice. Those articles irritated both Stuart and me. The job was getting done.

Very early on, Arkansas Night was conceived as a port in the storm. We had come from a community—at least it seemed so in retrospect. When you move on, you tend to remember the fond times and forget about the bad. There were people working in Washington now who had spent their entire adult lives side by side in the same office, or running into one another in the coffee shops and the restaurants, or meeting in the same courtrooms, or cheering for the Razorbacks in the stadium or at courtside. Now we never saw one another. Everyone was working too hard, too long, too late.

Even in the White House, where so many Arkansans now had their offices, it wasn't the same. We were in a new, more unforgiving league. There wasn't time to stop and chat. Even if you took time, someone harder would use that softness against you.

(For instance, if you left work at 8 P.M., someone would call a meeting and wonder why you weren't there.) But we Arkansans felt a need for companionship, for connection. Never mind that the Washington attitude was that if that's what you yearned for, perhaps you were in the wrong place.

Vince was especially concerned about me in those early days. "Are you okay, Hub? You're over there all by yourself." I told him I was fine, and I was. But I took note of his caring. He and I had gotten even closer over the past fourteen months while the campaign was going on. I had been swamped with POM's and my family's problems, and Vince had been buried in work. With Hillary gone, we had turned to each other. Now we needed each other's support more than ever.

I don't know for certain, but I think Deb Coyle was the person who started Arkansas Nights. Deb, assistant to Bruce Lindsey at the White House, had once worked for the Rose firm. Then she worked for Betsey Wright at the governor's office. When Mickey Kantor was looking for an assistant during the transition, I told him Deb was the best. She could bring efficiency to chaos better than anyone I knew. The White House dearly needed her. Deb also used her White House credentials to fine effect in reserving us a big table in a good restaurant. The very first Arkansas Night was dinner at Two Quail.

Vince was there, and Bruce and Deb, and Marsha Scott, and Nancy Hernreich, Sheila Anthony, and other Arkansans. This wasn't so much about geography as it was about making contact. Just as when, back in Little Rock, the litigators all got together at Brandyfest, this was a chance for us to stop working for a few hours and laugh and let off steam. Vince was as funny as I'd ever seen him. He told about his own drug test, a concept that was hilarious on the very surface—Vince Foster, of all people, taking a drug test. He was escorted to this cold, Big Brotherish building where a stern, no-nonsense nurse had handed him a plastic cup and pointed him to the bathroom. He stayed in there for what felt like *hours,* and when it seemed there was no hope, he timidly unlocked the door and quietly approached the nurse. "Pardon me . . ." he had said. She didn't want to hear it. She took one look at his empty cup and then shouted to a colleague across the room. "We've got another one who can't pee!" It was a big deal for him to tell a story like that. He rarely told funny stories about himself. We appreciated that he had deviated from his usual taciturn nature as much as we did the story.

I told the story about my beeper. My first day at Justice, I was briefed about the Justice Command Center, and how certain people are on call twenty-four hours a day. I had no idea that that meant me. I was fast asleep one night in my little bedroom in my cousin Ruth's basement. When the phone rang, I couldn't imagine that it was for me. Then Ruth was calling me from the top of the stairs. "Webb? *Webb?* The phone's for you."

"Hello." It was 3 A.M.

"Judge Hubbell?" said a crisp, official-sounding voice.

"Yes?"

"Judge Hubbell, there's been an airplane hijacking in Europe. The plane is going to be refueled before it leaves the Continent, and then it will fly to New York."

That was it. There was now a silence on the line. I was waking up to the realization that I was required to fill that silence.

"Uh, okay," I said. "What do you want *me* to do?"

"Judge Hubbell, we're required to inform you of any event of this magnitude."

"Um," I said. By now I had gathered my wits somewhat. "What time does the plane arrive in New York?" I said.

"Three o'clock this afternoon."

"Well," I said, "why don't you call me back at six in the morning."

My fellow Arkansans were practically on the floor laughing. It helped. We had all stumbled into an absurd world, and the only sanity was laughter.

One Sunday in early February, I spent the afternoon at the White House going over attorney general candidates with Vince and Bernie and Bruce. By then we had seen a second candidate shot down by the "nanny problem"—Judge Kimba Wood of New York. The media sensed a story building, and that was helped along by leaks within the White House. Washington's abhorrence of the information vacuum had sent leakers and leakees scurrying like rats in a wall. Because no information was forthcoming from Bernie or Vince, false stories surfaced and then were proved wrong. But the problem wasn't just the surreptitious whispering. In front of the whole White House press corps, George Stephanopoulos time and again seemed unable to utter the simple words, "I don't know"— even when those words described the truth. Instead, "information" was shoveled in to fill the vacuum. The advent of instant communications has deprived people of the opportunity to think. The media began enjoying the flip-flopping—that was a story in itself. But the Justice Department became a legitimate focus of suspicion. Who *was* Webster Hubbell, and what was going on inside those thick rock walls?

That evening the President and First Lady hosted the birthday party for Mary Steenburgen. After dinner, the President took us to see the Oval Office, and as Bernie, Vince, and I were leaving, President Clinton handed Bernie a piece of paper. "Check this one out," he said. In the hall, Bernie handed the note to Vince, and then Vince showed it to me. The name on the paper was "Janet Reno, Miami prosecutor."

A day or so later, Vince called me at the office. "Hub," he said, "I think we've got a live one." He asked if I could meet him at a law office outside the White House to interview the latest candidate for attorney general. "The President will want your reaction." He gave me directions to the office, but stressed that I should be extremely careful how I came. The media was all over the place, looking for any hint of a break in the story. I had a driver for official business during the day, but I took a cab. I leaned far back in the backseat and tried to make myself invisible.

Safely at the law office, I was shown to a room where Vince was waiting. "I'd like you to meet Janet Reno," he said, and I turned to find myself almost eye-to-eye with a very tall woman with short brown hair. She was smiling what I immediately thought of as a down-home country smile.

We visited for about an hour, and I went over the issues that she would have to grasp immediately. As Miami's prosecutor, she was well schooled in the crime issues—drugs, youth violence, and so on. She also was well versed in immigration issues. Though she had no federal experience, she had worked closely with Miami's U.S. attorney, FBI, and DEA offices. I liked her. She was human. When she left, Vince seemed pleased with the way the meeting had gone. He liked her warmth and her easy ability to handle herself in public. Now we just had to hear from the battery of lawyers who had been given the job of picking apart her personal life. I remembered something Bill Clinton had said to me on the golf course in Little Rock back when he was considering whom to pick as his running mate and what they would go through. He shook his head. "I'd hate to do it to any of my friends."

At Vince's call, at least ten attorneys filed into the room. Some of them were accountants, too. They had read all her clippings, reviewed her tax returns, and questioned her extensively about the fact that she was still single at age fifty. Later, the press would ask her the same thing. What Janet replied to that remains my children's favorite story about her. When a reporter asked why she was still single, she smiled and said, "No one ever passed my mother's potato test."

"Can you explain?" they said.

"My mother said, 'Janet, you'll know you're in love when your heart goes potato, potato, potato.' I just haven't found a man who makes my heart feel that way yet."

The vetting committee's worry was that she was "too clean." She had no debt, bought cars at sticker price so the dealer wouldn't be doing her a favor, and still lived in her family home. Her conviction rate as a prosecutor was normal, she had run for office several times and been elected by the multiethnic Miami citizenry, and although the city had had racial problems, she was supported by all groups. I was taken aback when the vetting committee decided that because of her lack of federal experience, they couldn't recommend her nomination.

Vince and I later met with Bernie to compare notes. Vince had really liked Janet. "You can't run for public office without being tough and resilient," he said. He thought she would be independent and would meet all the political criteria. Bernie could speak to that. He was especially sensitive to the charges that Bush appointees had had such close ties to the President. Bernie wanted the attorney general appointee to be seen as his or her own person. He and Vince both wanted to be able to tell the President that I could work with her. I assured them I could. The three of us sensed in Janet a strong-willed, independent woman. Though such a creature tended to intimidate much of official Washington, we had no problem with her at all.

The very next day, President Clinton announced that Miami prosecuter Janet Reno was his nominee for attorney general. I was there when the announcement was made. As the President escorted Janet to the podium to be introduced to the media, he whispered in her ear, "Don't screw up." They both laughed. It looked like they were off to a good relationship.

9

Dancing on the Head of a Pin

Suzy came to look at schools on February 12, the day after Janet Reno's nomination. It was also George Washington's Birthday, but Suzy wasn't in a celebratory mood. I was working, and the weather had turned nasty by then—snow, sleet, with a damp coastal wind that cut through to the bone. To Suzy, the harsh cold seemed to reflect the difficulty of our situation. We had been separated for three weeks and we were both getting tired of that. On the other hand, I was so busy that I didn't have time to think about it. Meanwhile, Suzy was in Little Rock acting as both mother and father, trying to sell the house, trying to pick up the chips that I'd let fall when I took this job and moved away.

I had no time to join her in scouting the schools, and she understood that. She rented a car and set out by herself. She didn't know the city, and wasn't used to driving in so much traffic, especially in snow and sleet. In her own words, "I was feeling very sorry for myself." The night before, we'd had dinner with Mike Cardozo and his wife, Harolyn. A vivacious brunette, Harolyn had grown up in Washington. Her father is Nate Landow, a prominent businessman, and Harolyn was property manager for her father's many apartment buildings. She knew the area in a way most of us transients would never achieve. Suzy and Harolyn talked about schools, and Suzy told her where she planned to be looking the next day—Stone Ridge, the Maret School, and a public school out in Montgomery County. Harolyn asked her for lunch, and Suzy accepted—with the caveat that she just didn't know how her schedule was going to work out. She had a lot of ground to cover.

The next morning she found herself stuck in sleet-slowed traffic. She was trying to find the Stone Ridge School out on Connecticut Avenue, but the weather had conspired against her. Finally, she made it, though she was running perilously late for her next appointment, way out at the Walt Whitman School in Bethesda. The weather was getting worse, and Suzy was getting frustrated. The final straw was when she reached the Whitman School and they had closed because of the storm. Not a soul was there besides Suzy. She sat angry, and in tears, in her lonely rental car.

Suddenly Harolyn drove up. She had figured out where Suzy was supposed to be and met her there. She told Suzy to follow her home, where she had a beautiful lunch laid out—silver, linen, the works. That gesture may well have saved my marriage. Mike had been my lifesaver in Washington, and now Harolyn would turn out to be Suzy's.

I tell this story because the life we found ourselves living puts a great strain on any marriage. In distance there's inconvenience and uncertainty. I know both Lisa Foster and Suzy got tired of hearing how hard Vince and I were working—especially when at other times we might say something like, "Oh, we had dinner at the White House with the President and First Lady, and watched a movie with Barbra Streisand." Suddenly our stories of fourteen-hour days sounded hollow.

Lisa was never comfortable with Vince off in Washington by himself. That was no secret—she told it to anyone who would listen. At first she'd planned on staying in Little Rock until the end of the school year, but within a month she was making plans to come to Washington. Meanwhile, Vince was enjoying himself in those first couple of months. He was still on a high. He was working extremely hard seven days a week, and because of his hours, he hardly saw the light of day. He drove the Pimpmobile back and forth between his sister's house and the White House, always in the dark. But we were all like that—I felt like a mole, going down beneath the street to take the Metro home at night. If it was after 10 P.M., I usually caught a cab. If the challenges we faced hadn't been so formidable, we might have succumbed to the bleakness of the world around us.

Vince did tell me once that a person "could get claustrophobic" in the little office he was in. There was room for only a small sofa, a small bookcase, a desk, and a chair. The one little window looked out on the parking lot. The focal point in Vince's office was a photograph he cherished—a picture of Bill, Hillary, Lisa, and Vince at the Arkansas Repertory Theater. He placed the picture on his bookcase. I think it was the only picture in the room.

I told him that he could have a much larger office if only he would move to the Old Executive Office Building. That's where Janet worked while she prepared for her confirmation. Vince said no, he would rather be where he was. Proximity to the President was crucial in the White House pecking order, and his tiny office was pretty close. It was even closer—across a reception area—to Hillary's office, and he was spending a lot of time working with her on health care reform. Her office wasn't large—it was more the size of Bernie's. But the sun streamed through her windows. Vince was exhilarated by the issues they were wrestling with together. They were the team he had always imagined they would be, he told me. The only thing wrong was that the third member of the old troika was six blocks away.

I think the beginning of Vince's downturn was when the Health Care Task Force was sued. That happened when those opposed to health care reform went into court to force all White House meetings on this issue to be made open to the public under the Federal Advisory Committee Act. It happened very soon, in early February, and though the effect on Vince was one that would build over time, the immediate effect was a subtle shift in his relationship with Hillary. Instead of a team working together toward a glorious goal, they were suddenly attorney and client. His legal advice was now front-page news. And with the pressure

Hillary was under to get a health care bill passed in the administration's avowed "one hundred days," she became a very demanding client indeed.

On the final weekend in February, two events occurred that would have severe repercussions on life inside the Justice Department. Terrorists bombed the World Trade Center in New York City. And the Bureau of Alcohol, Tobacco, and Firearms (ATF) staged an abortive raid on the compound of a cult in Waco, Texas. The cult was known as the Branch Davidians, and their leader was a charismatic figure named David Koresh.

President Clinton, furious at ATF for allowing the media to alert Koresh about the raid and devastated over the loss of lives, asked Stuart Gerson and the FBI to take over surveillance of the compound. Through Mac McLarty, he told Stuart he wanted to be advised if there was any change in status other than negotiation by the FBI.

I didn't have much to do with Waco initially. I was enjoying a rare visit to Little Rock when the ATF raid occurred, and only heard about the President's involvement when Stuart told me about it the following Monday. Stuart did keep me informed, though, and on one occasion, when I heard that the FBI was playing irritating records on loudspeakers outside the compound—sounds of rabbits screaming and God knows what other weird noises—I told Stuart I thought that seemed counterproductive and should be stopped unless someone could explain how it helped in the negotiation. Stuart agreed and later reported that he'd instructed FBI Director Sessions to stop the racket. This was just another check mark in the negative profile of Director Sessions that was revealing itself to me. I'd had several dealings with him by then, and I found him singularly unimpressive. It might have been the pressure he was under or just his manner, but he couldn't relax and he wasn't open to discussion or questioning. He didn't strike me as a leader. He wasn't anyone I would follow anywhere.

Janet was well into her confirmation preparations then, and I was meeting with her regularly to keep her abreast of the various issues developing at Justice. Waco was just one of them. Stuart was monitoring the World Trade Center bombing investigation, and he kept me informed. Stuart, Michael, and I were still working well together. At the start of each day, we would meet, and usually we would talk issues over lunch. Never did we leave at night without a handshake. We were usually the last three out of the building.

Stuart and I were both also dealing with the case of Congressman Harold Ford. The congressman had been indicted back home in Memphis on bank fraud charges. The first trial had ended in a hung jury. A week before the retrial was to begin, Ford tried to buttonhole the President about his case during a congressional reception. Mac rescued the President and suggested to the congressman that he get in touch with me. Mac warned me that he would be calling.

Ford phoned me the next day. I told him that it would be inappropriate for me to talk to him directly, but if he wanted his lawyer to call me, I would be glad to speak with him. His lawyer called and explained that, although Congressman Ford was upset about the way he was treated by the U.S. marshals, there was a bigger issue. He asked to meet with me in person. In all criminal cases, Mike Cardozo had warned me, I should make sure that someone from the Criminal Division sat in on the meetings so there would be no misunderstandings. A career lawyer named David Margolis was dispatched to this meeting.

Ford's lawyer explained that when the trial began the following week, a jury from Jackson, Tennessee, would be bused in to hear the case. Jackson is a hundred miles north of Memphis. The jury had already been selected, and of the eighteen jurors and alternates, all but one was white. Congressman Ford is black. The complaint was that the Justice Department, through the U.S. Attorney's Office in Memphis, was essentially saying that the U.S. government needed to bus in an all-white jury to try a black man in Memphis.

The situation offended my sensibilities, too, but I was careful not to make any commitments. There was a chance the case would be postponed, and I hoped that was so because it would give us time to gather more information. But I did report to Stuart

Gerson about my meeting. The next day, the Congressional Black Caucus asked to meet with me about Ford's case. I agreed to do so only when Stuart said he would like to meet with them, too. I told them we wouldn't discuss the specifics of the Ford case, but we would listen to their concerns about the jury selection and its ramifications nationwide. The caucus members were vocal in their demands, but respected my ground rules.

Stuart and I hoped the judge in the case would postpone it, but we soon got word that he would not. The career lawyers in Main Justice (which is what the Justice Department's attorneys in the field, such as U.S. attorneys, call the headquarters in Washington) were troubled by the way the Memphis U.S. Attorney's Office was handling the jury-selection issue, but they cautioned Stuart and me that it would be a mistake to step in at the last minute. Stuart called the U.S. attorney and asked that his prosecutors fly to Washington to present their side of this issue. We met with them on Thursday, and I could tell that although Stuart was asking all the questions, somehow they felt that I—this "Clinton person"—was behind it. On Friday, Stuart and I pondered the ramifications of stepping in versus taking no action in the case. Stuart was troubled by the whole thing. He talked not only to me, but also to his chief of staff and Ed Dennis, the Bush administration's assistant attorney general for the criminal division. He felt that if we allowed the busing in of an all-white jury to try a black man, it would have ramifications around the country—including the retrial of the defendants in the Rodney King case. For my part, I told Stuart I was bothered that the Justice Department that had broken so much ground in civil rights when I was growing up now seemed to be heading in the opposite direction.

Stuart asked me if I would support him whatever his decision was. It was one of those moments when I was clearly the Clinton administration spokesperson being asked to honor the institution of the Justice Department. I told him that he was the attorney general, and by then I knew he would do what in his heart he thought was right, and I was comfortable with that.

That Friday afternoon, Stuart decided that Justice should be color-blind, and he dispatched an attorney to Memphis to ask the judge to select a jury from Memphis, the defendant's hometown. Even though Stuart has written op-ed pieces in *The Washington Post* explaining his decision—and affirming that it *was* his decision—everyone believed that I had stepped in to protect Clinton's friend, Harold Ford. From the bench in Memphis to *The Wall Street Journal*, the question was, "Who is Webster Hubbell?"

Ironically, the judge refused the Justice Department request, and Congressman Ford was tried by an all-white jury and acquitted. My sister Patty, who lives in Memphis, called and warned me. "Brother," she said, "I love you. But if I were you, I wouldn't come to Memphis in the next few months. The U.S. Attorney's Office here thinks you're the devil."

I was also getting pressure from Vince to put together a top-notch team to defend the Health Care Task Force. Like me at Justice, Hillary was being assailed for having no official portfolio—she wasn't a federal employee, so on what grounds was she heading up this administration's health care effort? Since I had to see Janet at the Old Executive Office Building, I usually stopped off and said hello to Vince whenever I came by. He told me Hillary and others were quizzing him daily about the capabilities and loyalty of the career Justice Department lawyers who were handling the case. He admitted using me as a foil. "Webb is monitoring at Justice," he would tell them. "We're both involved." That would usually calm everyone down.

Another issue I had to brief Janet on was the question of U.S. attorneys. The ninety-five U.S. attorneys throughout the country are like the Justice Department's field generals—they and their subordinates investigate crimes, charge criminals, and make sentencing recommendations. Policy is set in Washington by the President and attorney general, but each U.S. attorney has broad discretion in interpretation of that policy. They're appointed by the President but serve a four-year term. Just before President Clinton was inaugurated, Mac McLarty asked the Bush transition team to have President Bush send a letter to all political appointees, including U.S. attorneys, advising them that they should expect to be asked for their resignations effective January 20. The

Bush letter went out, but instead of saying they "should" expect to have to resign, it said they "might" be asked to resign. For the U.S. attorneys, this left a glimmer of hope that they would be allowed to serve out their terms. On the day Zoe asked me to work with her, she dumped the issue in my lap. "We've got to figure out what to do here," she said. The question was, Did we ask them all to resign? Ask only those in troubled offices to resign? Or leave everyone in place until we had a confirmed AG?

I wrote out the pros and cons to each of these options. None was very pretty. I had discussed the issue with Vince and Bernie and others inside the White House and at Justice. The one consistent recommendation was that we ask the District of Columbia U.S. attorney, Jay Stephens, for his resignation immediately. The transition team and the career Justice Department evaluations of his office both said that it was in shambles. But if we singled him out, it would appear that we were trying to interfere with the politically sensitive investigation of Dan Rostenkowski, the Democratic chairman of the House Ways and Means Committee.

This quandary pointed to larger problems, of course—because of the snags with the attorney general nominees, the Justice Department was woefully behind in its internal staffing. Bernie was pushing Janet to interview candidates for positions even while she was preparing for confirmation. And the roster of U.S. attorneys was almost 100 percent white male. We were going to be very late in broadening the makeup of this important office. Democratic senators were calling daily about when they should send their recommendations to the President.

But in the end, we decided to wait for Janet. In Washington, everyone rushes—and by doing that they make mistakes or convey incorrect impressions. The mistakes take on lives of their own. At the White House, Vince was already frustrated with how the inability to say "I don't know" to the media was hurting Hillary and health care. At Justice, we were determined to do this right.

Stuart Gerson's final official act before Janet's confirmation was to write a letter to the President recommending the termination of FBI Director William Sessions. "I don't trust his judgment," Stuart said, telling me it was about time to hand over the Waco reins to me. He recommended that I not deal with Sessions at all, but instead consult with the deputy director, Floyd Clark.

As Janet's confirmation hearing was under way on Capitol Hill, I walked across Pennsylvania Avenue to FBI headquarters for my first meeting with Floyd Clark. I was taken into the "tank," a kind of war situation room where men wearing headsets monitored world events on scores of television screens. The walls in this room are lined with lead to prevent eavesdropping—hence, the "tank." When I was introduced to Floyd, I thought he looked exactly the way an FBI man *should* look—starched white shirt, shoes you could shave in front of, hair as unyielding as Jimmy Johnson's. He was a very serious man. My natural inclination is to joke a bit to put people at their ease, but Floyd was already at his ease. My attempts at humor failed every time. With a pleasant but hurried smile, he'd always say, "Judge Hubbell, let's get back to the situation."

Floyd and his team briefed me on the disastrous ATF raid. Then they told me how, once the FBI was called in, they had secured the perimeter and were now engaged in "negotiation strategy." The basic idea was to slowly tighten the circle around the compound while giving the people inside as much room as possible to negotiate their way out. Floyd described the tremendous firepower inside the compound, and also gave a detailed breakdown of the number and ages of the men, women, and children inside. He described the hold that David Koresh had on the people with him. Floyd's agents had interviewed the ones who had come out, and they had a pretty good psychological profile of everyone left with Koresh.

One major obstacle was the media. Floyd's team was convinced that the media's being tipped off had resulted in the deaths of several ATF agents. Now the cameras were as numerous as guns. Floyd told me that they believed that Koresh had portable generators and a year's supply of water and food. The FBI also believed that inside the compound the Davidians were constantly monitoring the media so that every move the FBI made was known on the inside. The media attention was giving strength to Koresh and his followers.

I asked many questions. Then I told them, in no uncertain terms, "You understand that before any decision is made to go in, the President has to be notified." They all nodded understanding. As I left, they were in the process of building a scale model of the compound. With luck, Janet Reno would soon be United States attorney general, and they would use that model to bring her up to speed.

On March 17, I finally moved out of my cousin's basement into an efficiency apartment in a high-rise building owned by Harolyn's father in Bethesda. It wasn't fancy, and Suzy said it smelled like old bacon. But I was grateful and glad to be moving. I felt guilty about abusing Ruth and Art's ongoing generosity—I know my strange hours disrupted their household. Ruth and Art had been fascinated by my doings at the Justice Department, and even when I would roll in at ten or eleven, they would be awake and ready to hear about my day. So I often sat up with them for an hour or more depriving us all of much-needed sleep. Mornings came earlier and earlier. My new apartment was in the downtown area of Bethesda, but I never saw any other people as I traveled to and from work. I left at 6 A.M. and got home late at night. I came from and returned to a ghost town.

Once Janet was confirmed, the pace of my mornings picked up even more. Attorney General Reno swept into office with a plan for her own management team, which included me. A wonderful Washington attorney named Chuck Ruff was her candidate for deputy attorney general, with primary oversight over the Criminal Divisions. She wanted me to be associate attorney general, with primary responsibility for the Civil Divisions. Civil law was my background. She felt very confident about her choices, and so did Bernie. Chuck gave Janet the Washington and federal expertise she lacked. And I, because of my connections to the administration, would help her weigh the scores of political decisions she would have to make daily.

That was the good news. The bad news was that I would be subject to Senate confirmation. Bernie was all for that—he said it would finally deflect all the "Webb Hubbell, Shadow AG" rumors that were flying around town. *The Wall Street Journal* had been particularly insistent about my role inside Justice: "The further action needed, if we can be blunter than is couth for Senators, is to choose between two respectable alternatives. One, get Webster Hubbell out of the corridors of Justice. Or two, get him out in the light of day through nomination for a confirmable post." I, of course, had no confirmation jitters about the work I had done at this point at Justice. I was worried only that the FBI, in their extensive background check, would uncover my billing practices at the Rose firm. But how could I say no? That would be even more suspicious. I was in the game to the end now, whatever that end would be. And there wasn't a soul I could talk to about it.

At our next Arkansas Night, I noticed how much the group had grown. People like Kevin O'Keefe had become honorary Arkansans. The real test of being invited to Arkansas Night was loyalty to Bill and Hillary, not where you came from. No one in this group would ever be a source of leaks or gossip about our friends. We had learned we were the exceptions in this town. Kevin grew up with Hillary in Chicago and was one of the few pure friends of Hillary in the White House. Just as at the Rose firm, her intellect and early success had brought on resentment and jealousies even within her own home, the White House.

Vince expressed concern that night about my standing for confirmation, but in hindsight, I think his reasons reflected the state of his own distress. By late March he had become increasingly angry about the incessant leaks, especially the ones about Hillary. The story had come out about her throwing a lamp at the President. "Vince," I said, "we've both seen her mad, but I can't imagine that she would do anything like that. And even if she did, who would've talked?"

That was precisely Vince's point. He told me of *course* the lamp throwing hadn't happened, but he was having a hard time dealing with stories like that. He was convinced that people inside the White House were conspiring to hurt the President and First Lady. When he told me that, he was on his way to see the head of Secret Service, to try to put a stop to leaks coming from that particular pipeline.

And in general that was the basis of his concern about my confirmation. He had read the "Who is Webster Hubbell?" pieces. He had heard the "Clinton crony" slurs. He was afraid, he said, that I would be "the first Arkansan" that "they" would try to destroy. He was also concerned that "they" would use my hearings as a way to ask questions about Hillary. I told him I wasn't the least bit concerned about that. "But, Webb," he said, "they can destroy anybody if they want to—no matter how good a person you are. It can be vicious."

His urgings touched that deep well of insecurity in me. "Do you have any reservations about me doing the job?" I said.

"Oh, Webb," he said, "you've been doing a great job *being* the attorney general. I'm not at all worried about that." He told me he thought Bernie was right, that I had to go through confirmation. But he could never do it himself in a million years, he said. "Don't let them get to you, Webb."

Later, after we'd had a couple of drinks, his whole demeanor changed. "Hub," he said, "who would've thought we'd ever be doing what we're doing? I could *never* go back."

Janet Reno was an instant hit. She took the country by storm, and was invited to speak just as often as she could make the time. I found her easy to work with. I had been using the big office usually reserved for the chief of staff. It was separated from her corner office by a small reception area and an ornate conference room, the latter of which had served as Bobby Kennedy's office when he was attorney general. The room had a beautiful fireplace and an elegant oriental rug. His children had roasted hot dogs and marshmallows in its fireplace, and Kennedy had often brought his dogs with him to the office. You can still see evidence of their presence in the stains on the rug.

I was prepared to move, but Janet asked me to stay where I was. We had a lot of work to do, and she wanted me close by. At the top of the job list was confronting the issue of Justice Department personnel, from replacing U.S. attorneys in the field to naming assistant AGs in-house. We also had a situation down in Waco, Texas, that just didn't seem to want to go away.

Ten days after her confirmation, I took on the U.S. attorneys. During Janet's preparation for her hearings, I had asked Nancy McFadden—who later became my chief deputy—to research how previous administrations had handled the problem. Predictably, she turned up a mishmash of tactics. But the overriding example was that of the Justice Department office in Washington. In past years, the political appointees resigned when the administration changed. The career deputies would step up as acting heads of their respective divisions. The U.S. attorneys had a similar wealth of career assistants, and the attorney general could review the qualifications of the various assistants and appoint one as interim U.S. attorney.

I explained all this to Janet. "Webb," she said, "if you think that's the right way to do it, then go ahead."

"You're likely to get a lot of irate calls from U.S. attorneys and Republican senators," I told her.

"No I won't," she said. "You will."

And that, in the proverbial nutshell, is the Janet Reno style. She surrounds herself with good people and makes them accountable. I told her that this would work if we did two things: First, every U.S. attorney was to be alerted by telephone on the same day that we wanted his letter of resignation. Second, if there was some unique personal circumstance that necessitated one of the U.S. attorneys staying on the job, I wanted to be able to make that decision. She agreed. I would keep her informed of course. We talked during that period at least twenty times a day. The reason for making all the phone calls in the same day concerned a pet peeve of mine. If you're going to lose your job, you ought to hear about it from your employer before you read about it in the newspapers. Once the letters went out, the press would have it.

I called Bernie, Vince, and Kevin O'Keefe, the person in the White House who would have to prepare the nominations of the successors. I told them to expect a firestorm.

On Monday morning, March 22, three people from our staff began phoning the U.S. attorneys. Before long I had a call from Senator Joseph Biden, chairman of the Senate Judiciary Committee. He didn't disagree with the action; he just expected to be informed first. I apologized for the oversight, explaining why we were trying our best to keep this quiet. He was right to scold me, because he was catching grief from his colleagues. But I also knew that Capitol Hill has more leaks than Hubbell's Folly.

Actually, the process went remarkably well. Most of the U.S. attorneys were expecting such news, and in many cases they did ask for a little more time. Several had big trials coming up. A few were just weeks or months from reaching their twenty-year mark for retirement. In every case, their request for time was granted. The only complaint came from Jay Stephens in the District of Columbia. He didn't call Janet or me, but instead held a press conference—at which he charged that we were trying to interfere with his investigation of Congressman Rostenkowski. I told Janet we should just sit tight and see how it played out. Before the day was over, Stephens said two things that seemed to cool down most of the cynics. He said he would resign that coming Friday. He also said there were a lot of good people on his staff who would take the Rostenkowski investigation forward and that his resignation would not affect the investigation.

I, of course, was widely accused of orchestrating the "Monday Massacre." But we were now poised to put the President's team in place. By the end of the year, we had filled some ninety of the ninety-five spots—many with women and African Americans. Janet interviewed every appointee. For my role in this episode, I was referred to in *The Wall Street Journal* as "Mr. Clinton's Hubbell Telescope."

Like most Arkansans, I had also been keeping my eye on the Razorbacks. So had the President. It was March madness, the NCAA playoffs. One afternoon I got a call from the White House. "Could you come watch the ball game with the President tonight?" Suzy and Kelley happened to be in town looking at schools. "By all means, bring them, too."

The truth is, movie or ball game nights at the White House tended to be another kind of Arkansas Night. Usually Marsha, Bruce, Vince and Lisa, Mac, and the McCoys—Grady and Ann, who worked in the social office—were always there. But the President often invited others—Bernie Nussbaum had become an honorary Arkansan, along with Vernon and Ann Jordan. If someone happened to be staying in the Lincoln Bedroom, they would be there, too. You never knew who you were going to run into at the White House theater.

It's not a huge room, but it's still surprising to find it in the stately house at 1600 Pennsylvania Avenue, behind one of whose imposing doors in the East Wing is this theater the size of a screening room at your local multiscreen complex. Of course, this theater is elegant—with drapes, flowers, and comfortable stuffed armchairs for thirty or forty people. There's no pecking order determining where you sit—except that the President gets the front row center. If Hillary or Chelsea are there, they sit next to him.

Neither was there that night. Hillary was traveling a lot at the time. Her father was seriously ill in Little Rock, and she went to visit him as often as possible. In the midst of her big public health care campaign, she was involved in her own personal health care drama.

When we arrived, the President was standing out in the hall next to the popcorn machine. Vince and Lisa were already there with their son Brugh. The President was wearing jeans and running shoes and talking to a small woman whose back was to us. Then Kelley whispered, "Dad, it's Barbra Streisand!" Kelley *loves* Barbra Streisand. She of course responded the way you would expect the typical twelve-year-old to respond—she panicked. She couldn't take her eyes off her, but she was afraid to meet her.

In a few minutes, Vernon Jordan showed up. Vernon and I had played golf a few times by then, and he came over to talk with us. I told him about Kelley's infatuation with Streisand. "Come on, Kelley," he said. "I'll introduce you."

In our house now we have a great photograph of the three of them—Barbra, Vernon, and Kelley—who looks like she's about to burst. Vernon later inscribed the photo for her. "To Kelley," it says. "I'll be your agent. Vernon."

* * *

Such nights had become bizarre interludes, frankly. Vince and I often reminded each other about the Mary Steenburgen birthday dinner—how *excited* Mary was, and how important it was for us to retain that excitement ourselves. But it was hard, and getting harder.

Chuck Ruff had what by now was regularly referred to as "a Zoe Baird problem." For Zoe's sake, I hated to hear her name used in that way. For a time, though, Chuck hadn't paid social security taxes for his household help. *The Washington Post* went crazy with the story. Bernie wanted to go forward and fight, but Chuck was enough of a Washington insider to decipher the handwriting on the wall. He knew that if two women had been disqualified for that, a man couldn't now be approved without massive—and appropriate—fallout. He withdrew his name from nomination. A good man, he is today the White House counsel. The President is well served.

In his place he recommended Philip Heymann, an official at Justice during the Kennedy and Carter years. Heymann, then in his mid-fifties, had been a member of the Watergate prosecution team and was now teaching at Harvard. Bernie knew Phil well. Janet asked me to call him, and he soon flew to Washington for an interview. We looked at others during that time, but Janet and I both felt Phil was the right choice.

In early April, she announced nominations for her management team—Phil for deputy AG, me for associate AG, and Drew Days for solicitor general. Drew had been an assistant AG in the Carter administration and was now teaching at Yale. The nominations were well received. I was gratified that, in an April 11 article, *The Washington Post,* noting that I had been "demonized to some extent," went on to say, "Assuming that his connections are not used to bring political pressures to bear where they shouldn't, the well-connected Mr. Hubbell could turn out to be an asset to the department. This appears to be a strong team."

I felt that the worst was past now. The FBI had turned up nothing about my billing irregularities. As part of their research into my background, they had interviewed members of the Rose firm. But apparently no one had suggested that the slightest thing was amiss. My spiritual side concluded that there was a plan for me here. I had been allowed to leave my old life behind in order to do *good*. I gave thanks, and resolved to do my utmost to live up to that purpose.

At that point, Suzy and I were comfortable financially. We had a lot of bills from our Little Rock days, but we also had more cash on hand than in times past. I had received a year-end bonus from the law firm, plus we had the proceeds from the sale of my portion of the Rose building and the money from the sale of our house. As soon as the kids started school, Suzy was going to go to work. Although my $124,000 salary at Justice wasn't as much as I'd made at Rose, with Suzy's salary and money in the bank, we thought we'd be okay for a while.

Bernie, Vince, and Mike Cardozo felt sure that I would face very tough questioning at my hearing, and we put together a confirmation team immediately. It was composed mostly of Justice lawyers, but, as one of his last acts before going back to his law practice, Mike arranged for a good friend of his to head up the team. He was Mike Berman, former chief of staff for Vice President Walter Mondale. The Rose firm also pitched in, helping research various Little Rock issues that might arise. My favorite lawyer at Rose, Amy Stewart, flew to Washington to help me prepare. Jerry Jones put together information for me at his end.

Meanwhile, I had to deal with the daily problems at Justice. None was as volatile now as Waco. In early April, Director Sessions asked for a meeting with Janet and me. He brought Floyd Clark and Larry Potts, also a deputy director. Where Floyd was stiff, Larry made me think of a cherub. He always had a nice smile on his face. We met in Janet's opulent conference room, and the discussion we had amid those civilized surroundings was as incongruous as any I've ever been involved in. Director Sessions had been keeping me up-to-date, of course, and I'd been doing the same with the others. But the FBI, Sessions said during this meeting, felt that negotiations with David Koresh were at a standstill. Their proposal was to shoot CS gas (an especially potent tear gas) into the compound.

My God, I thought. What had happened to cause such an abrubt shift in strategy? I wasn't sure what CS gas did to a person, but the idea of gas at all was appalling. Director Sessions explained that this gas was just a strong irritant and that this wasn't a change in strategy—that it was consistent with a gradual tightening of the perimeter by slowly applied pressure. He said it was merely part of the negotiating strategy. Janet was skeptical. I sensed she feared that Director Sessions was growing impatient. Sessions was from San Antonio and early on had wanted to fly to Waco and handle the Koresh negotiations himself. Within Justice, that was viewed as a grandstand move that would only derail the negotiations. Whenever Sessions would mention this idea, I could see Floyd Clark and Larry Potts roll their eyes. They were careful not to appear to contradict their director in front of Janet or me, but it was clear to me that Director Sessions had lost the respect of his troops. Neither Stuart nor Janet ever approved of his going to Waco. As all of us continue to relive the decisions we made in those days, I recently learned that Janet still wonders if things would have turned out differently if she "had sent Webb to Waco" before that fateful day.

One of the problems at Waco was that there appeared to be a turf battle brewing between the interim U.S. attorney in San Antonio and the assistant U.S. attorney who headed the Waco office. The cult members who left the compound were being held for the murder of the ATF agents. The FBI was concerned that if those Davidians were indicted right then, it certainly wouldn't help the negotiations. We dispatched a team to Texas to see what was up. Floyd Clark and Larry Potts went for the FBI, and a senior deputy AG in the Criminal Division, Mark Richards, went to represent Justice. Janet and I both had complete confidence in Mark's judgment.

A few days later when they returned, we resumed our meeting. The positive side of the briefing was that a career prosecutor named Ray Jahn had been put in charge of all Branch Davidian prosecution. But that was about it for good news. Inside the compound, they apparently had firepower to match the FBI's. Floyd and Larry described being in an FBI bunker and peering through a laser scope at one of the portholes inside the compound—only to have the beam returned by a similar scope from within. They told about a near-helicopter crash and the fear that other militia groups would try to join up with Koresh. They believed that the hostage rescue team had been in the field too long, and was losing its edge. The FBI was moving ahead with its plan to use the CS gas—subject, of course, to the final approval by Janet and the President.

Janet and I were still skeptical, but Mark was coming around to the FBI position. "If we do it," I said, "we have to tell the White House first." Director Sessions bristled at that suggestion. He was afraid of leaks, he said—the kinds of leaks that had caused the deaths of ATF agents. "The people I'll tell won't leak," I said.

I also told Sessions and the others that I wanted to speak with the negotiator. Were we to go forward with another tactic, we had to be absolutely certain that the negotiations had broken down. Finally, after viewing the FBI's plan for inserting the gas, I broached a protocol question with Floyd. I told him I didn't want to step on toes, but this was very important. "Is there someone in the military who can give us a second opinion on this?" He wasn't at all offended.

While Floyd set that in motion, I went to the White House to see Bernie, Vince, and Bruce Lindsey. I told them where things stood in Waco, and that it was a sad state of affairs that there were so few people in the White House that I could trust not to leak. Lives were at stake, I said. I knew the President wanted to be informed about this. Bernie and Bruce said they would tell him.

The U.S. Army still denies the existence of the Delta Force, so I don't want to do anything to undermine that. In fact, when Janet mentioned our consulting with them in a congressional hearing, someone joked that by even uttering the words she'd just violated the National Security Act.

Floyd called and said he had been in touch with an elite hostage rescue unit of the Army. He had also located the leading expert on CS Gas. The only condition for a meeting was that I call a certain general and authorize these people to fly to Washington.

"Can I do that?" I said.

Floyd laughed. "The Army knows who you are, Webb. If you call, they'll be here."

He was right. Very quickly we were back at the FBI again. We convened in Director Sessions's conference room to hear the Army unit's leader discuss the situation. He was a general, a man right out of a Tom Clancy novel—confident, articulate, in perfect physical shape. He walked through the FBI's plan as though it were his own. He explained that his unit had different "rules of engagement" than the FBI—in rescuing hostages on foreign soil, his men were authorized to "eliminate" the targets in order to free the hostages.

"What are our rules of engagement?" I asked.

"We can't fire unless we're fired on," said Floyd.

Janet asked about the CS gas and its effects. "Exposure to the gas is so irritating that you just have to get away from it," the Army general said. "Even with a mask on, it'll drive you crazy." Janet had him explain its long-term effects, and its effects on children. She wanted to know about possible explosions. There was a fire plan, we were told, but because of the media we couldn't very well pull a bunch of fire trucks around the periphery.

Finally, I asked the general, "Do you see any alternatives?"

"No," was the crisp answer. He was even more adamant than the FBI about the fatigue of the negotiators. He would have pulled his men out by now, he said. "Tired people make mistakes."

I asked the FBI if they thought their hostage rescue team was worn out. Not completely, they said—but the strain was showing on their faces.

When we got back to Justice, Janet asked the FBI and the Criminal Division to prepare a report on what was about to happen at the compound, and to answer the question "Why now." Director Sessions continued to stress that David Koresh was a fugitive holding women and children hostage, and that he was responsible for the deaths of several federal agents.

Meanwhile, I wanted to assure myself that we hadn't left a stone unturned. I wanted to talk with the negotiator directly. With Floyd, Larry, and Mark Richards, we set up a conference call to Waco. For two hours I quizzed, pulled, pushed, and searched for an answer that would keep us from doing what we were about to do. How about using religious experts? Could we call on the lawyers representing Koresh? What about using family members? My goal, I told all listening, was to at least save the children.

"Judge Hubbell," said the negotiator, "Koresh considers these women and some of these children his *wives*. He'll never let them leave." He said Koresh's lieutenant had confirmed Koresh's view that these little girls were his wives, and therefore sexual partners. After the tragedy, Janet would focus on the part of the FBI report that mentioned Koresh's beating his hostages. As the father of three girls—the youngest then twelve—I couldn't get the sexual abuse out of my mind.

The negotiator told me he had never been in a situation in which he felt negotiation was impossible—until now. "We haven't negotiated one person out of there," he said. "Anyone who's left, Koresh has let them."

I asked if he understood what the FBI was proposing to do. He said he did. I asked if he agreed with that strategy. "Judge Hubbell," he said, "I believe it's the only option left."

I thanked him. Then I asked for his promise that no matter what the attorney general decided, he would negotiate to the last minute to try to get those children out of there. He gave his word.

That night was Arkansas Night. It was a small group, and I must have been showing the strain. "You all right, Hub?" Vince said.

"Yeah. We're still holding firm, but all the doors seem to be closing."

"Trust your own judgment," Vince said. "You'll do the right thing."

We talked just between us about the issues that were now taking up our days. This wasn't just practicing law; this was life or death. Even I was losing weight.

Vince was unhappy. He told me that Hillary had snapped at him about the Health Care Task Force. "Fix it, Vince!" he said she had hissed. It hurt him deeply. The stress was getting to us all.

We talked about how we couldn't discuss these pressures with anybody else. Suzy had no idea what was going on about Waco. Lisa knew nothing of the problems Vince was wrestling with. Lisa was taking steps to move to Washington. They had been able to rent their house in Little Rock, and had found a small townhouse in Georgetown. Vince looked forward to having her closer, but it also put more pressure on him. Lisa would want him home earlier now.

The next day, Friday, I explored as many Waco options as possible. I kept thinking about Vince's words: "Trust your own judgment." My judgment told me we didn't want to gas those people. I felt it would touch off a disaster. While Floyd sat with me, Floyd said the FBI had to know about the gas by Saturday so they could begin deployment for a Monday go. Monday would be April 19.

At the end of the day, neither Janet nor I felt good about the plan. The FBI said that if we didn't go forward with it, maybe it was time to turn things over to the Texas Rangers while the hostage rescue team retrained. I could tell they didn't relish that idea. Janet and I said we would meet with them the next morning, Saturday. After sleepless nights, we each got to the office early that day. We were still in agreement—neither of us wanted to go with the FBI proposal. So it was settled, it seemed. We would continue negotiations. Janet went to her office while I phoned the FBI and asked Director Sessions and his men to come over.

They took the news about the way I thought they would. They listened stone-faced while I explained another new idea I had. "What about skunk oil?" I said. "In Arkansas, turkey hunters sometimes use skunk oil to keep the turkey from smelling the hunter. *Nothing* smells worse than skunk oil. Let's surround the building with skunk oil." Floyd gave me that polite smile and continued to explain the effects of a "no" decision. The hostage rescue team would be replaced with other law enforcement agents, he said. There were also risks that other cults might come to Waco to help the Davidians.

When we were finished, Director Sessions asked if he could discuss it with the attorney general. I said I would go talk to her. She agreed to come back to my office to hear their appeal. Director Sessions made a passionate plea to the effect that not only was Koresh holding women and children, he was destroying the credibility of the FBI. "Good men have died trying to arrest David Koresh. We *have* to go in." They went over their plan again for Janet. At the end of it came the inevitable moment of pregnant silence. Go or no-go. It was her call.

"Okay," she said. "Let's go ahead."

I was surprised by the turnaround, but I understood. I reminded her that she needed to speak with the President. She asked me to get in touch with him. I called Bruce and told him the story. In a few minutes, President Clinton called Janet. I only heard her side of the conversation, but it was clear from that that he knew how tough a decision she had to make here, and he trusted her judgment.

All day Sunday, the FBI and Waco agents were preparing for the Monday-morning assault. At Justice, we reviewed scores of documents and reports in order to be prepared to answer the questions most likely to be asked—Why now? and, Why did we have to use CS gas? Occasionally, I would pick up the phone and call the FBI to make sure the negotiator was still trying to get the children out of the compound.

Sunday night in my little efficiency apartment, I lay awake looking at the darkness. Sometime in the early hours, I came up with one more plan, and resolved to go directly to FBI headquarters first thing and present it to them. I was on the Metro before dawn. When I stepped off at Eleventh Street, the only people I saw were huddled figures sleeping on the heating grates of the massive buildings. I hurried down Tenth Street past Ford's Theater, then across to the FBI Building. And I couldn't get in.

I had to go across the street to Justice and ask the Command Center to call into the FBI tank and tell them I was coming. By the time I got there, they were already shooting in the gas.

*   *   *

The conflagration at Waco engulfed Washington, too. Inside the Beltway, the tendency is to run and hide when something so disastrous happens. Being "unavailable for comment" is the usual bureaucratic tack. Janet didn't handle it that way. That night she was on every television network taking full responsibility for what had happened. She was on *Nightline* with Ted Koppel. I watched it at the Cardozos' house. Mike had called as soon as he saw what was happening. "I'm going to pick you up," he said. "You shouldn't be alone tonight."

Even so, sitting there watching reruns of the horror with Mike and Harolyn, I was alone with my own considerable guilt. I kept reliving that day. When I'd reached the FBI tank that morning, Janet, Mark, and Carl Stern, Justice's director of public affairs, were already there. So were Floyd, Larry, and Director Sessions. They were all watching the insertion of the gas as broadcast by CNN. I got so tired of hearing the word *insertion*. It sounded so stiff, like bureaucracy-speak.

At first everything appeared to be going as planned, though no one was coming out of the compound. My mind flashed to the Army general's words, "They will come flying out of the building. No one can withstand CS gas." I thought, Something's wrong. We had a phone hookup with the commander in an armored vehicle. He kept mentioning the wind. We could see on TV that the wind was blowing hard. The wind was blowing the gas out of the building as fast as it was being pumped in, the FBI decided. That's why the people weren't coming out. The wind also tended to muffle what sounded like shots from the compound, but no FBI personnel were returning the fire. Good, I thought. Stay cool.

As they kept injecting the gas and no one came out, we began to speculate about underground tunnels. There had been talk about that possibility before. The FBI was convinced that the wind was the problem—that all they needed to do was insert more gas. The plan had been to insert gas, then pull back and negotiate. No one wanted to admit that the plan wasn't working.

A sign, written on a sheet, appeared in a window. RECONNECT THE PHONE, it said. Apparently an armored vehicle had severed the phone line that the FBI had run into the house. But the very fact that somebody inside wanted to talk seemed encouraging. George Stephanopoulos called for me. He wanted to know if the President knew about this beforehand. George seemed irritated that *he* hadn't been told what was to happen, but he calmed down when I told him I'd only told Bruce and Bernie in order to keep the security tight. I handed George off to Carl Stern, who brought him up to speed. Watching the screen, I wondered, Why hasn't anybody come out yet? I knew the phone problem was frustrating to those inside. The vehicles made another run at the house, inserting more gas. Then they pulled back. It was all going as planned, except much quicker than I imagined. And nobody was coming out. If that Army general couldn't stand the CS gas, how could these women and children?

The President called for Janet at 10 A.M. She told him we were hopeful. No agents had been hurt and we just had to be patient. He said let him know if anything changed. We wouldn't have to call.

Janet was scheduled to give a speech in Baltimore, and the FBI told her that if she canceled, it would appear that something was wrong. Koresh might even hear about it on TV and take it as a signal to hold on. Janet agreed. The FBI drove her to the site of her speech. Actually, it guarded her twenty-four hours a day. Janet had initially resisted having a security detail, but she quickly learned that every Cabinet officer undergoes a risk assessment and is assigned a security detail based on that assessment. The attorney general of the United States needs twenty-four-hour protection, a sad commentary on our country.

After she left, Mark and I watched awhile longer. We were told that the decision from the field commander was to pull back and let the gas work; it was just a matter of time. I was relieved to have even a moment of status quo. Mark suggested we take a few minutes and run across the street to Justice. When Janet got back, she would want to know who all had called and what else was happening.

When I got back to my office, I noticed my desk already littered with pink phone slips. I switched on the TV as background while

I checked my messages. But when I glanced at the TV screen, I did a double take—the vehicles were going in again. They were inserting more gas. I phoned the FBI tank. "What's going *on*?" I said.

"The gas wasn't working, so we decided to reinsert."

I called Mark and we hurried back across the street. When we got there, it was worse than we imagined. No longer were the vehicles "merely" inserting gas; they were now pushing down the walls of the compound. Director Sessions explained that the field commander was afraid Koresh was holding people against their will. They were opening an escape route. This, he said, was also part of the plan—it was just happening sooner than expected.

I stared at the TV. Where were the people? Why wasn't the gas working? Then I saw smoke coming from a window. "Oh, shit," I said. Everyone in the room turned and looked at me.

The field commander was saying, "There are flames! We see flames!" Oh, please God, I thought. *Get out of there!* We heard shots. I thought Koresh's people were firing at the vehicles, but that wasn't the case. Later I would learn that they were shooting one another. The flames were unbelievable. I watched one person on the roof struggle with an FBI agent who was trying to get him to save himself. He didn't want to do it. Another agent tackled a woman to keep her from running back inside. The flames were everywhere now. What power would make someone want to run back into that?

The White House was on the line; they wanted a report. I had to phone Janet and give her the news. "Instead of coming out, it looks like they've burned themselves up," I said. "We hope there are tunnels full of people." Director Sessions left the tank.

Watching all that replayed that night at the Cardozos', I couldn't help asking myself, What if? What if I hadn't left to go across the street—would the FBI have changed the tactics? Once we were gone, had Director Sessions gotten anxious and ordered a new insertion? Could I have prevented what happened? What if when I had gone there that morning, the building had been open?

We watched Janet on *Nightline,* and when Ted Koppel asked

if she had spoken to the President that day, she said, "No, but Webb Hubbell talked to him." Harolyn looked at me. "Is that true, Webb?" I told her it wasn't—that I had talked all day to people in the White House, but not the President. Janet had forgotten that he had called before things got out of hand.

As Michael drove me home, I was beeped. It was Janet. She wanted to know how I was. "I'm okay," I said. "Janet, you did great. Mike and I just watched Koppel." I asked how she was, and she said she was exhausted. But we would have a lot to deal with tomorrow, and she wondered if I could be in early. Of course I could. It's interesting, I thought, how people observe niceties even more in times of crisis.

"Webb, did I make a mistake when I said you talked to the President?"

"I talked to George and Bernie and everyone else over there, but you remember, he called you this morning."

"I was so tired I just forgot."

Naturally, that slight mistake caused more talk around Washington. Janet Reno didn't talk to the President, but Webb Hubbell did? Who's running the Justice Department?

When I got back to my apartment that night, I was beeped again. "Judge Hubbell," the man at Command Center said, "hold for the President."

"Hub," came the familiar voice. "How're you doing?"

"Fine, Mr. President," I said. "I'm sorry I let you down."

"Oh, come on, Hub. There's no doubt he was trying to commit suicide. He had an unbelievable hold on those people. You and Janet did all you could do."

"Thank you," I said. "How are *you* doing?" It was my usual way of dealing with pain—trying to help someone else.

"I'll be okay. Keep your head up. I'll talk to you soon."

It felt good to get a pep talk from my friend, but even that wasn't enough to keep me from feeling that we had failed miserably. Though I'm convinced that Koresh was the one responsible for the deaths of everyone inside the compound, I still have many sleepless nights when I second-guess every decision made. That night was just the first of many.

The next morning I arrived at Justice to find Mark Richards standing outside Janet's office. "I guess you're here for the same thing I am," I said. He nodded glumly. We knocked on her door and went in together. "I'm submitting my resignation," I said.

"Me, too," said Mark.

She looked at us and laughed a little, then shook her head. "I don't even want to hear about it," she said. "Sit down—we've got a lot of work to do."

Two weeks before my confirmation hearing, I was working at my desk when my secretary buzzed me with a message. "Judge Hubbell, Jerry Jones is on the line for you." Jerry was my former partner at the Rose firm. I assumed he had some more information relating to the upcoming hearing.

"Hey, Jerry," I said.

"How are you, Webb?"

"Doing fine, Jerry. Getting ready for confirmation."

"Listen," he said, "I need to talk to you about POM. Ron and I are coming to Washington, and we were wondering if you could have breakfast with us at the Mayflower." Since Bill Kennedy had left, Ron Clark had taken over as managing partner.

When we hung up, I had a sinking feeling. There must be some problem with Skeeter and his bill. Just what I needed.

On the appointed morning, I met them at their hotel suite. Breakfast was ready when I arrived. As I suspected, they explained that not only hadn't Skeeter paid what he owed the firm, he hadn't paid either of the experts we hired—the economist and the patent attorney. Their bills were now over a year old, and both experts were threatening to sue the Rose firm.

What impeccable timing, I thought. Here I am a couple of weeks before being confirmed as associate attorney general of the United States, and these guys threaten a lawsuit. They're trying to embarrass me. They figure either I or the firm will cough up the money.

"I'll talk to Skeeter," I said. "I'll see what we can work out."

"The firm is not going to pay these bills, Webb," said Ron. The mood in the room had just turned a corner.

"We're going to let the economist sue us," he said. "We're going to tell the patent lawyer the same."

I didn't quite know what to say. Now my old partners were engaging in pressure tactics themselves. They *knew* the contract for expert service was with the firm. And even though the bills were outrageously high—about $125,000—they owed the money. But they figured I would prevail on Skeeter—or Seth—to pay these bills. They figured I would do anything to avoid having such a sticky problem at this precise moment.

I felt terrible that Skeeter hadn't been able to pay the firm. For a year after the trial, Skeeter and I had worked diligently either to find a buyer for POM or to refinance the business so that we could pay for the expenses of the trial and keep POM afloat. We were just unsuccessful—nothing seemed to work. Even when I left to go to Washington, Skeeter was still trying to find a way to pay the firm the expenses they had advanced. If he'd refinanced POM, maybe he could have negotiated the bill down to a level that he could pay. But I knew one thing—if this hadn't been family, the Rose firm would have written it off as a business loss. It had happened a thousand times. These friends just saw an opportunity to put the squeeze on me.

Then they squeezed a little harder. "Webb," Ron said, "we've been looking at some of your old bills and there are some unexplained write-offs that we'd like you to take a look at." I'm sure I went pale. He handed me a list of about $30,000 worth of expenses that I had charged against my fees received from clients. My heart was in my throat. This is it, I thought. This is the day I've dreaded for five years.

"I'm sure there's some explanation, Webb," said Jerry. "We aren't singling you out. We've also looked at other partners. Some of them didn't have an explanation and just paid the money." The mood was warming again. These guys were good.

"Listen, Webb," Jerry continued, "we hate to raise this with you now, but if you can get POM to pay the economist and the patent lawyer, we can work out the rest."

There it was—the offer. The bottom line. I kidded myself into thinking I could still be home free. I knew what I had done, and

I thought I knew what the firm was doing. I would be in huge trouble if they really *were* auditing my expenses.

But this wasn't that, I decided. They were simply applying a little well-timed pressure to keep from eating that expense. It was hardball, and it was damned effective. But I still had a chance.

I was caught up, you see, in trying to dance on the head of a pin.

10

What If?
What If?

La Tomate is an Italian restaurant on Connecticut Avenue, a couple of blocks northwest of Dupont Circle. Sitting as it does on a V-shaped sliver of land between two streets, it feels like an island, and I always thought it would be a perfect place for Hillary, Vince, and me to have one of our long escape lunches. Unfortunately, we seemed to have left those in Arkansas.

The night after my confirmation hearing, Suzy and I had dinner there with the Cardozos, the Bermans, the Fosters, Bruce Lindsey, and my sister Terry. Suzy was up for the hearing, but since we'd just sold Hubbell's Folly she was also house-hunting. We had found a house we liked on McComb Street, just across from Sheila and Beryl Anthony. Washington prices were outrageous, of course, and this was a smaller house than we were used to. Inside, it was also drenched in paint the approximate color of Pepto-Bismol. But we could see through the paint. This house would work. Now I only had to get confirmed.

I had told my confirmation team about the lawsuit of the POM economist. They couldn't believe the Rose firm would let something so petty go to trial. But I hadn't told them about the billing inquiry. I hadn't told Vince. I hadn't told Suzy. I hadn't even told her I'd had a meeting with Jerry and Ron. I hadn't told anyone about it, and that was my mistake. At that moment, I committed the ultimate act of disloyalty to my friends—especially Bill, Hillary, and Vince. I knew that what I had done at the firm was wrong. I knew it at the time I was doing it, and I knew it as I sat before the Senate Judiciary Committee answering questions about my past. By being there I was compounding the wrong, and I knew that, too. It didn't matter what others at the firm might or might not have done. I should have seen that if they raised this issue with me, it would eventually come out somewhere. At that point, I owed it to everyone involved not to go forward with my confirmation hearing.

But I couldn't bring myself to face the consequences of my wrongdoing. I still thought I could escape. I thought if I could somehow resolve the firm's concerns about the economist and the patent lawyer, we could put the other issue behind us.

I met with attorneys for the economist, and they seemed in no mood to reduce the amount of their client's claim. They did say that if things could be resolved soon, a lower settlement was a possibility. I told them I would get back to them. I also met with the patent lawyer and asked him to hold off until I could meet with Skeeter and the firm. He had become a friend of mine over the two-year history of the POM case, and he needed the money badly. But unlike the economist and the firm, he didn't want to pressure me or use the timing to his advantage. He said he would wait a little longer.

I called Skeeter. He said he would do all he could, but he couldn't possibly stop the lawsuit in two weeks. I called the firm and told Jerry that I would guarantee that they would be reimbursed if they would resolve the lawsuit prior to litigation. I would pledge my retirement funds. Jerry wanted to help, but the firm would have none of it.

So the lawsuit was filed. Nobody seemed to notice. At the time, I thought that was a good thing. Now I know different.

I was scheduled to be in Little Rock to address the Arkansas Bar Association on June 11. While there, I would also help Suzy finish packing. The moving date was set. Hubbell's Folly was almost history. I called Jerry Jones and told him that after my confirmation hearing, I would come meet with them in person. At that time, I said, I thought we could resolve everything.

We were too superstitious to be celebrating that night at La Tomate, but I did feel that things had gone reasonably well the day before. As I'd met with the individual Judiciary Committee members prior to the hearing, the most ticklish issue was my membership in the segregated Country Club of Little Rock. In point of fact, the country club was no longer segregated—it had one African-American member. That certainly wasn't enough, but it was a start. And I had been instrumental in getting him into the club. Many of my friends who were black wrote letters to that effect. But I was proudest of two letters from men I hadn't seen in years. They came unsolicited.

Darrell Brown was the first black ever to try out for football at the University of Arkansas. He described in great detail how, during that difficult and frightening time, one large offensive tackle named Hubbell had gone to great lengths to make sure Darrell knew he supported and sympathized with him. The second letter was from a young black man I had represented when I first started practicing law. He recounted how he had expected a white, big-firm lawyer to be condescending, but that I had treated him with great respect. Those letters touched my heart. They made this whole controversy tolerable. More than once during the questioning, I thought of Fanny Taylor, who had taken care of me as a child. She would have been proud to see how far her little boy had come.

Even so, I found myself in the middle of a Senate turf war. Democratic Senator Carol Moseley-Braun of Illinois wanted me to resign my membership in the country club. But Senator Howard Metzenbaum (D-Ohio) said that because I had fully complied with the Senate requirements—by showing I had attempted to integrate the membership—I should most definitely *not* resign. In fact, added Metzenbaum, he would vote against me if I did. Senators Moseley-Braun, Dianne Feinstein (D-California), and Paul Simon (D-Illinois) would probably vote against me if I didn't.

My friends and family had commiserated with me about the

situation. I felt bad because my membership in the country club was also shining a big, bright spotlight on the fact that Mac McLarty, Vince Foster, and Bill Kennedy all belonged. If I resigned, why shouldn't they? Days before, I had told Vince I was sorry for causing a problem. "Bill and I've talked about it," he said. "We're ready to drop our membership if that'll help." Like me, they had maintained their memberships for the benefit of their families back in Little Rock. It seemed the least we could do, since while we were in Washington we were having so much fun hobnobbing with movie stars. Vince's family was now in Washington with him, but they planned to go back to Little Rock someday. That was one problem with resigning. The other was that it looked like you were apologizing for having done something wrong.

In the end, I decided to do what felt right for me in my unique situation. I resigned. I didn't think my membership in the club was wrong, but I didn't see how I could effectively head up the civil rights section of the Justice Department while there was any question about it whatsoever. I quietly resigned and announced it at the start of my hearing. Once the senators saw it as a *fait accompli,* they realized I had defused a potentially explosive situation. Many of them congratulated me.

That evening at La Tomate, Vince told me that he, Bill, and Mac had also resigned that very day. So I was feeling hopeful. I was with my family and my closest friends. The hard work was over—now whatever happened, happened. But Suzy and I both noticed that Vince wasn't himself that night. He seemed skittish, or maybe obsessed is a better word. Obsessed with what, I wasn't sure. He just looked like a man watching for the next shoe to drop. He was quiet, preoccupied. There seemed to be a gulf between him and the rest of us. "What was the matter with Vince?" Suzy said later.

Over the next few weeks, I would come to a kind of understanding, but that night I had no idea. When we were talking just between ourselves, I tried to probe good-naturedly. "So, Vince," I said, "I see in the paper that you guys fired the whole travel office." The news had hit that morning.

He looked at me with real dread in his eyes. Clearly, he didn't want to talk about it. "I think you're going to hear plenty about that one, Webb," was the only thing he said.

The next morning, a Friday, I was going through the stack of papers on my desk when I ran across a report saying that the White House had contacted the FBI about a possible misappropriation of funds. This was the very subject Vince and I had discussed just the night before—the travel office. I was about to read it when Janet called and asked me to come see her. She was extremely upset. "I just screamed at Bernie," she said.

"What for?"

"A reporter called me. He said the White House had contacted the FBI about the travel office. I didn't know a thing about it. I was cornered and he knew it."

"Well, you just haven't gotten to the report yet," I said. "I was just reading it. I'm sure it's in one of these stacks." She had several in-boxes. I rummaged around in them until I found it. "Here," I said.

Even though the attorney general had this report on her desk, what the White House had done was a violation of what we understood the working relationship between Justice and the White House to be. We hadn't formalized it into policy, but we had all discussed it. The White House wasn't to contact the FBI directly. They were required to go through the attorney general's office— Janet, Phil, or me. But I sensed that Janet's anger wasn't so much about a principle or a policy as it was about being caught off guard.

As she read the memo, she was horrified to find that it was worse than she thought—the FBI public affairs person had been consulting *with* the White House on a press release. The media was incensed by this incident. Criminal investigations and politics weren't supposed to be such cozy bedfellows.

Phil Heymann was drafting the policy on contacts with DOJ. But that was just one more thing at Justice that hadn't been formalized yet. I told Janet that Phil needed to finish the policy as soon as possible—and, meanwhile, he should try to calm everyone down on the Criminal Division side and at the FBI. I said I would talk to Bernie.

Bernie seemed to feel he had walked into a hornet's nest. He fully understood Janet's anger, though. I told him the quicker we could finalize this policy, the quicker we would all be able to head off such snafus. The major problem in this particular case was one of perception—it could appear that the White House was pressuring the FBI to investigate the travel office. In Washington, perception becomes reality upon delivery of the morning paper.

I didn't get to talk to Vince about all this until later—after I heard that Bill Kennedy was the one the FBI said pressured them. I told him, "Vince, this doesn't sound like the Bill Kennedy you and I know." Back in Little Rock in the offices of the Rose firm, Bill made Vince seem talkative. Vince told me that Bill had been working daily with FBI agents on background checks. When Vince dumped the travel office problem in his lap, Bill said to the agents, "Guys, if we suspect someone at the White House was stealing money, what do I do?" "You turn it over to us to investigate," they said. Which he did. Now I had read a report from the FBI to the AG saying that Bill had pressured the agents—to the extent of saying that if they couldn't help, he would go to the IRS. I told Phil Heymann I thought the FBI was covering its backside—if there turned out to be problems at the travel office, they were just doing their job. If not, they would blame Bill Kennedy.

"Welcome to Washington," Phil said. It reminded me of the time almost a decade and a half ago, when I had just become mayor of Little Rock and was accused of having an affair. "Welcome to politics," Hillary had said. There was something terribly wrong when such good people accepted duplicity as standard operating procedure.

This White House–FBI confusion happened partly because we were still in transition at Justice. Janet was in a hurry for Phil, Drew, and me to be confirmed—we couldn't even go forward with our assistant AG nominations until then. But the confirmation process quickly proved as sticky as most business in Washington.

One night I got a call from Senator Bob Dole, the Senate minority leader, asking that I write him a letter attesting to the fact that I had no involvement whatsoever in the travel office firings. I dispatched the note the following morning. Then something else came up. In addition to the country club issue, one senator had produced a hearing witness who suggested the committee look into whether I had engaged in insider trading. The witness was none other than my erstwhile neighbor Roy Drew, a former broker at Stephens, Inc., who had split off from that company and aligned himself with Sheffield Nelson. Roy hated the Stephenses too for some reason, and he also took on Sheffield's vendetta against Bill Clinton. Roy's testimony concerned an investment club that I was in in the early 1980s.

Back when everyone around us seemed to be making so much money, Vince, Hillary, another Rose partner named Ken Shemin, and I decided to pool our communal "expertise" to see if we could get rich, too. We called ourselves the Midlife Investment Club, and we were hopeless. Each of us kicked in $5,000. Overall we lost money, as our tax records later showed. But at one point I personally—not as part of Midlife—bought five hundred shares of Arkla, the regional gas utility, and ended up making $3,000 on that deal. Roy implied that Hillary was somehow involved in a plot with me—she called him every day, he said, asking how Arkla stock was doing. He was careful not to accuse me of a crime, but he did suggest to the senators that they might want to check into whether I might have engaged in "insider trading."

When Bernie heard that, he burst out laughing. He had defended scores of Wall Streeters against accusations of insider trading. "Webb," he said, "if you had inside information and only bought five hundred shares and only made three thousand dollars, then you aren't *smart* enough to be associate attorney general."

Still, it was another cloud over my head. Senator George Mitchell of Maine, the majority leader, phoned me once from the floor of the Senate. He said Senator Dole wanted to hear from my own lips that I hadn't engaged in insider trading. I dutifully and truthfully spoke the words into the receiver.

According to Senate rules, each senator can employ a tactic

called a "hold" to delay a nominee almost interminably. It soon appeared that Congress was ready to confirm Phil and Drew, but we had been presented as a package. I received word that some senators wanted me to agree to being split off from my colleagues. My confirmation team advised against that—they had watched too many single nominees dangle in the wind. The committee was playing games with me, they said, just because I was the President's friend.

But I felt terrible holding up Phil and Drew—and therefore Janet. The senators don't have to tell who's holding up which nominee. Sometimes, in fact, to disguise their strategy one senator will hold up a nominee for another senator. It's all about horse trading, of course. But sometimes you can't even figure out who wants to trade, or for what.

Before the Memorial Day recess that Friday, I got a call from Senator Mitchell. "I hate to ask you this, Webb, but I've got thirty-seven people waiting to be confirmed. If I agree to let them hold you, they'll confirm the other thirty-six before recess."

My advisers told me no, but I couldn't go along with them. "Senator," I said, "I can't hold up the government. What they are doing is wrong. But if I said no, I'd be wrong as well."

I thought it was all over. I asked everybody to please leave my office. Here I had given up my law practice, moved to Washington, sold my home, bought another house—and now I wasn't even going to be confirmed. There was no way I could stay at Justice. Everybody would assume I was exactly what *The Wall Street Journal* had called me—a nonconfirmable shadow attorney general. I was as depressed as I had ever been in my life, and that was saying something.

In a few minutes Mike Cardozo showed up. He had heard the news and figured I needed cheering up. While we were talking, Gail Hoffman, who had been the confirmation point person at Justice, came running in. "Webb! You've been confirmed!"

I was incensed. "Listen, Gail," I said. "I love you—but I am not in the *mood* to be kidded. I know what's happening. I talked to Senator Mitchell."

"No, it's on TV!" We flipped on C-Span and there, scrolling

across the bottom of the screen, was a list of people who had just been confirmed. "Webster Hubbell, Associate Attorney General," was one of them.

Gail gave me a lesson in Washington politics. "Senator Mitchell knew he could make a deal with Senator Dole," she said. "You had consented to be held, so he ran a bluff. He told Dole, 'We're going to stay in session and vote one by one on each nomination all Memorial Day weekend.'" Dole and the Republicans relented.

Soon Senators Mitchell and Dole called, both of them very gracious. I thanked them for their support. I also congratulated Senator Mitchell on his superb ability at horse trading.

My Arkansas trip went better than I had any right to expect. Of course, I was already soaring when I got there. Just two days before, I had been formally sworn in as associate attorney general of the United States. In the imposing Great Hall at the Justice building, Attorney General Reno had given a very glowing introduction of me. She had finally gotten her team together. There's a wonderful photograph of that event that I cherish. I am standing at the lectern delivering my acceptance speech, and Suzy is looking at me lovingly. I had made her proud, my children proud, myself proud. I thought many times of my father and mother on that day. I would have given anything for them to be there.

So when I arrived in Arkansas, it was with a new level of confidence. My speech to the Arkansas Bar Association was less than memorable, but I had a good time seeing so many old friends from around the state again. They were all effusive in their congratulations.

Even the Rose firm meeting went well. I had met with Skeeter and he knew the lawsuit was a problem, but he hoped the firm would come around to taking some of the responsibility for the exorbitant fees. So I went to see Jerry Jones and Ron Clark. After some pleasantries (they congratulated me, too), they told me they had decided to pay the economist. "Are you really willing to guarantee that we'll be reimbursed by POM?" Ron said. I told him I was. They handed me a guaranty and a pledge agreement for my retirement account. One small part of it bothered me. The way it was drawn, I would have to guarantee whatever payment was made to the economist and patent attorney. I could persuade Skeeter to repay them, or it would come from my retirement. But there was no incentive for them to try to negotiate the fees down. I suggested we rewrite it, and they agreed. We also went over their list of billing questions, and they said they were satisfied with my explanations. I left the office feeling that a great burden had been lifted from my shoulders. After I returned to Washington, I received a note from Jerry Jones. "Sure did enjoy being able to spend a day with you," he wrote. "Hang in there and change America."

Aside from helping Suzy, only one other piece of business remained. I still had the "Betsey files" along with mine in the little office in my bedroom. I took some of mine to a rented space in a warehouse, and asked Walter to personally take the others with him to D.C. I didn't trust the movers. So when Walter was ready to leave, he stacked the file boxes in his 4Runner and drove them to our new house in northwest Washington. We would then figure out what to do with them from there.

Our old friends threw a wonderful going-away party for the entire Hubbell clan. The invitations were emblazoned with the headline WHO IS WEBSTER HUBBELL V? We laughed and told stories and got sentimentally drunk. If I could have frozen my life at that moment, I would have had it all—adoring family, dear friends, professional success, unlimited promise. But the night finally ended, and the sun came up the next day. I boarded an airplane and headed back to Washington.

I happened to speak to Hillary soon after I got back. I told her the files were in my basement. I told her about walking away from Hubbell's Folly for the last time. I also told her about my weekend—the Bar Association convention, the going-away party. She'd spent a lot of time in Little Rock with her mother since her father's death a couple of months before. Hugh Rodham had died around Easter, and Vince and I both had gone to the funeral. During the service I thought of Hillary and her dad and a trip Hillary, Vince, Ken Shemin, and I had taken to visit Hugh and Dorothy in Chicago. We had a client who was a professional baseball player, and he had arranged for us to have six tickets to see the Chicago Cubs play the San Diego Padres in the National League playoffs. It was probably the first and only time that the Cubbies had gotten that close to a World Series. I had been around Mr. Rodham very briefly only a few times before, but as we cheered the Cubs and sipped our ballpark beers, I felt like we became friends. Vince and Dorothy really seemed to hit it off, teasing each other the way Hillary teased Vince. Hugh talked easily about how proud he was of Hillary. I could tell she was one of the lights in his life. We spent some time in the home she grew up in, and I found it wasn't too dissimilar from the ones I had known as a boy. It was filled with pictures of the Rodham children and their achievements.

Following the funeral, Hillary and her family went to the Little Rock airport to take Mr. Rodham home for burial in his native Pennsylvania. It would have been a crowd scene with only Hugh's immediate family in attendance—the President, Dorothy, Hillary, Chelsea, Hillary's brothers Tony and Hugh, and Hugh's wife, Maria. But of course there was the usual White House entourage of young people speaking into cell phones. And then there were Vince and me. At one point, I got a sense of how exhausted Hillary felt. She was standing next to Vince while all the usual confusion was happening around her. Suddenly she leaned her head over gently and rested it on his shoulder. It was a sweet moment of friends comforting friends.

Now I thought Hillary seemed a little homesick hearing my stories from Arkansas. Living in the White House wasn't any different than it would be living in any public building in Washington—of necessity, they're all fortresses. "Listen, Hub," she said, "as soon as Suzy gets here, let's all go someplace fun for dinner. I miss y'all. I miss being able to just go out and have fun. You and Suzy, Vince and Lisa, Bill and me—let's all go eat Italian. It'll be like old times."

I mentioned it to Vince when I next spoke to him, which was probably the very same day. He and I talked at least once daily, and usually much more often. Mostly we just dealt with business. He was swamped, and so was I. Gays in the military, health care,

Cuban and Haitian policy, immigration reform—where once we had talked Razorbacks and lingerie style shows, our conversation had now taken on the weight of Washington issues. There was hardly time for anything else. Arkansas Night was designed to let us get away from all that and just be ourselves, but Vince didn't come as often now that Lisa was in town. Sometimes the two of them came together, but Arkansas Night was mainly for those of us who were still waiting for our spouses to arrive. It was a Lost Boys and Girls Club. We tried to catch up during the business day, but there was always Bernie calling him, or somebody on the other line.

I remember that we got to spend a little time visiting on two successive days in late June—at the announcement for Doris Meissner as director of the Immigration and Naturalization Service, and the next day at the announcement of the nomination of Ruth Bader Ginsburg for justice of the Supreme Court. Bernie was upbeat, but Vince was troubled. On June 17, 1993, *The Wall Street Journal* had published an editorial entitled "Who Is Vincent Foster?" It said, "the most troubling thing about the Clinton administration is its carelessness in following the law." But the thing that made Vince irate was that the White House press staff hadn't sent the *Journal* his picture—so instead the paper ran a big question mark where the handsome face of Vince Foster should have been. I later wondered if the question mark felt too close for comfort.

Vince told me he was concerned about the internal review of the travel office situation. He was worried that Congress would have a hearing. He said he felt the FBI had lied about Bill Kennedy pressuring them. Vince seemed to feel about dissembling Washington the same disgust he had felt for the slippery Jim McDougal so many years before. He had standards, scruples. Now, every single day they were being called into question. Vince had never been overweight, but he was getting very thin. At the time, we laughed about the fact that Bruce, Vince, and I were all losing weight. We called it being on the Stress Diet. It doesn't seem so funny anymore.

Hillary saw us and came over. She linked arms with both of

us, the way we had that spring day in New York so long ago. "When are we going out, guys?" she said. "Let's go eat Italian." I volunteered that since we'd just moved into our house, they should come by for drinks on Saturday night. We could go to a restaurant from there. Hillary said that would be great, and Vince and I gave her a hug. He seemed genuinely excited now, almost the polar opposite of the way he had been just moments before.

For my marriage's sake, I should mention here, even though Suzy was unnerved to hear that we were entertaining the President and First Lady while the house was still littered with boxes, she handled it like the trouper she is.

On Saturday morning the Secret Service came and checked out our house and neighborhood. As I helped Suzy clean and unpack, the agents peered into every room and closet. They flashed lights into the attic and along the basement floor. I have no idea what they were looking for—whatever they hoped not to find, I suppose. They stayed with us the rest of the day.

Once they had cleared us, Kaki came over to help us put the finishing touches on the house. I hung pictures. I made sure we had vodka for Hillary and Diet Coke for the President. After cocktails, we were all going to I Matti, Vince's favorite Italian restaurant, in the Adams-Morgan area of the city. The White House had made the reservations, so a wonderful big table was waiting for us. I'm sure that life inside that restaurant was even more stressful than life inside our house that day. When the White House calls, they usually do not tell the restaurant management that it's the President and First Lady who are coming. But then the Secret Service inevitably shows up, and the speculation tends to reach critical mass shortly thereafter.

Late in the day, Lisa and Vince came over. They lived only a few miles away in a rented town house. It was like so many Washington town houses, small and compact—a sliver of living space elbow to elbow with others just like it. It was a pretty place, on a narrow and shaded Georgetown street. But living there was a big change for Lisa and Vince. They were used to their large house and swimming pool in The Heights. Vince was a tall man—six feet three—and he felt cramped there, just like in his White House office. Washington houses tended to be outwardly elegant but inwardly oppressive—reflecting the personality of the city's primary industry.

Vince, Lisa, Suzy, and I were having drinks when the phone rang. "Hold for the First Lady," a voice said. When she came on, she told me *Parade* magazine was planning to run a story on a supposed half brother of Bill's who had just surfaced. Hillary had talked with Betsey, who told her that one of the files I had was on Bill's father. She asked if I knew where that file was, and I told her I guessed it was downstairs. I said I would go look and call her back. While Suzy, Lisa, and the Secret Service waited upstairs, Vince and I went to the basement to search through the boxes. I couldn't find the file. I called Hillary and told her—saying I would find it and call her back. She said tomorrow would be soon enough. (The next morning I did find the file. Hillary asked me to bring it to her office on Monday.)

But on Saturday night, that breaking story disrupted our planned evening together. "Webb, you all go on to the restaurant," Hillary said. "I'll still try and meet you. Bill is a little stressed out and I doubt if he'll be coming."

We went to dinner and Hillary soon called to say she just couldn't make it. Vince hardly said a word the rest of the evening. Suzy, as much as she loved Vince, thought his behavior was extremely bizarre. "He was sulking," she said. "It was so uncharacteristic of him." He pulled his chair back and turned himself away from the rest of the table. He was like a child who had been promised quality time with a parent, only to have the parent renege when business had called him away.

I tried to talk with him about it the next day, and he opened up some about what was bothering him. He was upset about Hillary. "It's just not the same, Hub." He told me again that she'd said, "Fix it, Vince!" or "Handle it, Vince!" Someone asked me if Vince was angry at Hillary about that. I said no. His feelings were more in the nature of a lament. "She's so busy, Hub," he said, "that we don't ever have any time to talk."

I don't mean to give the impression that Vince worked only for

Hillary. His days were filled with tasks relating to many White House issues. He was also worried about the impending internal report on the travel office firings. He felt responsible because he had asked Bill Kennedy to take care of it. He was thinking of hiring a lawyer, though I couldn't tell whether he meant for himself or for his department. "Talk to Bernie, please," he said. "Try to convince him to hire outside counsel. He trusts your judgment." He worried that there would be hearings on the Hill. He couldn't bear the thought of being made to sit there under the hot lights of the cameras, being grilled by caustic congressmen who had no idea who the real Vince Foster was or what he stood for, and who didn't think twice about dragging him and his good name through the mud for their own ends.

He was repelled by the Rose firm's plan to open an office in Washington—repelled by what it said about the firm he had once loved. He yearned for the old days, back when Rose was still professional, when William Nash and Gaston Williamson and Phil Carroll provided a standard of excellence, of *behavior*, that set us above all other firms. He remembered the firm's retreat after Mr. Nash had retired and Gaston had become less influential, when we all asked ourselves the question, "How do we want the Rose firm to be known?" Watt Gregory spoke up: "I want the Rose firm to be known as the firm that can *get deals done*." And that's what it had become. Vince felt trapped. He hated Washington, but he couldn't see himself going back. In his mind, there was nothing left to go back to.

Since Waco, Janet's confidence in Director Sessions had dropped to zero. She told Phil and me that she was ready to recommend to the President that a new director be appointed. I kept to proper channels. I told Bernie Nussbaum, who told the President. Many people were interested in the job, but Bernie wanted someone with impeccable credentials who was very independent. Bernie was proud of Janet. She was increasingly seen as someone who stood on her own two feet, who brooked no interference—from any quarter—in her handling of her duties.

Janet had interviewed potential candidates, and both Phil and

Bernie kept coming back to one name—Judge Louis Freeh. A Republican appointee to the federal bench and a former FBI agent who had investigated many important cases, Freeh looked like the perfect candidate. Janet's only concern was that Judge Freeh looked even younger than his forty years. The FBI was assigned the background check on Judge Freeh. It was to be carried out in the strictest confidence.

As that project was under way, Phil called me and said there was a meeting I might want to sit in on. Once he began explaining, I remembered the articles in the newspapers. It had been in April. While former President George Bush was in Kuwait to receive that country's honors for his role in leading the allies in the Persian Gulf War against Iraq, a bomb had been found. Nobody was hurt, but Tony Lake, head of the National Security Council, wanted the FBI to work with the CIA in investigating whether the Iraqi government was responsible. We were sitting in the attorney general's conference room, and it was filled with people from the FBI, CIA, and Justice. There were about fifteen people in all.

"What if we find out Iraq *was* responsible?" I asked.

"We have a responsibility to retaliate," said Phil.

"What does that mean?"

Mr. Lake didn't want to tell what form of retaliation was being considered—"it might affect the decision."

This is where Phil Heymann really earned his stripes. The FBI did get involved, and soon they came back with a report saying that the device found "was consistent with a device used by Saddam Hussein and his government." The CIA wanted to issue a report saying that Saddam was behind this, but—as I would learn through this experience—when the CIA talks in terms of "knowing" that someone is behind a bombing, they are relying on confidential sources and past conduct that no one knows about. That is hardly proof "beyond a reasonable doubt." The FBI and Justice Department try to speak in terms of hard evidence—and when they don't, they identify that which isn't as "belief." I was learning firsthand how important each agency is in keeping world peace. Phil was very, very careful. He insisted that we weigh every single word, time and again, until we got our report exactly right. Tony Lake and the President eventually received two reports, one from the CIA and one from the FBI. Both concluded that Iraq was behind the attempted bombing, but one was based on "knowing" and the other on hard evidence. Janet was finally comfortable with both reports, though she didn't envy the President's task upon receiving them. One evening as we were leaving, she said, "I wouldn't want to be in his shoes right now."

As it happened, I was invited to the White House to watch a movie that night. During intermission, I found myself in the bathroom standing at the urinal next to the President. "I read the FBI and CIA reports," he said. "It was good work."

I had read both reports. "Yes, sir. Phil, Jim, and the others deserve a lot of credit. I was impressed."

"Have you looked at the evidence?"

"Well, I think that to the extent there is hard evidence, the conclusion is right."

"You know what I'm going to do, don't you?"

"No, Mr. President. I just know international law authorizes you to retaliate."

"I've decided to send missiles to Baghdad."

Oh shit, I thought.

"And, Hub, when I do this, there'll be eight hours before we know the results. Can you play golf with me tomorrow? I doubt my game will be any good."

I told him I would bring my clubs whenever he said to.

"Tomorrow morning."

"Fine, Mr. President."

When we went back to the White House theater, everyone was upset. "You guys were holding up the movie," they said.

The next morning I showed up at the White House with my clubs. When the President came down, he was surrounded by a swarm of very serious looking aides. One of them, George Tenant, said, "I'm glad you all are doing this. We're just waiting, and he needs to get it off his mind."

There were more carts than usual following along with us that day. Many of them looked like miniature situation rooms, with phones and screens and radios and such. As the President predicted, his game wasn't as sharp as it usually was. But I considered it my role that day to compliment his good shots and get his mind on easier days back in Little Rock.

After our round, we returned to the White House in the presidential limo. On some days after we had played golf, I would stop in and say hello to Hillary. Not today. The President and I said our good-byes and he was soon surrounded by aides. I watched him walk off through the Rose Garden to the Oval Office, and then I hoisted up my clubs and headed down the driveway toward the southwest gate, where I would catch a cab. I glanced to my right once and saw him standing at the window looking out from the Oval Office. Maybe he envied me at that moment. I sure didn't envy him.

I exited the gate and walked toward Seventeenth Street to hail a taxi. While I was waiting, a couple and their two children approached me. "Have you been playing golf in there?" they said.

I smiled. "No, there's no golf course in there. But I just got back from playing golf."

"Are you somebody?" their little girl asked.

"No. My name is Webb Hubbell, and I work at Justice."

"Do you know Janet Reno?"

"Yes."

"Wow!" said the little girl. "Is she great?"

"Yes—yes, she is."

"Do you know the President?"

"Yes again," I said.

"He's really a nice man, isn't he."

"Yes he is. He's just about the nicest man you'll ever meet."

The father spoke up. "Can we take your picture with our children? You at least *know* the President."

We posed, and somewhere in this vast country there's a snapshot of two cute kids with a sweaty Webb Hubbell, in his golf clothes outside the White House gate.

The travel office firings continued to generate waves of bad publicity. In mid-July, *The Wall Street Journal* published two editorials that hurt Vince to the core. One was entitled, "Who Is William Kennedy?" and the other was "FBI Director Rose." The latter speculated on the existence of an evil cabal of four former Rose firm partners (Hillary, Vince, Bill, and I) manipulating the FBI for our own dastardly purposes. "Ms. Reno is of course the latest media darling," the newspaper said, "and we might even join the praise if she ever really gets control of the Justice Department. For the evidence so far is that control has in fact rested with appointees from Little Rock's Rose Law Firm." It went on to say, "We know now Mrs. Clinton inquired about the travel office affair with Mr. Foster, and that she was prominently carboned on copies of crucial memos." It chastised Kennedy for contacting the FBI without telling Reno. It concluded with this cutting sentence: "A Rose clique from Little Rock that has already shown a willingness to cut many legal corners needs adult supervision."

Prior to those pieces, FBI Director Sessions had written to Senator Dole accusing Bill Kennedy of threatening to call the IRS on travel office employees if the FBI didn't investigate. When the White House internal report that Vince had been dreading came out, it strongly reprimanded Bill Kennedy and David Watkins, another Arkansas transplant, the deputy in the White House in charge of the travel office's administration. Vince was upset about that. He felt that neither should have been reprimanded—but that if either was, then Vince himself should also have received a share of the blame. He had delegated the handling of this unpleasant task to Bill Kennedy, partly in an effort to show Bernie, who didn't know Kennedy, that he was a capable, trustworthy person. Vince didn't think Bill had done anything wrong, but he knew that from now on Bernie would always be looking over his shoulder at Bill. Aside from feeling for Bill, Vince now believed he had to do everything himself. He felt guilty about having been spared that. In some sense, I think, he now saw himself as both the betrayed and the betrayer.

He told me he no longer trusted telephones, even the ones in his office. He seemed to be buying into the growing belief that somehow the Secret Service or burrowed-in Republicans were monitoring phone calls. Once we were talking on the telephone and he told me, "Hub, we do need to talk, but I can't on the telephone." We agreed to "go to a park bench and just talk" sometime soon.

By mid-July, I was immersed in all sorts of crises at Justice. We were close to a final decision on Judge Freeh. Ruth Bader Ginsburg was scheduled to be interviewed before the Senate. One of the universal fears of the administration was that a vast immigration emergency was building in south Florida. Castro, they worried, was going to let everyone who wanted to leave Cuba—and suddenly a mass invasion of Miami would take place. On July 14, I flew to Miami to supervise the finalization of the "Mass Immigration Emergency Plan," in which all branches of government were participating. It was my first official trip representing Janet and the President. I would get a chance to tour the Immigration holding facility that was housing some of the HIV-positive Haitians. I would even get a chance to have dinner with Hugh and Maria Rodham.

Just before I left the office, I got a call from Vince. He wanted just the Hubbells and the Fosters to go somewhere for dinner Friday night "and just talk." I told him great—that I would be back on Friday afternoon.

I was in Miami for three days, and while I was there I had a message to call Vince. "Hub, we're going to have to reschedule our dinner," he said. He and Lisa had decided to get away for the weekend. His sister Sheila had recommended the Eastern Shore of Maryland. I thought it was a great idea. "You two need to get away," I told him. "We'll get together when you get back."

Janet beeped me to find out when I was coming home. "It's time to deal with Director Sessions," she said. I told her I would come straight to the office on Friday when I got in.

Then Suzy called with good news—we had been invited to Harolyn Cardozo's family home on the Eastern Shore. I told Suzy I had a meeting Saturday morning, but we could head out right after that. I also mentioned that Vince and Lisa were going to be somewhere over there.

"I'll call Lisa and see if they're anywhere close," Suzy said.

On Friday afternoon I returned to the office to find Janet and

Phil deep in discussions about Director Sessions. He had dug in his heels and refused to step down. We all felt that he had served his country for many years and deserved to be treated with dignity, but he was not making it very easy. Janet was willing to consider just about any retirement package he wanted to put forward.

Then Director Sessions called. He wanted to come over. When he got there, he said he had been thinking about it and here was his bottom line: "I will not resign. The President will have to tell me to my face that I'm fired." He then went on and on, as he was wont to do. I glanced at Janet and could tell that any sympathy she'd had for the man had just drained away. When the director left, Janet said, "And he wonders why nobody has confidence in his leadership."

It was suggested that I call Bernie and tell him what Director Sessions wanted. "He can't do that," Bernie said. In Bernie's opinion, a face-to-face meeting would accomplish no useful purpose. Bernie asked me to arrange for the director to meet with the three of us the following morning in Janet's office.

Bernie showed up ready to handle the situation. "Judge Sessions," he said as soon as Sessions got there, "the President has received the recommendation that you be fired. My understanding is that you want a face-to-face meeting. There will not be such a meeting." Sessions was visibly shaken. He kept repeating that it was important that he not resign. It was as though he had rehearsed and rehearsed those words—but had never thought beyond them.

"Judge Hubbell," Sessions said, "you understand why I can't resign, don't you?"

"No, I don't," I said. What I wanted to say was, *Why are you doing this?* But what I did say was, "You have a lot to be proud of. I think your term should end some other way. You are much better off by simply resigning."

He left the office, but because it was Saturday he had to leave by a door where a battalion of press was waiting. They'd obviously gotten wind of something. As Director Sessions stepped out the door, he tripped. He fell and broke his arm while the CNN cameras caught the whole ignoble scene. I truly felt for him. I hate to see anyone fired, but it was clear that the FBI needed a new infusion of energy.

It was great to see my swimming trunks again. I had been working so hard for so long that I couldn't quite picture them as still part of my wardrobe. Suzy and I packed tennis gear, too, and I loaded up my golf clubs. I also carried a briefcase filled with reports to read in the sun.

Other than flying to Little Rock and playing golf with the President, I hadn't been out of the District of Columbia for six whole months. Now in one week I had been to Miami and was leaving yet again. Suzy and I reveled in the beautiful drive over to Easton. I thought about my old Austin-Healy and wished I hadn't wrapped it around a telephone pole. A top-down Healy would be perfect for a summer day on the Eastern Shore, except for one thing. I hate driving across bridges, and the one spanning the Cheasapeake seems to go forever. Suzy always kids me once we get right in the middle of the bridge. "Look at that!" she says, pointing to things in the water. But I grip the wheel and stare straight ahead (when my wife lets me drive).

Suzy had talked with Lisa, who was really looking forward to her getaway with Vince. I wondered aloud if it was a good idea to mention to Harolyn that the Fosters were nearby. They needed this vacation. "They're grown-ups," Suzy said. "If they want to be alone they can say so."

The Landow family home was beautiful, and all the more so because we were among such good friends. Harolyn introduced us to her father, Nate, and to "Uncle Nick"—who turned out to be Nick Bollettieri, the famous tennis coach of such stars as Pete Sampras and Andre Agassi. Suzy couldn't wait to get changed and hit the court. Mike and I took it easy around the pool. Suzy had obviously mentioned to Harolyn that the Fosters were close by, because she was soon on the phone inviting them over. They showed up much sooner than I expected. Lisa was immediately whisked to the tennis court—they were playing doubles, and Nick was giving them lessons as they played. I told Vince I was sorry if we interrupted their getaway. "It's okay," he said. "I just wanted to get out of Washington." He told me they had explored the area where they were staying, even taking a ferry across to an island in the bay. "But we were already running out of things to do," he said.

Vince and I watched our wives out on the tennis court. It was almost a case of déjà vu, a flashback to a time that seemed familiar and safe. How many times had we sat under a canopy at the Country Club of Little Rock, watching our wives stretch and lunge for well-placed shots. I told him we were going to have a couple of tired babies on our hands that night.

Vince seemed in his element, too. He loved hats, and his favorite was a black New York Yankees cap with a white logo on the front. It wasn't one of those mass-produced caps with a plastic fitting strap across the back. Vince was, if anything, a meticulous man. His cap was wool twill, perfectly fitted, and formed like it had been made especially for his handsome head. He'd had it for years and it still looked new. He was wearing swimming trunks, a golf shirt, and running shoes. When I close my eyes today, that's the picture of Vince that I hope comes to mind. Back in Little Rock, before we went away, that was the weekend Vince. Sitting around his pool, usually with legal briefs in his hand.

They came again the next day and Lisa and Suzy were hitting balls soon after breakfast. Vince went on a long jog around a course that Harolyn had mapped out just for him. Michael and Nate were teaching the Cardozo children how to water-ski. I was sitting by the pool reading the morning paper when Vince came back. We went for a swim together, and while we were in the pool I asked if he wanted to talk about what was bothering him.

"Webb, we really need to talk, but not here, this feels too good," he said. "You and Sheila are the only ones I can talk to. But it's so nice here. Let's wait till next week. We'll have lunch. We'll go outside to a park somewhere."

Monday proved to be a tough day. I had been gone most of the previous week, and nobody had taken up the slack. I got in early and rolled up my sleeves.

That morning I was scheduled to meet with Mac McLarty about all the leaks from the White House alleging that Janet and the President weren't getting along. That was news to Janet, and she hated it when such stories were spread to the media. Mac and I had talked early the previous week. He had said he also wanted to talk with me about Vince. "I'm worried about him," he'd said.

When I got to Mac's office, he was running late. So I went upstairs to say hi to Vince and Bernie. Vince was sitting in his little office working on some papers. "Hey, wasn't that a great weekend?" I said.

"I can't tell you what that did for me, Hub. I'm already looking into someplace to go for next weekend."

He started talking about the one month that he and Lisa used to spend in Michigan every summer. It had refreshed him, renewed him. He had come home ready to tackle the problems of life. This past weekend had reminded him of that.

I got a message that Mac was ready, so I said good-bye to Vince.

After Mac and I finished our Janet business, he brought up what was bothering him so much. "A lot of us are worried about Vince." I told him I had been, too—but then I described the weekend we'd all just had. I told him what Vince had just said to me about looking forward to the coming weekend. I mentioned that I knew Vince was upset about the travel office report, a document that had come from Mac's office. He knew it, too. But he seemed to take as much encouragement as I did from Vince's joy in his weekend on the Eastern Shore.

"We all need to take care of each other, Hubbell," Mac said. "Let's both look out for Vince and talk again soon."

I spent the afternoon catching up on paperwork. Late that afternoon I got a call from the White House asking if I could watch a movie with the President that evening. I was tired, but I never turned down an invitation to the White House. (Vince did that night, which was highly unusual.) I expected a crowd scene, but it was only the President, Bruce Lindsey, and me. Hillary was in Little Rock visiting her mother. The movie was *In the Line of Fire* with Clint Eastwood; it was about a tired old Secret Service agent trying to protect the President of the United States from a bomb-wielding psychopath. It was eerie watching that movie with the real President. There wasn't a lot of talk or laughter during the movie, and I went home as soon as I could.

The next morning Judge Louis Freeh's nomination was being announced in the Rose Garden. I got there late and Janet and the President were already talking to the TV cameras. Usually I would have run upstairs to see Vince, but I had so much to do at the office that I headed right back and spent the rest of the day trying to catch up from the week before.

That evening, Suzy and Marsha Scott and I were scheduled to have dinner with my children and some of their friends. We went to the Lebanese Taverna on Connecticut Avenue. We'd been there just long enough to be served drinks when I felt my beeper vibrate. "Why don't you wait till dinner's over," Suzy said. I looked at the number on the pad. It was George Stephanopoulos.

"I better see what George wants," I said.

I asked the waiter if there was a private phone I could use, and he directed me to the kitchen. I dialed and an assistant answered. "This is Webb," I said. "George paged me." I expected to wait. Usually when I phoned George, he was tied up with some other call. More than once I had stood holding the receiver for five minutes or more.

This time he came on the line immediately. "Webb, I have some terrible news." He didn't sound at all like himself. "They've found a body in a park in Virginia."

I couldn't for the life of me figure out why George would be calling me about a dead body.

"Webb," he said, and then he paused. I'll never forget that. In a movie, it would be long enough for a lifetime's reflection. "It's Vince Foster."

"No way," I said.

"It's an apparent suicide."

I couldn't grasp it. Every rational bone in my body said, Anyone but Vince. But somehow I knew it was true.

"George, I'm at a public phone. In a restaurant."

"Get to where you can talk and call me back."

I hung up and went back to the table. As I approached, I could see Marsha and Suzy looking at me, studying my face. For some reason I leaned over to Marsha first. "Marsha, you and Suzy and I have to go." I handed Walter my credit card and keys.

Suzy heard and started to ask questions.

"Suzy, we have to *go*!" I said, and she read in my eyes that she should silently get up from the table.

11

Rumblings

Marsha remembers that I couldn't seem to talk. We went to the basement garage to get her car, and I was catatonic but moving, looking straight ahead, pushing forward.

"What's going on?" Suzy said. I didn't answer.

"Is the President all right?" asked Marsha. I still didn't say a word. We got in the car, Marsha driving, Suzy in the backseat.

"We have to go to our house," I said. "I need a secure phone."

Marsha began heading toward McComb Street. "It's Vince," I said. "They think he's dead."

They started asking a million questions, none of which I had the answer to. I told them everything I knew. "A body was found in a park in Virginia. They think it's Vince."

When we got to our house, I realized I had left the house key with Walter. We were locked out. Ordinarily, I would have dashed across the street to Sheila and Beryl's, but not this time. Not yet. I had to know for sure before I saw Sheila.

I knocked on our next-door neighbor's door. We hardly knew these people and now this. They weren't home, but a house-sitter was. She must have made a great leap of faith to open the house to three people looking the way we did. I called George.

"Webb, it's not a mistake," he said. "They found his jacket and his White House pass." He told me Bill Kennedy was en route to

Virginia to identify the body. I asked him about signs of a struggle. All the way home I had tried to piece together some logical explanation—he was carjacked and murdered; he was the victim of a robbery gone bad.

"There's no evidence of a struggle," George said. "None. The Park Police and David Watkins are on their way to Lisa's to tell her. You need to get there as soon as you can."

"Is there anybody besides the police who can break it to her?"

"I don't know, Webb. Try to catch them."

Then I thought again of Sheila. "Oh God, George—*Sheila*. Has anybody told her?"

"I totally forgot about Sheila."

"She lives right across the street from me."

"Webb, you've got to go do it. Right now."

"Listen, George—Lisa is Catholic. Please try to stop this suicide talk until you're absolutely certain."

"I'll try, but word is going to spread." Then, before we hung up, he said, "Webb, I know this is tough. Are you okay?"

"Yeah, George," I lied. "I'll be all right. Thanks."

Suzy and Marsha had heard my side of the conversation. They both were crying. "I have to go tell Sheila," I said. "Go get in the car. After Sheila, we have to go right to Lisa's."

I ran across the street and walked right into Sheila's house. It was midsummer and the windows and doors were open. She was on her back porch having a drink with someone when she saw me walking through the house. I didn't realize that Marsha and Suzy had also gotten out and followed me. Suzy stayed at the front door while Marsha came in right behind me. She remembers the scene in slow motion. Sheila and the other person rise, smile, say, "Webb." The other person turns out to be Vince's other sister, Sharon Bowman, visiting from Little Rock. Almost immediately the smiles drain from their faces. "What?" they say. Their hands rise slowly to their mouths as I force the words from my lips. "It's Vince. I don't know how to say this. They think he's dead."

I could hardly believe that both Vince's sisters were here. What fate. I told them the rest as I knew it, and said I had to get to Lisa's house fast. "Go!" said Sheila. She said she and Sharon would try to get hold of Beryl and follow as soon as they could.

The Fosters' town house was on a narrow, curving one-way street. Marsha stopped just long enough to let Suzy and me out; then she went and found a parking place. I got there just as two Park Police officers and David Watkins from the White House were walking up to the doorstep. David's wife, Aileen, was there, too. "David!" I said. "Can't I do this?"

He wheeled around. "Webb! I asked the same, but they say they're trained." David and I held back while Vince's daughter Laura came to the door. She went to get Lisa. I heard one of the Park Police officers murmur low, and then Lisa's bloodcurdling scream: *"Nooooo!"* I hurried up the steps and into the town house. Lisa was folded up on the stairs, and Aileen helped her up to the bedroom. David and I asked the Park policemen if they needed to stay. I say police*men,* but until months later I didn't remember that there were two of them, a male and a female. I only remembered the man.

He said he knew it was a terrible time, but he needed to speak with Lisa if at all possible. I think he was as overwhelmed as we were. He never said that he was or would be conducting any type of investigation. I questioned him about the possibility of someone taking Vince to the park, but he said there was no doubt that this was a suicide. Later I was taken aback when, at the Senate hearing on Vince's death, the Park Police officer said I had been rude to the female officer and had shoved her away from talking to Sheila. As I say, I didn't remember her even being there. Suzy and Marsha remember that she was questioning Sheila, who looked as if she needed rescuing. They asked me to help, and I went over and gave Sheila a hug and escorted her away. People asked if the Park Police officers needed to stay, and the man said in official tones that he had important questions to ask. Eventually they left and never came back. If they had an investigation to conduct, why didn't they return? I'm still angry when I read that somehow we weren't all candid about Vince's being depressed. When a tragedy like this happens, you simply go into shock. Yes, I knew he was depressed, but I never once considered that he was depressed enough to kill himself.

Lisa asked me to come upstairs, where we just held each other for the longest time. No words can describe the array of emotions I was feeling: *My best friend was dead, the world had gone crazy, all bets were off.* She and I talked about the past couple of days. He had gotten some antidepressants from their family doctor. We looked in the medicine cabinet—they were all there. She checked in the closet for a gun Vince had kept there. I was surprised. I'd never known Vince Foster owned a gun. Lisa swept her hand around on a shelf, and it was there. But there was another one, she said. Vince also had an old gun he had inherited from his father. She couldn't find it. I wanted to take the one gun out with me, but she wouldn't let me. She wasn't thinking clearly. Later I sneaked back upstairs and wrapped the gun in a towel and gave it to Beryl for safekeeping.

Later that night, Lisa said, "You took the gun, didn't you? I wasn't going to do anything stupid."

I smiled. "Humor me, please. I just don't want any more guns around." She didn't argue.

There was only one phone in the house, and it was ringing like mad. My beeper went off so often the batteries died. Marsha Scott has another vivid memory of that night. After Lisa and Sheila were told, Marsha says, the men and the women reverted to some kind of primitive rituals. The men walked around talking into telephones, taking charge, asking questions, giving orders. At one point, Marsha recalls, David Watkins had a cell phone to each ear, and when a battery went dead he threw the phone across the room. The women, on the other hand, were curled into shapes of caring, of nurturing, of holding and consoling.

The little living room was filling up fast. Senator David Pryor and his wife, Barbara. Beryl and Sheila and Sharon. Bruce Lindsey. Mickey Kantor. Mac McLarty. My son Walter had heard and came to be with us. Cars were jammed in the tiny street outside. At about 11 P.M., the President arrived. Hillary was in Little Rock with her mother. And this is something else Marsha remembers.

While the other men were barking into telephones, the President of the United States came in, wearing casual clothes, and he walked around the room hugging everybody there. At first he didn't even say anything. He just hugged.

I asked David to get a doctor to prescribe something for Lisa. I was on the phone trying to stop the suicide talk. Then, while I was on the phone with my friend Mike Schaufele in Little Rock, he said, "Webb, it's on television right now." I flipped on CNN and there was Vince's picture. They said he was an apparent suicide.

I talked with Phil Carroll, Vince's mentor at the Rose firm. Phil, a Catholic, said, "Webb, tell me he didn't commit suicide."

I told him I still didn't believe it myself. Now I wonder why I said that. Maybe it was because I knew it would crush Phil. Or maybe it was because of all the people I ever knew, Vince had seemed the most cool and collected. I know that seems to contradict the stories I've told in this book, but at the time I thought those were just incidents, not a pattern. I now know a lot more about depression. I know that it kills like cancer if it isn't treated, but as a society we aren't trained to recognize the symptoms.

Bill Kennedy showed up and reported the inevitable—it was Vince. He had placed the pistol in his mouth and pulled the trigger.

As the night went on, I helped Lisa deal with the hundreds of decisions that need to be made at a time like that. Being busy helped me, too. I called my old friend Tom Wittenburg, the funeral director who had buried both my parents, to find out the details of getting Vince back home. I called the Catholic bishop in Little Rock about a service. I called a D.C. attorney to see about getting the body released from the Park Police. I told David Watkins that I thought it very important that Vince's office be locked. Lisa and I had looked for a suicide note at the town house, but to no avail. Maybe Vince had left one at the office.

Sheila stayed with Lisa and Laura that night. I told them Suzy and I would be back first thing in the morning. When we got home, there were at least fifty phone messages. Friends from all over had heard the news and called to see how we were doing.

Harolyn, thoughtful Harolyn, had come over to be with Caroline and Kelley while Suzy and Walter and I were at Lisa's. Walter was still awake when we got back. I sat on the couch next to him. When he said, "Are you okay, Dad?" that's when I finally cried.

The Park Police gave a briefing the next day at the White House, which I attended on Lisa's behalf. Before that, Suzy and I had driven back to the town house, where Lisa and I had made yet another search for a note. Questions were rushing to Lisa's mind now: Where had Vince been all the previous afternoon (he hadn't returned to his office after lunch)? Had he taken the pistol with him that morning, or had he come home to get it? Whom had he talked to on the phone? I found out he had spoken to attorney Jim Lyons about representing him in the travel office mess. He had also talked with Brant Buck from the Rose firm. Why? I wondered. God forbid, did it have anything to do with my problems? Brant later said his conversation with Vince concerned the Clintons' blind trust. Vince was Bill and Hillary's personal attorney. There would be later speculation, however, that Vince had somehow found out about my crime and couldn't stand it. I hated hearing that, but it wasn't true. When I was in Little Rock for Vince's funeral, Jerry Jones told me that the few people at Rose who knew about my billing problems had taken great care not to mention it to Vince.

The meeting with the Park Police took place in David Watkins's office. Two senior officials explained that even though this was a suicide, there would have to be an investigation. They wanted to question his family, friends, and colleagues about his state of mind. David and Bernie assured the police that they would have total cooperation. After introducing myself and stressing that I was there not in my capacity as a Justice official, but as a friend of the family, I asked about jurisdiction. "I would assume that the Secret Service, or Justice, or perhaps the state of Virginia would have jurisdiction." The police officers weren't at all offended. They explained that most people don't know the Park Police have jurisdiction over any investigation of crimes committed in federal parks. Vince's body had been found near an old cannon at Fort Marcy Park, a Civil War–era outpost on the Virginia side of the Potomac.

As the meeting broke up, I tried to catch Bernie, who seemed flustered and in a hurry. "Bernie, I think your office ought to stay out of the investigation," I said.

He looked at me quizzically. Apparently, such a thought had never occurred to him. "Really?" he said. And then he dashed off toward the door. "Let's talk about it soon."

The President asked me to stay and sit in on his briefing of the White House staff. It was held in the White House auditorium, which is in the Old Executive Office Building. By the time the crowd assembled, everyone had heard the news. Every eye was red; mascara was running. People wept silently, sitting in their chairs. I stood to the side holding Marsha's and Deb Coyle's hands. Mac spoke first, telling about growing up with Vince in Hope. Then the President stepped up. His eyes were puffy and red. He told the staff about playing mumblety-peg with Vince back before either of them was even school age. That's how far back that friendship went. Maybe it's terrible to say, but Bill Clinton is at his best in moments like this. He is a healer. He gives eloquent voice to the emotions his listeners feel but can't seem to utter. I almost cried when he talked about Hillary that morning— "her two best friends were Vince Foster and Webb Hubbell." I say I almost cried—but I didn't. I held it in, the way southern men are taught to do. The President concluded by saying that tragedy was part of life, and we had to learn to deal with it. We all needed lives outside the White House, he said. And we needed to watch out for others, as well as ourselves.

When he mentioned Hillary, I remembered having spoken briefly with her sometime in the past fifteen hours. I wasn't exactly sure where or when—probably at Lisa's the night before. Hillary was at her mother's house, and I could hear the pain in her voice. "I'm okay," she said. "How are you holding up?" There wasn't much to say. I told her we would talk when I came to Arkansas for the funeral. As we hung up, Hillary said, "Take care of Lisa and the kids, Webb. But hurry home."

David Watkins told me Vince would be flown to Arkansas on a military plane, and I asked to escort the body home. David said there were two seats available, if Suzy wanted to go. I imagined us sitting on jump seats in a cold C-130, and Suzy opted to take a commercial flight. Walter said he would ride with me. Our plane turned out to be one of the Air Force One jets, with the presidential limo in the cargo hold. We were met at the Little Rock airport by old friends of mine and Vince's. Many Rose partners were there. I hugged them all. They said the whole state was in shock. What was so tough about Washington that it could kill a Vince Foster? Later, by myself, I watched Vince being placed in the hearse. I put my hand on the box that held my friend and said, "You've come home."

I dropped Walter off at a friend's house and then went to see Hillary. Her mother's house had seen a lot of grief over the past few months. I hugged her and we went back to the room she was staying in. She dabbed at her tears as we talked. "Webb, did you have any idea he was that depressed?"

I told her I knew he was upset about the travel office—but no, there was no way I saw anything like this coming. I listed the things I knew were troubling him—*The Wall Street Journal* pieces, the paranoia about the telephones, the guilt over Bill Kennedy's reprimand. But I also told her about the weekend on the Eastern Shore, and about my conversation with Vince on Monday. None of it made sense. I didn't tell her what he had said about not being able to talk to her anymore, but somehow she seemed to know. "With health care and my dad's death, I didn't have time to see him on a personal basis as much as I should have." She had obviously been going through the same what-ifs that all of us had.

She asked who had come to the town house the night he died. She asked about Lisa, Sheila, and the children. She asked if his face "was messed up." I didn't know at the time, but I would later view his body privately. The way he shot himself the bullet had exited through the back of his skull, so there was little visible damage to his face. "We shouldn't have asked him to come to

Washington, Webb." She was now getting to the core of what had been eating at her for days.

"Listen," I said, "it would've destroyed him if you *hadn't* asked." I told her about the pact he and I had made—if invited, we would go to Washington with our friends. I told her how energized he had been during the transition, and how proud he was of his White House pass. "This is gold, Hub," he had said, tapping the laminated card. And I told her how proud he was of her.

We were interrupted with the message that Bill Kennedy was on his way. "How's Bill doing?" she asked. He was aware of how upset Vince had been about the travel office situation. Someone later told me Vince had said it was "too late to save Bill and me, but maybe I can still protect Sheila and Webb." To this day, nobody understands what that means.

Before I left her, Hillary brought up something she needed my help on. It concerned a bizarre rumor she had heard. "I know there are some crazy stories out there," she said, "but Bill has been approached by a reporter whose father is Bill Harrison, the writing professor at Fayetteville. The son claims to have proof that there's a Navy hit squad that murders people and makes their deaths look like suicide."

"That's nuts."

"I know, Webb—but both Harrisons swear that Vince was investigating this and was about to report back."

"Well, okay. If they call me, I'll talk to them."

"Thanks, Hub."

We hugged one more time. As I was going, she said, "I know you're being a rock for everybody else right now. But don't hold it all in forever."

"I could offer you the same advice," I said. She gave me a sweet, sad smile, and we promised to talk when the next few crazy days were over.

We laid Vince to rest in Hope, where his journey had begun. It had been barely two years since Vince and I stood on this same ground burying his dad. Now father and son were together again.

A few days later, I went with Lisa to the Rose firm to discuss Vince's estate. After that meeting, Jerry Jones and Ron Clark pulled me aside. They told me Skeeter hadn't yet resolved the matter with the patent lawyer. I was offended at their insensitivity—couldn't they at least wait until we took care of their former partner's widow? But I said nothing. I told them I would deal with the POM problem. I was using their bad timing to avoid facing my own true problems.

As Suzy and I flew back to Washington, I felt an aching emptiness in my chest. Nothing would ever be the same. The excitement Vince and I had felt just six months before—even if I could regain a shred of it, how could I ever trust it again?

Prior to my leaving for Arkansas, Phil Heymann had told me that in fact both the Park Police and the Justice Department had jurisdiction over Vince's death. I had felt better about that. I trusted Phil's sensitivity to the family's needs and concerns. But when I got back to Justice, I found that trouble had come from an unexpected direction. "Glad you're back, Webb," Phil said. "We almost had a problem with Bernie, but I've taken care of it." He told me that Tom Collier, chief of staff at the Department of Interior, had called to complain that the Park Police felt Bernie wasn't being as cooperative as he should be. He then told me about the search of Vince's office. Phil thought they had an agreement to jointly review any documents there, but Bernie had gone in and conducted the review the way he would have done a corporate litigation discovery back home in New York. In other words, you use every tactic you can to avoid turning over documents. One of Bernie's associate counsels, Steve Nuewirth, even accused an FBI agent of trying to look over Bernie's shoulder when the agent stood up to stretch.

The last thing anybody needed now was even the *appearance* of noncooperation. "You want me to call Bernie?" I said. Phil told me no, that I ought to stay out of it. He said he thought things were now under control.

Then I got a call saying the press was going wild—they'd heard a rumor that a suicide note had been found. That was what I dreaded most—that information would be leaked before the family had been informed. I called Phil. "Look," I said, "I'm going to stay out of the case. But if there's a note, I think somebody ought to tell me about it." After checking with David Margolis, the career deputy who had recently joined Phil's office, Phil called me back. "David says it's okay for you to see the note. In fact, maybe you can interpret it."

I went down to David's office, where he held out to me a hand-written note on a sheet from a legal pad. As I read it, I had the eerie feeling that I was hearing Vince Foster speak to me from the grave. I also was becoming sick to my stomach, because this wasn't Vince's handwriting.

"What do you mean?" Dave said when I told him. The color was draining from his face.

"Dave, I practiced law with Vince Foster for twenty years. This is not his writing."

He told me to wait a minute and disappeared. When he came back, he was smiling again. "I'm sorry, Webb," he said. "The original note was torn up in his briefcase. The officer copied it over as it was pieced together."

Somehow that still didn't make me feel better. What if the officer's handwriting had been released as Vince's? And how could such a mistake have gone this far? We had to be very, very careful here. I deciphered what I could of the note for Dave. When I first read the note, I thought it was Vince carefully preparing to resign. When he made a presentation to a court, a client, or to the firm, he always carefully articulated, in writing, the points he wanted to make. This note read to me like he was going to see the President or Mac and tell them why he was resigning. I've later read that Lisa had encouraged him to write down what was bothering him. Either way, he probably finished the process and tore it up. Not trusting that the trash wouldn't be rifled through, he stuck the note in his briefcase to throw away at home. He killed himself before he could throw it away. This wasn't a suicide note.

But I recognized immediately the words that would cause a firestorm. They made up his very last sentence: "Here, destroying people is considered sport."

I asked Dave Margolis if there was any evidence that this was anything other than suicide. He shook his head. I told him about the reporter with the Navy hit squad theory. (Later I received a visit from the reporter and his father, and I passed their materials over to Dave. He checked, and said there was nothing to it.)

I told Sheila about the note, and she already knew about it. In fact, she said, so did Lisa. I later learned that Bernie had delayed releasing the note to Justice until Lisa and Sheila could be advised. Of course he was criticized for that. "Webb, Lisa has asked the attorney general not to release the note's contents," Sheila said. I knew Janet wouldn't be happy about that. The family hoped to put Vince's death behind them by refusing to discuss it further. The Justice Department didn't want to appear to be suppressing evidence, and that's why Janet finally decided to release it. So there was no right way to handle the situation. Even so, I doubt anyone could have predicted the morbid and widespread fascination with the death of Vince Foster.

When I think of how the conspiracy industry boomed, it makes me ill. Vince would have been mortified. Naturally, there were those who indulged for political reasons. There always are. But the worst of all turned out to be the U.S. Congress, which, in its misguided effort to find the rational reason for the irrational act, justified numerous investigations on the basis that one of them had to "explain" why a troubled man killed himself. Everybody jumped on some scapegoat bandwagon—Whitewater, Madison Savings and Loan, "Travelgate," even bizarre international cabals (Vince, Hillary, and I were accused of having something to do with the notorious Italian BCCI scandal—it must have been the *Vincenzo* story). Unwittingly, my depressed friend had helped numerous irresponsible people further their selfish causes. It's not fair. It's not fair to Vince, to his family, or to the millions of people who suffer from this disease we ignore because we can't understand it.

I think Vince felt trapped. Lisa eventually told *The New Yorker* that they were fighting about going home. I'm sure he wanted to go, but felt he couldn't. He also wanted to stay in Washington, but felt he couldn't. He couldn't do either because of that thing inside him that demanded he not fail—that he always march proudly forward toward excellence and never turn back in defeat. The White House had disillusioned him. No longer could he hold it up as a noble symbol of glory. He had been inside it, and life was less than noble there. In all of this, Vince Foster finally discovered that he couldn't control his world no matter how many hours he spent behind closed doors meticulously rehearsing talking points. Once he stepped from behind that closed door, he found that everyone else had been rehearsing their shouting points, or hissing points, or lying points, or leaking points. They overwhelmed him.

I really don't think Vince killed himself over his relationship with Hillary in any way. I know he loved her, as I do. I call this workplace intimacy. I think Hillary, like many others of us, questions whether, if she had spent more time with him, she could have affected the outcome. I'm sure she loses sleep over it, as I do. I still wonder what would have happened if I had stopped to see him that Tuesday morning before he died. The truth, I believe, is that there is nothing we could have done. He was suffering from a disease called depression.

Vince Foster was a good husband, a wonderful father, a loving brother, and a fine friend. He was also a sick man. Maybe when people stop using his death for their own purposes, we can focus finally on the disease that shortened his life and has killed so many others.

One immediate result of Vince's death was that many people in the administration, from the Clintons on down, realized that we all needed to be taking more time away from the office. At the end of the summer, Vernon Jordan and his wife, Ann, invited me to spend a few days with them on Martha's Vineyard. The President and First Lady were to be vacationing there, and Vernon thought it would be good for us to relax with some much-needed golf.

I flew up on a tiny commuter plane, arriving just in time to be baptized into the glamorous life of late summer on Martha's Vineyard. From the airport, I went straight to a dinner party at the home of Katharine Graham, owner of *The Washington Post* and

Newsweek. Though I was tired, hot, and wrinkled, I was ushered directly into an elegant dining room where several tables were set for dinner. The guests were just being seated. Kay Graham saw me and came over to take me around for introductions. I couldn't believe who was there—Henry Kissinger, Larry Eagleburger, Nicholas Katzenbach, Barbara Walters. Everywhere I looked, there were celebrities.

Kay showed me to my table, which happened to be *her* table— and the President's table, and Eagleburger's and Kissinger's. But next to me was a tall, striking woman wearing a low-cut and revealing pants suit. It was Carly Simon. I hadn't the slightest idea of what to say to her. I knew her music well, and that of her ex-husband, James Taylor. We just talked about my trip up and the beauty of the island for a few minutes. And then we settled on a topic that both of us found irresistible—our children. We were consumed with our respective stories, when suddenly I heard someone speaking in my direction. "Webb! Carly! *Hush!* The President is talking." It was Kay Graham, being the perfect Washington hostess. The President looked amused, and then continued his dialogue with Henry Kissinger.

We did play a lot of golf over the next few days, and when the President wasn't available, Vernon drove me around the island in his red Cadillac convertible. I told him about my boyhood in the South, and he told me about his early days in the civil rights movement. Vernon and I became real friends that week. He talked about some of the tragedies in his life, and something his mother told him has stayed with me and helped me through my darkest days. She said, "Vernon, the good Lord doesn't give you a load you can't tote."

Life almost felt fun again for those few days, and I wish I could say that everything eventually returned to normal. But Vince's death was the watershed. It was the pivotal moment. Before, there was hope. To me, the astonishing thing was how fast everything began to unravel. At first it was unraveling *out there* somewhere, beyond my radar scope. Once again, the pattern would only show up in hindsight.

After Vince's death, I plunged into my work just as he used to do. That was partly because I needed to for me; but also, there was just so much work to be done. My days were filled with issues like the reauthorization of the Legal Services Corporation, the lawsuit against the Health Care Task Force, and NAFTA. We were constantly trying to respond to pronouncements from Congress on issues like the use of the National Guard to patrol our borders. I was learning to be an expert in immigration policy, environmental policy, and war powers. Janet wanted me to review any letter going from Justice to Congress. So besides doing my own work, I read every letter to Congress from every other person at Justice.

I think it's no wonder, then, that in August when I got a call from Bill Kennedy asking if I remembered any connection between David Hale and Madison Guaranty Savings and Loan, I said no. "Why?" I asked.

And Bill said, "Oh, we got a question and I was just checking." That was it. I hung up the telephone and plunged back into the pile on my desk. Of course, Hale had approached me about Madison, as I noted earlier. But because it hadn't led to anything, I had long forgotten it. But this was just the first incident in the eventual pattern.

One of the things I had to deal with after I returned from Martha's Vineyard was an issue that was taking forever to complete. Within a month of my arrival at Justice, I had been visited by the acting head of Justice's Office of Legal Counsel, Dan Kofsky. The Office of Legal Counsel actually issues legal opinions throughout the executive branch. It is staffed with some of the brightest legal minds in the country—for example, both Mike Cardozo and Zoe Baird trained there.

When Dan came to see me, he brought along a lawyer named Jon Rogovin, who had been assigned to help me until he could be placed permanently, as well as another man who was head of the independent Office of Government Ethics (OGE). The three of them had a problem. A few weeks before the Bush administration political appointees left Justice, the Office of Legal Counsel issued a letter ruling stating that the one-year ban on lobbying the department of government you had left did not apply to signing legal briefs. Some high-level attorneys are paid handsome sums to sign legal briefs for other firms or entities. The Rose firm once had a case before the U.S. Supreme Court and we hired a former solicitor general to help. He signed the brief and argued the case. We knew that having his name on the brief increased tenfold the chances of our case being heard.

According to the letter ruling, a senior official could leave Justice and immediately be opposite the U.S. government in a lawsuit signing briefs unless it was a matter that the lawyer had substantial involvement in during his tenure. This wasn't a published opinion, so neither Dan nor OGE knew who in Justice had received the opinions. OGE was also concerned that other lawyers who left other divisions of the executive branch, such as the Departments of the Interior or Education, were operating under the belief that they *couldn't* sign briefs opposing the United States until the one-year ban was exhausted—while a select group of Justice lawyers could use this private letter to their advantage.

The bigger problem was that they all thought the letter opinion was wrong. I saw a political problem and a legal problem. The legal problem was that if the opinion was wrong, we needed to change it. The political problem was a bit stickier. I didn't want a change of a month-old rule to look like the new administration was punishing lawyers from the previous administration. I asked for a thoroughly researched memo on the subject.

The memo took a while to prepare, and one evening I sat and read all the points for and against. Dan had been unbiased and fair, but it was clear to me that we had to reverse the previous opinion and inform everyone that signing briefs violated the one-year ban. When I told Dan and Jon, I said we needed to get the word out to all recipients of the previous memo. Jon warned me that I was about to make a lot of people mad. "Ken Starr gets paid a million dollars a year to sign briefs," he said. He said that no matter how hard I tried to be fair, I would be seen as "messing with people's livelihood."

I never heard back from Jon on Ken Starr's reaction. The problem was compounded when the Criminal Division heard about the opinion and opened a criminal investigation—despite my pleas that this was surely a case of an honest difference of opinion on the law, not a criminal matter. The investigation found no criminal conduct. This issue came up again when in Ralph Nader's book, *No Contest: Corporate Lawyers and the Perversion of Justice in America*, he criticized Starr for signing briefs. Some of my friends have suggested that perhaps because of my actions Ken Starr has a vendetta against me. I don't believe that. I committed a crime, and every time someone tries to take me down that path of blaming others for my actions, I try to dissuade them. I can't take one step in that other direction ever again.

The second event in the eventual pattern came in September. After the August exodus when everyone goes on vacation, Washington picks up again with a vengeance. Now Phil and Janet were wrestling with a major crime bill, trying to shape its direction so that it was consistent with the President's agenda, Janet's agenda, and the political realities of the time. I was supervising the Justice appointments, the U.S. attorney appointments, the judicial appointments. Immigration issues were becoming an administration priority. I was running from meeting to meeting, discussing crime with Janet and Phil, discussing Cuba at the State Department, and then stopping off at the Office of Management and Budget to try to get money for more border guards.

Every day at Justice, in the midst of the regular barrage of mail, were pieces of correspondence known internally as Urgent memos. There was a stamp—URGENT—that marked these papers. Usually they were reports from U.S. attorneys' offices alerting everyone to a politically sensitive case—status reports on the Rodney King beating, for example, or criminal investigations of former congressmen (or current ones, for that matter). As I was sifting through my stack one day, I found one that said the Resolution Trust Corporation (RTC) had referred possible criminal wrongdoing by Jim and Susan McDougal at Madison Savings and Loan. The memo, like all Urgent memos, was addressed to Janet with an FYI copy to me. I probably wondered why they were still going after old Jim McDougal, once found not guilty and now destitute, divorced, and living in a trailer in rural Arkansas, getting by on social security disability. After that, I never gave it another thought.

In the early fall of 1993, the news stories started about David Hale's allegation that then-Governor Bill Clinton had pressured him to make a loan. My reaction to those stories was the same as that of almost everyone I knew—nobody will take him seriously. I really didn't know David Hale well, and now my impression of him is tainted by all that I've read about him in the press. But when I heard what he was saying about the President, I figured he had gotten into trouble and had cooked up this story as a way out. When the first article appeared, I phoned Bill Kennedy. "Now I know why you asked about David Hale," I said.

"Yeah, he called me. But we wouldn't touch him with a ten-foot pole." Bill meant that Hale had wanted the White House to interfere in the indictment against him, but there was no way anybody was going to even consider that. You can imagine how that would play—everyone would believe David Hale knew something about Clinton.

"Well, everybody'll see through this," I said.

And Bill said, "I hope you're right, Hub."

I was out of the loop on this at Justice, as well I should have been. One day soon after I had that conversation with Bill Kennedy, Carl Stern stopped me outside the AG's office. "Webb," he said, "I'm really starting to get a lot of calls about 'Whitewater' and Madison Savings and Loan. Can you help me figure out who's who in all this?"

Before I could answer, Irv Nathan, Phil's chief deputy, said, "Webb, you need to stay completely out of this. Your firm used to represent Madison." I thank Irv Nathan to this day for that sage and timely advice. The Justice Department's ethics adviser, Janis Sposata, told me I didn't need a written recusal—in fact, she preferred oral recusals because they usually kept the issue from being highlighted. But after a few weeks, David Margolis said he thought I needed to make my recusal not only more formal but more sweeping. David and I didn't want a single piece of paper on the Madison issue crossing my desk. We didn't even want it crossing the desks of any of my staff. Everyone at Justice thought such actions were so extreme that they would surely allay any suspicions that I was involved in any decisions regarding the case.

At the time, I was only seeing the tiniest tip of the iceberg. From that glimpse, I couldn't fathom what was happening, nor where it was happening, nor why it was happening. I only knew that suddenly people inside Justice were getting nervous about this issue and my relationship to it. Much later, I would be told what was going on. Several months before the 1992 election, the RTC made a criminal referral to Chuck Banks, the Republican U.S. attorney in Little Rock. A referral is a memo or information sent to Justice or a U.S. attorney by a regulatory body, such as the RTC or the EPA, suggesting possible criminal wrongdoing. What I was told was that Jean Lewis of the RTC sent Banks a referral concerning Madison and Jim McDougal. That document suggested that the Clintons were potential witnesses, not criminals. Banks saw this as political, so he did nothing about it until after the election, and once the election was over, he sent the referral to Main Justice in Washington with a recommendation that the investigation be declined. Because of the changeover of administrations, the recommendation floundered at Main Justice. Normally it would have been sent back approving Banks's recommendation, and the RTC would have been notified of the decision.

By the time it was sent back, however, Chuck Banks was gone. The U.S. attorney's staff waited until Paula Casey was confirmed. When she finally got around to looking at the first referral, the RTC had sent a second, expanded referral. My understanding is that Jean Lewis at RTC, frustrated by the delay, feared a political cover-up. From what I've read in the newspapers, Jean Lewis was hardly a Clinton lover.

But there I go again, believing the newspapers.

Throughout the autumn, the pieces kept falling into place. Like the red and golden leaves drifting around us, they seemed to land randomly. But though I couldn't see it, there was a definite pattern forming.

I received a phone call from my former Rose partner, Rick Donovan. "Webb," he said, "April Breslaw wants to talk to you about the circumstances of our firm being hired in Madison versus Frost. Did you disclose Hillary's prior representation of Madison?"

"Sure," I said, and then pointed out that it was no big deal anyway because we—Rose, Madison, and FDIC—were on the same side against Frost.

"Well, April wants to talk to you."

"Fine. By the way, Rick, there should be letters in the file about this."

"I know, Webb."

I called April and she said she didn't recall my disclosing Hillary's prior representation of Madison.

"Well, April, I think I did." And I told her essentially what I'd told Rick. "It wouldn't have been a big deal because we weren't in a conflict position."

The next piece to fall came from Jim Lyons, one of the attorneys who had grilled Vince and me during the campaign. Jim and I met when he came to Little Rock in 1987 expecting Bill to announce his candidacy for President. When Bill did run in 1992, Jim came to Little Rock several times during the campaign, and we would visit. After the election, he was one of the transition counsels. He and I also worked on the Clinton five-year lobbying ban. It was Jim who wrote the memo for the transition team saying that the Betsey Files should be in the possession of an attorney.

In October, on my way to California to look into a rash of hate crimes, I stopped over in Denver to give a speech. I stayed the night at Jim's house. We caught up with each other's lives and laughed about the media's fascination with Whitewater. "When will it all end?" we asked.

Later that month when the news stories started heating up, Jim called me and said he was coming to town to brief Bruce Lindsey on the work he had done on Whitewater during the campaign. Jim had hired an accounting firm to review the Whitewater records, which showed that the Clintons lost $60,000 on the Whitewater deal. Bruce was the point person at the White House on

Whitewater issues. He asked me to pull the files he had given to Betsey on the subject. He said he would pick them up before his meeting with Bruce.

The "Betsey files" are the Clintons' personal files, the ones collected by Betsey Wright on issues that Bill's opponents were expected to use against him during the campaign. They contain all the documents surrounding the draft issue, and records on Clinton's father and mother and his brother's criminal case for possession of cocaine. Some opponents had accused Hillary of not being "a real lawyer," so we compiled summaries of all the significant cases she had worked on. Of course, there are files on the claims by various women that they had had affairs with Bill. When the press called Betsey on one of those subjects, she pulled the file and gave them the correct information. She hoped that would put an end to the issue.

Mac, Hillary, Betsey, Bruce, and Vince all knew I had the files in a safe place. They were not files anyone wanted to turn over to the White House press corps to rummage through. Besides, we believed that as long as they were in the possession of a lawyer, the lawyer-client privilege attached to them. But since Vince's death I had become somewhat uncomfortable with having all those files in my basement. In the summer I had talked with Bob Barnett, the Clintons' Washington attorney, and told him I wanted to turn the files over to him. He said we had to wait. Bob's wife, CBS reporter Rita Braver, was about to be assigned to cover the White House, so Bob was trying to get an attorney named David Kendell to take over the First Family's business. Once David came aboard, then he could take the files.

Bob and I touched base on this several times during the fall. Then in November, he called to tell me David had finally been hired. David and I had lunch in mid-month, and I gave him some files that related to Madison. The next Saturday, David showed up at my house in a van and loaded up the files that had been in my basement since June. I figured that would be the last I would ever have to think about them.

Not only was I not seeing red flags about my own vulnerability, I was increasingly filled with enthusiasm about my work. Since

Vince had died, until Bernie got a new deputy he was consulting with me. I was Justice's representative on the President's management council, and I was meeting in that regard with the second-highest officials in most governmental departments. I attended meetings on issues I had never dreamed of, such as Cuba policy and various subjects under the purview of the Joint Chiefs. I had become known as someone you better talk to if Justice was involved.

At Justice, I was the confidant of both Janet and Phil concerning each other. After four months, they were beginning to have their problems. Janet's style was to dish out the work and expect you to be on top of it immediately. Phil's style was to accept those assignments from Janet and delegate them to people in his department whom he trusted. But in meetings, when Janet asked about the status of a particular issue and Phil said so-and-so hadn't gotten back to him yet, that wasn't the answer Janet wanted to hear. She was frustrated and so was he. Because of that, she had begun giving many of what were typically deputy AG tasks to me. I was asked to sit in on meetings and play a more major role in formulating the crime bill. Budget became my issue, though I'm sure Phil didn't mind handing that one over to me. Some of Phil's staff weren't comfortable with what they viewed as a "co-deputy" system that Phil and I had devised, and the press picked up on that and reported rifts at Justice. Phil and I talked about them, we had a good working relationship, and we were frustrated that once again the media were trying to create a story where there wasn't one.

As Christmas season arrived, I recommended to Janet and Phil that they have a heart-to-heart talk before they went their separate ways for the holidays. They did, and both said they felt better. I felt like a matchmaker as Suzy and I headed over to the annual White House Christmas party, the very first *Clinton* White House Christmas party. After the year we'd had, I was ready to put aside my differences with everyone on the planet and just have fun. Christmas has always been my favorite season.

Bill Kennedy had told me the Rose firm had chartered a plane to bring the partners and their spouses to the White House holiday festivities. There appeared to be no reason for me to dread seeing any of them. I had spoken to Skeeter earlier in the fall, and he told me he'd paid the patent lawyer half of what what was owed, and had agreed to give him a note for the rest. I'd reported this to Ron Clark, who welcomed the news. I was relieved enough about the situation to wish Ron well with his plans for the new D.C. office.

But at the White House Christmas party, I couldn't help noticing that many of my former partners seemed as frigid as the December frost. Some were cordial, but many were anything but. I didn't know what to make of it. Then Jim Blair, counsel for Tyson Foods and an old friend of the Clintons, sidled up to me and confirmed what I was feeling. "Webb," he said, "several of your old partners are apparently mad at you. If I can do anything to help, let me know." I thanked him and went off to get Suzy so we could have our pictures taken with the President and First Lady.

Several days later I called Jerry Jones. I told him I couldn't help noticing that some of the partners seemed a little cool toward me. Was there something wrong?

"Well, Webb," Jerry said, "I think we ought to talk about it. Are you coming home for Christmas?"

"Yes."

"Well, let's get together right after the holiday."

"Fine, Jerry," I said. But it wasn't fine. What could be the problem? I tried to put it aside. I didn't want to ruin this Christmas. I hadn't seen Rebecca or Walter for months. Our friends were having parties. It was Christmas, time to be joyous. Time to go home.

A few days before we left, I got the call from Nancy Hernreich. "The President wants to know if you're going shopping?"

"Sure," I said. I was thrilled. I had hoped this year in Washington wouldn't change the tradition we had built up since 1979.

To be honest, it wasn't the best Christmas shopping trip ever. We went a few days early because he and Hillary were having their families to the White House for Christmas. Then the First Family was leaving for Little Rock and Fayetteville between

Christmas and New Year's. The President and Marsha Scott and I went shopping, and though we laughed and told stories, the Secret Service kept a pretty tight rein on things. We went to the shops at Union Station, and usually there was a crowd waiting outside each store wanting an autograph from the President. We didn't stay long. We wished one another Merry Christmas, and I hailed a cab and headed home. The President and I planned to see each other again right after the holidays, when we would go to a Razorback basketball game together. Meanwhile, Suzy and the kids and I had to catch a plane for Little Rock.

It was my first trip home since we buried Vince. Now, with something apparently brewing at the firm, I headed west with some trepidation. It was a low-lying anxiety that, over the next few days, I tried to quell with food and drink.

We enjoyed the parties, hugged our children, laughed with our friends. For old times' sake, I made the rounds of The Heights stores that Bill and I had always gone to together. I even stopped by the country club to say hello and take a gentle ribbing about my decision to resign my membership.

On Christmas night at the Wards', Skeeter told me something that made my heart sink. He had decided not to give the patent lawyer a note for the remaining money he owed. That meant he wouldn't be getting a release for the firm. I thought I knew why Jerry Jones wanted to talk to me.

Skeeter and POM were struggling. The case was now over two years old, and he had spent a lot of money on a losing cause. I'm sure he was second-guessing the decision to file the lawsuit and to hire the experts. Since I was gone and not around to help him, I'm sure he was saying to himself that everybody else involved was paid a lot of money while he got nothing at all out of it. Why should he pay any more? I was partially sympathetic, in spite of the problems it was causing me. Had we won the POM case, the Rose firm would likely have received a fee of more than $3 million. For such an upside, risks are often taken. I also felt guilty about letting the experts' costs get out of hand.

Right after Christmas I called Jerry Jones, who invited me to come to his house for a meeting. After the usual pleasantries, he told me what I had already heard from Skeeter. We talked about what could be done, and I assured him again that the Rose firm would not be out another dime. If Skeeter wouldn't or couldn't pay, I would somehow pay the patent lawyer personally. People have asked why I would do such a thing. First, the Wards were my family, even though Seth had little use for me since I had "abandoned" him to go to Washington. Also, I felt obligated to the Rose firm. If I had still been there, we would have written off the costs and I would have paid for them in my fee allocations over five years. Now there was no one to eat the expenses. I had lived with those guys for twenty years, and I well knew the resentments this was causing.

Then Jerry changed the subject. He told me the firm had been going back over all my expenses and now had some $60,000 to $70,000 worth that they wanted substantiation for. My stomach turned. But it wasn't over; it was just beginning. "Webb," Jerry said, "there are some partners who think you can't justify these expenses. Some people think you stole from the firm." We locked eyes and I tried to remain calm. He handed me a list.

I told him I would do my best to get documentation for the expenses listed, but that I needed some records from the firm. Then I said, "If I can't document these to your satisfaction, I'll pay the firm back, if that's what you want."

He was noncommittal. "I'll get whatever records you need," he said, "but we also want you to order your credit card records."

His final sentence sent chills through me. "Webb, I can't emphasize how serious this is."

I left his house a dazed and desperate man. I had no idea what to do. Did I tell Suzy? No. Did I think of hiring a lawyer? No. Did I think about resigning from my position at Justice? No. What possible reason would I give for my resignation? And would it help, anyway?

Amazingly, what I did that very afternoon was get on an airplane with the President, the First Lady, Chelsea, Suzy, and Rebecca, and flew to Fayetteville to watch the Razorbacks play. My mind was anywhere but on that basketball court. I'm sure I appeared to be a zombie. And yet I talked with the President about the game, with Hillary about her mother, with my Fayetteville friends about everything under the sun except what I cared about most. We stayed in a hotel that night. Suzy slept, but I couldn't stop obsessing. I sat up most of the night trying to figure out what to do.

What I figured out to do was exactly nothing. How could I *do* anything? How could I face the shame? Instead, the next day Suzy and I flew to Little Rock and then back to Washington. Soon I was lost in my work again, and I could pretend for entire minutes at a time that I wasn't a man on the brink.

By the beginning of 1994, the newspapers were unrelenting in their coverage of the story known as Whitewater, which had ballooned to include assorted allegations about the interconnected business dealings of President Clinton, Hillary Clinton, Jim and Susan McDougal, David Hale, Jim Guy Tucker, the Rose Law Firm—and Seth Ward. The Republicans were also calling for a special counsel. They had fought tooth and nail to try to prevent passage of a new independent counsel law. Now that the shoe was on the other foot, they couldn't wait to dance on Bill Clinton's toes.

Throughout the campaign, Seth's name had never come up in connection with any issue. I was stunned to see him drawn in now. I was still staying away from it all at my perch in Justice, but because of my extreme closeness to several of those whose names were now appearing in the press, I said to Phil Heymann, "I don't want to wake up one day and have everybody calling for my head." In other words, if I should resign now or later, please tell me. "Webb," Phil said, "nothing we're looking at involves you."

Then suddenly the newspapers were reporting that the Rose firm was shredding records. I called Bill Kennedy. "Have they lost their minds?" I said. He'd had the same thought, but had assumed that there was no truth to it. I wasn't so sure. No law firm wants its skeletons held up for public inspection. I never found out what they were shredding.

The President's mother, Virginia Kelley, died in January 1994, and I soon found myself heading back to Hope, Arkansas, to bury another friend. I guess there was a message in that. Suzy and I flew with the President and First Lady on Air Force One. On the way to Hot Springs, the President and I sat across the table from each other playing hearts—at the same time he talked on the phone, held conversations with various aides about his upcoming Brussels economic summit, and concentrated on the card game. I had also seen him read books and do all those other things at the same time. I thought again, What a mind. It is astonishing to be around him.

On the way back to Washington, Mac, Bruce, and the President were talking about "Whitewater." As a Justice official, I didn't want to be part of it. Bob Barnett, Mrs. Kelley's attorney for her autobiography, suggested that Suzy and I sit in the back of the plane while everyone else discussed what they should do. We had picked up some of the legendary McClard's barbecued spareribs in Hot Springs, so while the President and his staff talked about special counsels, I gnawed on tangy ribs, picked at fat french fries, licked my fingers clean of the succulent sauce. And when it was all gone, I still felt empty.

Since before Christmas, I had been primarily occupied with planning and coordinating the U.S. attorneys conference, scheduled for January 19 in Washington. Finally, we were bringing all the new U.S. attorneys together. It was a new year, and we wanted to get the Justice Department off to a blazing start. At the conference, I told them that Hillary had once said that if she could have any job in the world, she would be a U.S. attorney. Later, at the White House reception for them, she told them the very same thing. I felt good about the meeting. I even had a chance to greet Paula Casey. We'd never talked before that moment, but later I would be accused of having conspired with her to stonewall the Whitewater investigation.

After the U.S. attorneys conference was over, Janet pulled me into her office and said, "Webb, I've had it with Phil." I wasn't surprised. I had suspected the Christmas peace was a fragile one. "I don't think I can appoint you deputy, so I want you to get me Jamie Gorelick." Jamie was the first female president of the D.C. Bar Association. She served as the leader of both Zoe's and Janet's confirmation teams and was currently serving as the general counsel to the Department of Defense. I had worked with her a lot on both the gays in the military and A-12 fighter issues. She was energetic and incredibily organized. "Whatever it takes with the White House, I want you to get her," Janet said.

Janet told Phil it wasn't going to work and that she wanted his resignation. He wasn't surprised either, but he was disappointed. He had come back to Washington with high hopes of developing policies to undo what he considered to be the serious mistakes of the past twelve years. He also felt Janet wasn't honest with him when she came back after Christmas. When the news of Phil's resignation was out, some articles blamed my access to the White House as part of the reason for his stepping down. Phil quickly came to me and said that wasn't the case. He did wish he'd had better access to the White House, but he didn't blame me. He thought (as did I) that we had worked well together, and he hated that the press was trying to create an issue where there wasn't one. What his resignation did—until Jamie Gorelick was confirmed in early March—was to increase my workload all the more.

On January 25, 1994, my assistant told me Janet had received a letter from the President asking her to appoint a Whitewater special counsel. Bernie later told me that he had opposed the appointment, but that the President's other advisers were adamant that the issue would never go away until some independent counsel, not Clinton's Justice Department, looked into it.

Janet appointed Robert Fiske, an outstanding lawyer and former prosecutor from New York. After the announcement, Bernie called to tell me he knew Bob Fiske. "He'll be very, very tough—but fair," Bernie said. Phil later told me that Fiske was the person he'd had in mind the whole time—and that when Fiske met with

Janet, he wrote out his jurisdictional statement by hand. A jurisdictional statement is the basis under which a special counsel operates. It describes what he will investigate and whether he has both criminal and civil jurisdiction. Usually, it takes weeks of research to prepare such a document. When he finished writing it, he pushed it across the desk to Janet. "That's what I'll require," he said. Janet agreed on the spot.

Right after Phil's resignation, I had had a phone conversation with Jerry Jones. "Jerry," I said, "I know the firm wants me to give them my credit card records. But where are the firm records I asked for?" He told me the Rose firm had retained the Washington office of Vinson and Elkins to represent them in the Madison investigation. "Webb," Jerry said, "we've turned over your billing matter to them, and they recommend that we not send you any records."

I couldn't believe it. Why? What was the point? "Well, Jerry," I said, "I guess we'll have to talk through lawyers now."

"Yes, I guess so."

After hanging up, I tried to see this new development from all angles. The firm was asking me to provide them evidence of my crime without giving me anything from them that could help me justify those expenditures. I supposed it was possible that a third-party lawyer would make the firm realize that you shouldn't throw stones in glass houses. Maybe they would work something out with me. Again, I didn't tell anyone about this—not even the lawyer I later hired to represent me in the Whitewater investigation.

The White House was insisting that anybody who had ever had the slightest thing to do with Madison now needed to retain counsel. Bob Fiske was also going to investigate Vince's death. Somehow, he seemed to think that one thing had to do with the other. Bernie recommended that I hire John Nields, former counsel to the House's Iran-Contra investigation and former Supreme Court clerk. In early February, Bernie set up a meeting between John and me. I liked him immediately, and he had come universally recommended. But already, I wasn't being forthcoming with him.

I couldn't bear for anyone, even my attorney, to know who the real Webb Hubbell was.

The night of the day I first met with John, I went to the White House to watch the Arkansas-Kentucky game with the President. He cheered like a teenager. I tried to be the pal he wanted, but I couldn't summon the enthusiasm.

12

"All Hell Done Broke Loose"

In February, Hillary told me she wanted to create a small memorial on the White House grounds in memory of Vince. She wondered if Suzy, who now worked at the Department of Interior, could look into the regulations regarding such memorials. Suzy checked. The National Park Service said a tree could be planted, but that was about it—there could be no plaques on the grounds of the White House. For Hillary, that ruined the reason for the gesture.

It was a disappointment to us all. Vince's absence created a huge void. Soon after his death, the Arkansas Night dwindled to the occasional handful of lonely diehards. Partly this was because by summer, most spouses and families had joined their loved ones in Washington. But also, Vince's suicide meant Arkansas Night could no longer be the happy time it had started out being. We exchanged Vince stories for a while, but then they left us more sad than happy. Finally, Washington swallowed up Arkansas Night. Like the rest of the town, we succumbed to a force larger than we were.

In early March, I made a trip to Oxford, Mississippi. The Justice Department had intervened in a lawsuit that had the potential of dismantling the predominantly black colleges of Mississippi. The judge involved had called a conference with the principals, with the authority to settle the case. Ordinarily Justice opposes having high-ranking officials attend settlement conferences, because it would force us to fly all over the country every day. This time I said, "I'll go."

I flew to Memphis and drove the hour and a half to Oxford. It was a drive I had made often as a young man, visiting my maternal grandparents in the small town of Water Valley, just south of Oxford. This time I spoke at the University of Mississippi Law School, and I had a great dinner on Oxford's picturesque town square. But I failed to achieve a settlement in the case I had come for. Driving back to Memphis, I thought of my boyhood, and of the changes—and the lack thereof—in states like Mississippi over the ensuing years. I had hoped to make a difference. I had hoped to unleash some energy for *good*. And yet, when I got back to Washington, I was going to have to face the decision to resign from Justice.

There is a line in the film *The Natural,* as the Robert Redford character, Roy Hobbs, lies in a hospital bed facing the end of his baseball career, all because he was shot early in his playing days. He looks at his childhood sweetheart, Glenn Close, and laments that he "could've been the best that ever played the game." But, he says, "there are some mistakes you just keep paying for."

I thought of that line a million times over the next two years. It came to me first in that car between Oxford and Memphis. My old mistakes were self-inflicted, but they were there nevertheless. And I was going to pay for them for the rest of my life. This was when I finally realized that.

When I got back to Washington, Carl Stern alerted me to the fact that stories were circulating about "billing irregularities of Webb Hubbell at the Rose firm." Leaks were coming out of the firm itself, he said, to the effect that they were going to refer my case to the Arkansas Bar Association. Then my lawyer called. John had learned from a private source that the firm was in fact going to refer what they called "dishonest billing practices" to the bar. John had tried for weeks to resolve the matter quietly. He had told the firm we would do anything to resolve it. John was totally frustrated by the firm's unwillingness to settle—or even to talk.

By now John and I had discussed my resigning as a way of "offering the Rose firm my head." But I had also heard a rumor that Vinson and Elkins was concerned about Rose's destruction of records and the conflicts surrounding our representation of Madison. In tandem with a public relations firm, Vinson and Elkins had devised a strategy of blaming Hubbell for everything. I didn't and don't know if that rumor was true, but at times it sure seemed like it. It seemed as though the strategy was to save Rose by focusing the independent counsel on me—and thus away from other lawyers.

On Friday, March 11, I got word from John that the Rose firm was going to make the referral to the Arkansas Bar the following Monday. It was time, I knew, to resign. I had grown to love the Justice Department, where I felt I had done the best, most important work of my life. I wanted to save Justice, as much as possible, from being scathed by my mistake. That Friday when I headed home, I faced the worst weekend of my life. I would have to tell Suzy about my crimes.

She knew something was up—for days the newspapers had mentioned my name in conjunction with billing irregularities at Rose. When she'd asked what all that was about, it was easy for me to say, "Honey, you know those jerks at the Rose firm." My friends were the same way—they called and said, "Dammit, Webb, they can't do this to you. I'm going down there to chew them out."

"No, no, no," I said, ever the noble injured one. I was trying to please my family and friends by helping them believe I wasn't guilty. Every time I did that, I hurt them more.

Now it was time to tell Suzy. All these years I had let her sail along, proud of her husband and family, enjoying a life of relative comfort and ease, and now I had to confess that I had stolen to afford such a life. We were in our den off the kitchen when I made my first halting attempts to bring it up. "Suzy," I said, "we have to talk." She knew what was coming. She sat down on the couch while I leaned forward in my big easy chair. I couldn't say it. I danced around the absolute truth. I had become so caught up in a life of lies that I couldn't make my mouth utter the unvarnished words. I told her only enough for her to get the picture. "We were living way beyond our means. There were things I did to keep us afloat financially. . . ." She just stared at me in total disbelief. I told her I had to think seriously about resigning. I could fight this thing, but it would be easier if I weren't quite so much in the public eye.

We talked about it that night and during the next day. Then Saturday night I got a call from Jim Blair. As counsel for Tyson Foods, Jim was one of the Rose firm's most important clients. I had worked with Jim on many cases. He and his wife, Diane, were also close friends of the President and First Lady. I believe the Rose firm had gotten word to him for some reason. "Webb, there are bad stories coming out of the firm," Jim said. We talked very briefly. He asked if he could help. Then he told me he thought I couldn't possibly stay at Justice and deal with this, too.

That cinched it for me. I told Suzy, and she agreed. If it was that bad, then we had to do something. I called Mickey and told him what I was going to do. I wanted him to tell the President that I was submitting my resignation. Mickey argued vehemently against that. "If you resign, your career in government will be finished." He urged me to have a meeting at my house the next day to see if we could come up with a way to reason with the firm.

Suzy told me we had to talk to the children. Walter and Rebecca were away, but Caroline and Kelley were there. Caroline was seventeen, Kelley thirteen. Sunday morning we told them. I said I was having a disagreement with my old law firm about billing, and I didn't want to embarrass the Justice Department while the awful old Rose firm dragged me through the mud. So I was going to bite the bullet and resign. I had to always appear noble to my children. Kelley was too young to grasp all the ramifications, but Caroline was devastated. For a second. Then she was angry. Caroline is very much like her mother. She was angry at the whole situation—me, the firm, nasty Republicans, everybody. Suzy didn't express any anger at me, though I'm sure she felt it. And I hadn't even told her the whole story yet.

That afternoon, Mickey, Mike Cardozo, John Nields, Suzy, Caroline, and I sat in our living room exploring the options. No one but I knew just how guilty I was. This was another sham, this elaborate discussion of how to make the Rose firm see the error of its ways. Nobody asked me directly whether there was anything to the allegations, and John wouldn't have let me answer, anyway. Even he didn't know at that point, but I think he suspected. It's hard to explain why I hadn't been able to tell John. For one thing, it would have put him in an ethical dilemma if I had later decided to fight the charges. But also, I wanted desperately to buy into the rumors about my being a scapegoat for the firm. It helped me feel like a victim, even though I wasn't. I had a long, long way to go in confronting myself and admitting what I had done, but that day I took my first baby steps on that journey. "Guys," I said more than once, "nobody's perfect in their billings." I would use that line for a long time to come.

We decided that John would call the firm and tell them I would submit all of my records to an independent auditor. Whatever sum that auditor came up with, I would agree to pay to the Rose firm. The firm could still refer whatever they wanted to the Arkansas Bar. The only condition was that the firm would also have to open up its records to the independent auditor. On Monday morning, John conveyed that message to the Rose firm's lawyer. By noon, he had received their response: There would be no agreement between Webb Hubbell and the Rose firm.

Only I was not surprised. At all costs, the Rose firm wanted to avoid having the light of day shone on its own practices. That's what I thought then. That's what I encouraged others to think. It would be a long time before I would let go of that crutch and face the truth.

But I knew it was time to resign. Once John gave me the firm's answer, I called my deputy, Nancy McFadden, and my assistant and right arm, Kathy Gallagher, and told them what I was going to do. I would issue a simple statement, and I needed their help with logistics. Mike Cardozo and John Nields came over to help, too. While they waited in my office, I walked down the hall and knocked on Janet's door. "Janet," I said, "I've tried to work out my problems with my law firm, but I can't. I would be doing you and the President a disservice to stay. I hate this, but I'll be submitting my resignation today."

"I'm sick about this, Webb," she said, but she knew it was the right thing to do. The exchange was exactly that brief. Janet and I were very close, and I suspect that if either one of us had tried to talk about it much more, we would have become very emotional. I knew how much my leaving was a blow to her. Like everyone who knew me, she didn't want to believe I could have done something wrong.

I went back to my office and called Mickey and asked him to deliver the message to the President. Then I sat down and composed my resignation statement. Of my many regrets at that moment, I remember thinking that I hadn't accomplished something the President had asked me to do when I was first elected. "Webb," he had said, "if I put you over at Justice, I want you to find the answers to two questions for me. One, Who killed JFK? And two, Are there UFOs?" He was dead serious. I had looked into both, but wasn't satisfied with the answers I was getting.

Janet held a press conference that afternoon, but I didn't go to it. I made phone calls and began to tie up as many loose ends as possible. We had told the press I would have nothing more to say beyond the statement I had issued that day: "It is with deep regret that I have seen private issues between me and my family and my former law firm elevated to public speculation . . . ," I said in that statement. "It is my sincere hope and belief that by devoting sufficient time and energy now to my family and other personal matters, I will reenter public service in the future."

Late in the day, when I was ready to go home, I caught the elevator to the first floor. Someone there said, "Judge Hubbell, before you go, could you please step into the auditorium." When I did, the room erupted with applause. Almost everybody at Main Justice was there. I was incredibily touched by this show of support. A year before, I had come into these people's lives as "Bill Clinton's crony." Over that year I had gained their respect, just as they had gained mine. They didn't care what problems I had back in Arkansas—I had become one of their own, and they knew that at my core I was a good man. I hugged my friends and shook their hands. There would be other farewell fetes in the coming weeks, but this spontaneous display of affection will always be one of my dearest memories.

Over the next few months I learned a lot about friendship. I'm proud of a newspaper headline an Arkansas paper ran when I was being considered for Justice: HUBBELL LOYAL TO FRIENDS IN POLITICS AS WELL AS LIFE. My daughter Caroline pasted that article into a scrapbook, and wrote beside it, "Tell us something we don't know!"

What we knew, but didn't want to face, was that not everyone is so loyal. When the pressure is on, when the spotlight is hot, some people—maybe most people—duck and run. Washington seems to attract such people. I know from experience that there are many workers in government who are there because they care deeply about their country. But many others are there because they care about power. In a town in which proximity to power *is* power, then proximity to disgrace becomes too dangerous to chance. Initially I didn't hear anything from the President or First Lady. It hurt, and when I finally received a letter from the President accepting my resignation, I felt that it was pretty reserved. I never heard from Hillary at all. Yet I understand that they too were under heavy fire by then. They had to stand back until they had a chance to see what happened. I suspect that if I had been advising them, I would have told them to handle it exactly the way they did. But it still hurt.

Shortly after I resigned, I received a nice note from Arthur Liman, the famed attorney for the Watergate Committee whom I had met the previous fall on Martha's Vineyard. He passed along a quote from Edward Bennett Williams, one of the deans of Washington lawyers: "Washington is like Salem—a new witch is created and burned each week."

I needed to go to work—I had no idea when this investigation would end, and it was important for me to look as though I expected to get through this. But I needed to work for other reasons. The only money we had coming in now was from Suzy's job at Interior. It was a good salary, but it wasn't nearly enough. The truth is, we would have been in financial trouble soon, anyway. When we left Little Rock, I got my bonus for the previous year. I also received a little cash from the sale of our house and my share of the law firm building. But we had an expensive life in Washington. All my children were in private school, and we had a nice house and two nice cars. Most of the money we got when we left Little Rock went to paying some of the bills we had run up before we came to D.C. I had over $70,000 of credit card debt, much of it at around 20 percent interest. Even minimum payments on that much takes a lot every month. Now I was stepping away from my $124,000 salary at Justice and starting to add lawyers' fees. I needed to earn a lot of money fast.

Suzy and I discussed going back to Little Rock, but where would I work? Certainly not at Rose. With the investigation, my best chance at making money was in D.C. Plus, we had sold our Little Rock home, our kids were in school in Washington, and we had close friends like the Cardozos, Kantors, and others who were very supportive. We needed that. My friends said that people in Washington would pay a lot for advice. A high-powered lobbyist I talked with had no qualms about charging clients large fees. "You never know when one phone call you make will make your client a ton of money," he said. Considering that, he billed his clients on a retainer basis. For that he was available whenever they needed him. I wasn't interested in lobbying Congress, but consulting sounded very promising.

I left Justice officially the first of April. Mike Cardozo let me use an office in his suite at Nineteenth and M streets, and I started networking. I talked to old friends like Mickey Kantor, Vernon Jordan, and Beryl Anthony. Most of all, I talked to people who worked in D.C.—lawyers, lobbyists, and consultants. "You're well connected, Webb," they said. "You know everybody in the administration, and they love you. Get out there and let people know you're available to consult." Before long I was taking clients to lunch several times a week at Sam and Harry's, a restaurant across the street from my office. Nobody knew I had committed a crime. Many people believed—and I let them believe—that the Rose firm was upset over the money Skeeter owed the firm, and that if I got out of the spotlight this matter and all matters between me and the firm could be settled on a civil basis. People were more than happy to be working with me. They wanted to know who was who in the Clinton administration, and who should be contacted—and how—depending on the reason. As you've no doubt read in the newspaper, I lined up a lot of business very fast. Several Washington law firms started talking to me about joining them. I thought, If I can do this for a while, I can get out of debt. And then another thought crossed my mind: I'm starting business relationships on a dishonest basis.

I've said on several occasions that who my clients were and what they paid me is confidential. I regret that most of them have been dragged before grand juries and congressional committees. I have declined to talk to Congress about them, and I don't intend to now tell my clients' secrets in a book. I never once dreamed that my doing legal and consulting work could be viewed as some sort of "hush money." Does this mean that every time someone comes under investigation, he must stop working? You perhaps have noticed that the special counsel's investigation is in its fourth year. That can put quite a dent in someone's ability to make a living and support a family. This is getting ahead of the story, but I understand that Kenneth Starr, who took over the Whitewater investigation from Bob Fiske, has *had* to investigate once an issue has been raised. Otherwise, he would be criticized. At Justice, I dealt with the never-ending investigative mentality of Washington with the Inslaw case. Inslaw was a company that provided software to the Justice Department during the Reagan administration. The company later claimed that Justice stole the software programs and wouldn't pay for their continued use. This led to a twelve-year investigation, complete with congressional hearings and an independent counsel. When the IC reported that nothing was there, I had to reinvestigate the case. I agreed with the independent counsel—there *was* nothing there. But there are still people in Washington who grumble that it was all "a cover-up."

But as for the allegation of hush money, consider several things. One, I didn't hush. For three years I answered every question the independent counsel put to me. Two, no one knew back when I got those consulting contracts that I was going to be indicted and then pressured to say something bad about my friends. Finally, how do you prove a negative? Were you paid hush money, Webb? The answer is no. But how do I prove I wasn't? I can say that all my life, I obtained business through friends, acquaintances, and colleagues who respected me and my work. This isn't unique to me or to Little Rock. It's been the way lawyers have gotten work since the legal profession began. Frankly, I don't like lawyer advertising. I think that most of the ads are unseemly and hurt the profession. So was it wrong for friends of mine to look at me and see a friend and former colleague whom they thought of as a good and ethical person, but who was now down on his luck? Should they have turned their back on someone who had just resigned his job, had a wife and children to support, and needed work?

Even with hindsight, I don't have a good answer regarding what I should have done, except in one area. I should have found a way to be more candid with my friends. I should have given them a greater chance to *not* help. I should never have acted the victim. I hurt a lot of people because of that. I cost them fortunes in legal fees, and in some cases destroyed trusts and friendships. My stomach turns and my heart aches every single time I hear that so-and-so is appearing before the grand jury or Congress to answer questions about Webb Hubbell. Even some of my wife's friends have distanced themselves from her because of me. In some ways I know how the President and First Lady feel when their staff people are dragged before Congress. Yet Bill and Hillary didn't commit any crimes. I did, and I continue to pay for them. So do my friends. But, bottom line, it *wasn't* hush money.

While I was picking up consulting work, John was meeting a total stone wall at the Rose firm. From one of my first consulting checks, I paid the POM patent attorney and got Rose released from liability. Along with the release, John and I sent a check to

Rose and proposed that I start paying them quarterly until we could determine the amount I owed. The check was returned.

Suzy and I were invited to the White House several times in the late spring and summer. We still went to movies and ball games, and to parties such as Mike Berman's birthday party. I have a beautiful photograph of Suzy dancing with the President at that event. In mid-June we went to a reception on the lawn for the emperor and empress of Japan. Everyone was handed miniature Japanese and American flags to wave. By this time, the news stories had died down. As with termites, the damage was happening below the surface. The special counsel had subpoenaed my credit card records, and John Nields had sent for a copy for himself. The investigation was continuing. Meanwhile, no word of such unpleasantness passed between me and the President or First Lady, but I felt a slight distance. There was something unspoken standing between us. I'm sure they had been cautioned not to get to know too much. I know they felt for me—I could see it especially in Bill's eyes. They probably felt a little guilty because they had asked me to come. They had lost one friend, and now another had had to resign. It was a sad fact of life in the era of politics by investigation.

Over the Fourth of July, the President asked me to come to Camp David to play golf with him. Suzy didn't go with me, and that wasn't at all unusual. Only guests who were specifically invited came, and that didn't automatically include spouses. Besides, it was primarily a golf outing.

The Clintons hadn't used the camp much. For one thing, Chelsea was of the age that she wanted to be with her friends doing other things. Another reason was that there was no golf course at Camp David. There's just a chipping and putting green. The permanent staff at Camp David, determined to lure the President to his unused retreat, scouted golf courses within thirty minutes of the camp. They found four good ones, and the President wanted me to go with him to try them out.

The President, First Lady, Chelsea, and Hillary's mother, Dorothy Rodham, were going for the long weekend, so I drove up

Saturday morning expecting to play eighteen holes and come back that night. Camp David is tucked into the rugged countryside near the Maryland and Pennsylvania border. Cruising through that beautiful wild tangle of mountains and forests and rivers, I thought of what Vince had said on the Eastern Shore the weekend before he died: "I just wanted to get out of D.C."

We played a round of golf at a resort in Pennsylvania, and both the President and I were impressed with the course. "Why don't you stay over and we'll play one of the other ones tomorrow?" he said. I couldn't say no. That night we sat around the big den watching a movie, and the next morning the presidential caravan headed out early for another round of golf. As we drove by the little chapel, I remembered a welcome sheet I had gotten the night before when I decided to stay over. The sermon that day was on the "Sacrament of Failure," from Mark 1:13. The President attended before we played golf.

After another fine time on the course, we returned to the First Family's lodge and plopped down into the easy chairs on the back stone patio. From there we could look out at the mountains, a putting green, the swimming pool. It was just the two of us, old friends from far back. As we sat there, the President said, "I need to talk to you."

"What about?"

"You don't have to answer this if you don't want to, but all this stuff about your Rose firm billings—did you do anything that's going to get you in trouble?"

He was looking at me, but I turned to squint at a bluff far away. I couldn't do it. I couldn't tell him for many reasons, not the least of which was that if I did, he would then be a witness. He would be obligated to turn me in. "No," I lied to my old friend, the President of the United States. "I can work this thing out."

"Good," he said. "I'm glad to hear it." And we never talked about it again.

Driving home that afternoon, I felt sad about that conversation. In some ways I felt sad about the whole wonderful time I'd just had. I loved playing golf with Bill. We had great times needling each other, kidding about bad shots. Sometimes, as I would line up a putt to win the hole or match, he would say, "You know, if you make this, you'll have beaten the leader of the free world." A little added pressure. I still had the scorecard from that round we played right after he was elected President. He shot well that day, and he wrote a message to me right below the scores. "Webb—Thanks for all the rounds we've played, but especially this one. Bill." Over the years we'd had serious conversations on the course—the Hillary name issue, the Mickey Kantor conversation, even a talk about the pros and cons of potential vice presidential candidates. But most of what we had discussed fell into the category of guy stuff. Once after the campaign we laughed about a story he'd heard. A woman had been identified as someone who'd had an affair with Bill, and the press had gone to the woman's husband for a quote. The husband denied the rumors about his wife. "I know all the men my wife has slept with," he said, "and Bill Clinton isn't one of them."

Another time Bill and Vernon Jordan kidded me unmercifully the day after that big Martha's Vineyard party at Kay Graham's house, where there were so many stars I couldn't believe it, and where I was soon in intense conversation with Carly Simon. "What in the world were you and Carly talking about?" the President said on the golf course the next day. "You sure were getting close." Vernon chimed in, "He's just jealous, Webb. You got to sit by Carly, and he had to sit by Kissinger." I smiled like the Cheshire cat while they giggled like schoolboys.

We had a lot of memories, and I cherished them. But as we pulled up to a golf course in the midst of a caravan of Secret Service agents, inevitably the photographers would shoot our pictures. When I was at Justice, I was the person in charge of telling the White House counsel which people the President shouldn't be seen with. Now I was one of them.

Later in July, Lisa Foster came to Washington for the first time since Vince's death. It had been a whole year. When Hillary heard she was coming, she invited Lisa, Sheila and Beryl, Marsha, Michael and Harolyn, Kaki, and Suzy and me to spend the day at

Camp David. The day before we went, we had drinks at the White House. Harolyn took the Clintons homemade ginger snaps. Lisa and Hillary met privately for a time.

Lisa looked good, happy even. We spent a nice relaxing day at Camp David, but I could tell right away that this trip was a mission for her. She was here to put this chapter of her life to rest. When we got back to Washington, Lisa asked Suzy and me to drive her around to see the places she and Vince had been to. She wanted to see their old town house, and when we drove by it she asked me to stop. She went to the door and knocked. The woman who lived there knew who she was, and Lisa walked through the house looking in all the rooms. Suzy went with her, but I stayed in the car. I just couldn't go in. When she came out, she was carrying a bag that the woman had given her. It was stuff that had been left in the house. Lisa didn't want to look in the bag, so I looked for her. It held shaving cream and things like that. Ordinarily, new owners would have thrown that away, but this was obviously a perceptive woman. She knew Lisa would someday be back.

That afternoon Lisa went to Fort Marcy Park, where Vince had died. She wondered if I wanted to go, but if I couldn't set foot in the town house, I sure couldn't go there. When we dropped her off I had a sense that Lisa had confronted her final demon. She was saying her good-byes. I didn't know it then, but she was dating a Little Rock attorney, Jim Moody. I knew him and he reminded me of Vince. His wife had died soon after Vince did, and Lisa and Jim eventually began seeing each other. I was glad when I heard that. She deserves happiness. She deserves a second chance. We all do.

In August the independent counsel (IC) law was reenacted in Congress, so Robert Fiske's appointment expired. Under the IC law, a three-judge panel appointed by Chief Justice William Rehnquist was expected to name Fiske to be the independent counsel investigating Whitewater, continuing his role. Instead, Kenneth Starr was named to the job. Starr was the former solicitor general in the Bush administration. My lawyer, John Nields, had clerked with him on the Supreme Court, and initially felt that Starr would take a very limited view of what matters should be investigated by his office. It was a major surprise when Starr was appointed. There later were doubts placed on Starr's independence when it was disclosed that the chairman of the panel, Judge David Sentelle, had lunched with archconservatives Jesse Helms and Lauch Faircloth the day before the appointment.

In September my daughter Caroline and some of her friends met with the President in the Oval Office and had their photograph taken with him. The next month Suzy and I made our last visit to the White House. The occasion was Hillary's forty-seventh birthday party. Hillary loves costume parties. The year before, Suzy wore a flowing blue dress and went as Devil in a Blue Dress (Mitch Ryder and the Detroit Wheels). I wore all blue jogging attire (including blue tights) and went as the Deep Blue Sea. Together, we were the Devil and the Deep Blue Sea. Bernie was a gladiator, and Bruce came as a nun in a full habit. Vernon Jordan showed up wearing Michael Jordan's basketball uniform.

In 1994 the theme was "Sock Hop." The invitation was in the shape of a 45 rpm record. Suzy wore a poodle skirt and put her hair in a ponytail. I wore jeans, a starched white shirt, and my favorite black Chuck Taylor Converse tennis shoes. I've had them for twenty-five years. When you go to social events at the White House, you enter through the East Wing. The place was decorated like something out of *Rebel Without a Cause*. There were Harley-Davidsons in the rotunda and hoods lurking everywhere. Mickey and Heidi, Vernon and Ann, Jim and Diane Blair, all Hillary's staff, friends from Arkansas—they all slouched around in jeans and white T-shirts with packs of Marlboros in their rolled-up sleeves. A deejay spun the platters while white socks bopped and twisted to the hits of the 1950s. At the appointed time, the President and First Lady made their entrance. He wore jeans and had his hair slicked back like Elvis. Hillary looked like Sandra Dee. The date was October 11, 1994. I haven't seen Bill and Hillary since.

But we did talk to them a month later. It was Thanksgiving Day, around noon. We were having guests for a big midday dinner—Marsha Scott, Bruce Lindsey, and others. Suzy and I were scurrying around trying to get everything ready when the phone rang. Caroline answered and whispered that it was the President. They talked for a long time. Then she called me to the phone. The President seemed to be in a good mood. He didn't sound any different than he ever had. He hoped we were well and wished me and my family a happy Thanksgiving. He then said Hillary wanted to speak with me.

"Webb," she said, "it's on CNN that you're going to be indicted next week."

"What?"

"You and Jim Guy both. He's on TV right now saying it's a mistake because he hasn't received a target letter." Before any indictment, the prosecutor is supposed to send you or your attorney a letter officially informing you that you are a "target of an investigation."

"Well, Hillary," I said, "I haven't gotten one, either."

"You've got to fight this, Webb. You've got to get tough." She wished me luck and we hung up. And that was the last time I spoke to either of them.

I have no idea who leaked to the press that I was to be indicted, but it had to have come from Starr's office. As you can imagine, that wasn't the best Thanksgiving we've ever had. I tried to call John, but he was out of town for the holiday. As our guests came, I told them the news. I told them I hadn't received a target letter, so it had to be wrong. Somehow, I pulled it all together one more time. We laughed and made toasts and ate well that day. My friends and family were around me. I tried to count my blessings.

I couldn't find John the next day, either, but by then the press was hanging around outside my house. I told them the story wasn't true, that I hadn't received a target letter. One of the reporters said, "Webb, I'm sorry to tell you this, but we've got a very reliable source. This is going to happen."

John and I finally connected on Saturday. When I mentioned the target letter, he said, "Webb, you got one." He had received it the day before Thanksgiving, and was hoping to spare me the news until after the holiday. I understand why John hadn't told me about the target letter, but it bothers me to this day that the last time I talked to Hillary, I told her something that wasn't true.

We had only one week to decide how to respond. The power of an indictment is awesome—"The United States vs. Webb Hubbell," it read. When you receive one, you have to plead one of two ways—not guilty or guilty. And if you plead guilty, you try to work out a plea agreement. Under the federal sentencing guidelines, you get a much longer sentence if you fail to accept responsibility. John was aware by now of what I had done. But I had never told him myself. It was crazy to plead not guilty—I knew it, he knew it. But if I could work out some kind of deal, maybe I still wouldn't have to go to jail. I was grasping at anything by then.

Regarding the IC's jurisdiction, most ICs have the latitude to prosecute crimes they discover while investigating the specific matters they're pursuing. I was a very juicy plum to fall in Starr's lap. We asked for more time, but the independent counsel said no. This was the deadline, take it or leave it. I wanted to fight, but it was time I came to grips with reality. During that week I had to tell my children. That was the hardest thing I've ever done. I had started seeing a counselor, and he helped me get through it. When I said I couldn't bear to let them know their father wasn't perfect, he said, "There's no greater child abuse than a perfect parent." Then he said, "Are they perfect?"

"No."

"Do you love them any less for it?"

"No."

"Well, then. Just tell them you need their help. You'll be surprised."

Walter was still at Sewanee, and Suzy and I drove down to see him in a play. The next morning, after breakfast, I said, "Son, I've got to talk to you. There's a chance, a good chance, that I'll be indicted and probably have to go to jail." We were having this extraordinary conversation at the local Waffle House. I repeated that to each one in turn. Rebecca was at the University of Arkansas at Fayetteville, where she's now a senior. Caroline, now a junior at Davidson, was a high school senior. Kelley, now a junior at the Maret School in Washington, was in junior high. All of them felt a little guilty for what I had done. We'd all been living beyond our means. But I reassured them that *they* hadn't done anything wrong; I had. "I need your help," I told them. Walter said he would drop out of school right then if I needed him to. Each of them said they were ready to help in any way they could. I was never any prouder of them than I was that week.

With that behind me, John and I worked out with Starr's office an agreement by which I would plead guilty to one count of mail fraud (I used the U.S. mail to send my fraudulent checks) and one count of tax fraud (I didn't report the money I stole from my firm and clients). And I would agree to cooperate with the IC on his further investigation.

In the criminal code, there is a statute known to lawyers as "5K." It refers to the part of the law allowing a defendent, on the prosecutor's motion, to receive a reduction in sentence "for substantial assistance" to the prosecution. In real life, this almost always means you serve somebody else up to them to save your neck. Obviously, the IC was ultimately interested in the President and First Lady, and I didn't know of anything they had done wrong.

But John went to them and presented it this way: Webb doesn't know of any wrongdoing. But you, Mr. Independent Counsel, you have a different duty than that of a normal prosecutor. Your charge is to investigate and determine if any wrongdoing occurred. In other words, you have as much responsibility for reporting that *no* crime was committed—if that indeed was what you found—as you do for reporting that a crime was committed. Considering that, Mr. Hubbell is agreeing to cooperate completely in your investigation. But if he provides "substantial assistance," we want you to consider going to the court and asking for a downward departure of his sentence. I was looking at two years for the counts against me. We were hoping that my cooperation would get that down to a year or less in a halfway house.

The independent counsel agreed to consider what John said. I say "the independent counsel," but I really mean his staff. Ken Starr has never questioned me, but he met with John on my plea and on the downward departure issue. It was only the questioning where he was never present. I've only seen him twice, actually— once, in the courtroom the day I pled guilty. He came over and shook my hand. The other time was the day I was sentenced.

Having made the excruciating decision to plead guilty, I finally began facing myself. I had gotten past telling my children. Now I had to apologize to my friends and other family members for letting them down. I wasn't just the wonderful Webb Hubbell they knew and loved. I was also somebody else. Now I had to pay for it.

I don't mean to say that I had faced my guilt a hundred percent. That's been a process that continues to this day. But I knew I could no longer let myself let my *friends* believe I was innocent. My old friend and accountant Mike Schaufele came to Washington during that time, and on a morning walk I told him, "Mike, I've done some bad things." It hurt but it also felt good to say it.

Some friends allowed me to tell more than others did. Chris Piazza, a circuit judge in Little Rock by then, called as soon as he heard I was thinking of pleading guilty. He couldn't believe it. "Webb, I'll resign from the bench and come represent you," he said. I had to say, "Chris, thanks. But I've done some things I shouldn't have." He told me later that after he hung up the phone he cried.

I told my sister Terry sitting in her living room with both of us crying. I told my friend Charlie Owen while he was driving me to the airport. I'll never forget it—we were going around a long curve, and I said, "Charlie, I've got to tell you this. I've done some bad things and I'll probably have to go to prison."

He didn't say anything for a few seconds. Then: "Well, I'm sorry. But I love you, anyway." Both of us held back tears the rest of the way to the airport.

The day before I entered my plea, Suzy, Rebecca, and I went to the Wards' house to tell them what I was about to do. I apologized to them for what I had done and for the fact that this would hurt them as well. They're a proud family, and I knew they were embarrassed to have a son-in-law who was guilty of a felony. It's only my impression, and it may tell something about the shame I was feeling that day, but I believe the Wards thought we were coming to tell them we were getting a divorce. They were surprised to learn that Suzy wasn't leaving me.

On December 6, 1994, I stood before Judge Bill Wilson—the former lawyer who kidded Hillary about being "Hillary Sue Clinton"—in Little Rock. I thought about how many times I had tried cases in that very courthouse. I was a prominent lawyer, a former mayor and supreme court justice then. This time I was an admitted felon, pleading guilty to two crimes. Kenneth Starr came over and shook my hand, and then the dance began.

For the next seven months, I spent much of my life in the independent counsel's offices in West Little Rock. My main interrogator was a former U.S. attorney from Memphis named Hickman Ewing. He first took me through my own crimes. I think his strategy was to see how open I was about my own guilt before we went on to other subjects. He made it as hard as he could. "This American Express charge," Ewing said. "Is that business or personal?"

"It's personal."

"And yet *you*"—here he looked at me with disdain—"you paid it with a Rose firm check."

"Yes, I did." This was painful, but in a perverse way therapeutic.

That went on for hours at a time, and the hours turned into days that became weeks and then months. We combed through every false bill, every little lie. When Ewing and his people were satisfied that I was baring my soul, they began questioning me about Hillary's billings on Madison, about Vince's suicide, and about the personal lives of the President, Hillary, Vince, myself, and my friends. I answered every single question, told them everything I knew. I could tell, at times, that they weren't happy with my answers when the questions were about Hillary's billings. "Webb, you're getting defensive," they said. All those years that Hillary was at the firm, I had defended her. During Bill's gubernatorial and presidential campaigns, she was always under attack. My father-in-law and many of my conservative friends don't like the Clintons' politics. Now, when the IC's questions turned to Hil-

lary, I was again defending her. By then it was a Pavlovian reaction. I tried to explain that to them, but I'm sure my natural
instincts were conveyed by my tone and body language. I contin-
ually said I knew of no wrongdoing on the part of the President
and First Lady. Because of that, I believe some of Starr's staff felt
I wasn't being forthcoming.

Near the end of June 1995, I stood before Judge George Howard, Jr. Judge Wilson recused from the case after accepting my
plea. Since I hadn't served up the President and First Lady, I knew
I wasn't going to qualify for the 5K motion. But there's another
method by which a defendant can receive a downward departure
of sentence. It's a long shot, just recently accepted by the courts.
In this case, it's all up to the judge. He can decide to be lenient
on the basis of the defendant's "extraordinary public service."
Hoping for such a decision, John solicited letters from people well
acquainted with my many years of service to the community, and
we had them put together in a booklet for the judge to read. One
letter called me "a tireless and dedicated worker for community
causes." Another said I was "a man for others." One called attention to "the sacrifice on his part which he was always willing
to make." Another extolled "the truly generous and outstanding
character of this gentle man." In all, we gave the judge nineteen
community service letters to read. We also gave him letters from
my friends, family, and colleagues at Justice.

On the day of sentencing, Kenneth Starr stood and told Judge
Howard that he didn't agree with departing sentences based on
extraordinary public service. On the other hand, he didn't oppose
the motion. "If there's anyone who would deserve it based on
public service," Starr said, "it's Webb Hubbell."

So the decision was in the judge's court. He told those gathered
about the letters he had read—how glowing they were, how they
attested to a life dedicated to others. He even read from several
of them. As my friends' eloquent words of praise rang through
the courtroom, I could see my family's and friends' expectations
rising. *He agrees. The judge agrees.* People began looking around,
meeting one another's eyes. Some even dared to smile. I think I

was the only person in the courtroom besides the judge who knew what he was doing. At the last minute, then, when he abruptly went in the other direction, I was ready for it. My family wasn't.

Those are wonderful letters, Judge Howard said. But then he had a quote of his own. It was from Luke: "To whom much is given, much is expected." The judge let the words sink in. The smiles vanished; the tears began to come. Much had been given to Webb Hubbell, Judge Howard said, and Webb Hubbell had abused it. He then asked me to stand. He denied the motion for downward departure and then asked if I had anything to say prior to sentencing. My daughter Caroline was sobbing. She wasn't by herself. I was later told that even one of the IC lawyers was crying. I turned to console Caroline and to calm myself before I spoke.

"My attorneys have told you that to some extent my plea was a relief," I said. "I need to elaborate briefly. For many years I felt like Saint Paul when he wrote, 'I do not understand my own actions, for I do not do what I want. But I do the very thing I hate.' I was miserable on the outside. I continued to function, even at times in the most visible of arenas, with apparent ease, calm, and competence. But on the inside I was torn apart, separated from the values I knew were important. I tried to help all except the one who needed it most—me. I have a friend who described exactly how I felt. He was driving in Washington, in Georgetown, a confusing neighborhood, when all of a sudden he realized he was lost. He said, 'I knew where I was, but I was lost.' That was me—I knew where I was, but I was lost. . . ."

The court listened in total silence. When I was finished, the Judge said, "Mr. Hubbell, I hereby sentence you to a term of twenty-one months in a federal facility." He also ordered restitution to the Rose Law Firm and three years of supervised release after the prison term. I knew that under federal regulations a twenty-one-month sentence meant serving at least eighteen months in a federal facility. My lawyer then requested that I serve the sentence in a federal prison camp in Pennsylvania so I could be close to my family in D.C. Judge Howard declined to make that decision, saying he had concerns about my personal safety and wanted that decision to be made by the Bureau of Prisons.

The judge had one more order for me. After serving my time, I was to speak in prisons once a month for a year, traveling to Arkansas at my own expense to talk about the importance of friends, family, education, and the necessity of accepting responsibility.

With that, he banged his gavel down.

Part III

THE AFTERMATH

13

The Big Easy

A few days after my sentencing, we learned that I was ordered to self-report on August 7 to the Federal Prison Camp in Cumberland, Maryland. The reasons for Cumberland were proximity to my family and proximity to Congress and the IC for further questioning.

A couple of weeks before I was to surrender, Suzy and I drove up to Cumberland to see the place. The devil you know is better than the devil you don't know. At first, we took a wrong turn and came upon a big, brooding abandoned tire plant. "Oh my God," Suzy said, thinking that was the prison. Then we saw a dark old Pittsburgh Plate Glass warehouse and thought that was the place. By the time we saw the camp, we were relieved. The camp is a collection of stone buildings around a central square with no surrounding fence. Down the hill out of sight was the medium-security prison the camp supports. It is what you think of as prison—surrounded by chain-link fences, razor wire, and lights everywhere.

I was due to report at noon on August 7. The morning I was to leave, the press was camped in front of my house. I went out and asked for consideration for me and my family. Soon Suzy and Marsha Scott and I headed out on what would be the grimmest drive of my life. I was nervous and tense, and the weather was unbearably hot. We missed a turn and by the time we discovered our mistake, we realized the quickest way to Cumberland was to drive right past Camp David. The irony wasn't lost on any of us.

As we pulled up to the camp, the press was waiting at the entrance. We drove on through and I walked into the reception area at 11:59 A.M. "I'm Webb Hubbell," I said. "I'm here to report." The camp administrator was all business, suggesting that Suzy, Marsha, and I say quick good-byes while she told the press they could leave now. I hugged them both and they walked out the door. Later, the press accounts would report that I was driven to prison by two gorgeous blondes in a gold Lexus. Suzy failed to find humor in any such accounts. They were both blondes and gorgeous, but Suzy didn't drive a Lexus.

For the next three hours, I went through the admissions process, beginning with a Breathalyzer test and a strip search. That morning I'd fleetingly thought about bolting back a couple of Bloody Marys to calm my nerves, but it was a good thing I decided against it. If they find any alcohol or drugs in your system, it's a ticket straight to "the Hole." That's the dreaded solitary-confinement cell. There you spend twenty-three hours a day locked up, with limited phone and other privileges. I would soon learn that much of what passes for good behavior in prison life is essentially an abject fear of the Hole.

In 1995 some federal prison camps allowed you to bring in a few personal items; they've since stopped that. Inventorying my belongings, they checked off two pair of sweats, a pair of running shoes, an inexpensive watch, some papers and pens, a portable radio, a jacket, and one final item. Despite my twenty-two years as a lawyer, my term as chief justice of the Arkansas Supreme Court, and my time as associate attorney general of the United States, when I went to Cumberland, all I knew about prison was what I had seen in the movies. Two scenes stuck out in my mind. One was when Steve McQueen played catch with a ball bounced off his cell wall in *The Great Escape*. The other was the rape scene in *The Shawshank Redemption*. Hoping for something more along the lines of the former, I had packed my softball glove when

I went to camp. I took it as a bad sign when they said I couldn't bring it in.

I had been told I could bring five books. That was an interesting decision, choosing only five books as you head off to twenty-one months in prison. I finally settled on my Bible, my Episcopal Book of Common Prayer, a book called *The Return of the Prodigal Son* by Henry Nouween, Ronald Steel's *Walter Lippman and the American Century,* and, finally, Thomas Wolfe's *You Can't Go Home Again.*

A psychiatrist interviewed me to find out if I was suicidal. I told her I was fine, but I suspect she could tell I wasn't. Everyone was polite but direct. I understood that one of the goals of the admissions process was to dehumanize and depersonalize. The reception center was hot and I was wringing wet, but more from the stress than from the heat warming up my 320 pounds. I entered prison weighing more than I ever had in my life. By 3 P.M., I had been interviewed by a counselor, examined by a doctor, had shed my civilian clothes for a poorly fitting blue inmate jumpsuit and slippers, and had been issued my three green khaki uniforms and a bedroll. I was ready to make my first walk across the compound.

The Cumberland Minimum-Security Camp is essentially a group of stone buildings arranged in a square. Two L-shaped, two-story dormitories make up the top of the square and jut down each side about halfway. Completing the sides and cutting inward across the south end are two other L-shaped buildings—the education building/gymnasium on one side, and the administration building/hospital on the other. Across the bottom, a single-story dining hall completes the square. Just outside that tight perimeter are a softball field, the powerhouse, and a warehouse.

But the focus of prison life is that area in the center of all the buildings. That's called the Compound. It has sidewalks starting at all four corners and meeting in a circle at the center. When you take your first walk across that space, it feels like it goes on for a hundred miles.

Carrying my new clothes and my bedroll, I stepped out of the administration building and into the open. I could feel eyes boring into me from everywhere. Though I didn't know it then, rumors of my arrival had been circulating around the camp for days. The inmates at the Cumberland camp—the majority of whom were nineteen to thirty, black, and in prison for offenses involving drugs—were expecting a prima donna. I was the big-shot friend of Bill and Hillary. I was to receive special treatment. The two dorms are divided into four- and six-man cubicles. The day before I arrived, two men in a four-man cubicle got in trouble and went to the Hole. A whole cubicle was then empty, and rumor had it that I would have it all to myself, along with a private telephone. There were even stories saying I was being given a private bed in the guards' office. Rumors spread fast inside a prison. Very quickly they become reality.

The prison officials had anticipated that. They knew that the very last thing any of us needed was a congressional investigation into why I got special treatment. So they bent as far as they could the other way. I was escorted to a six-man cubicle on the second floor of my unit. I was the only white man out of the six. Fortunately, there was a bottom bunk available. And fortunately, nobody complained. Maybe they saw that it wouldn't be fun for anybody to have me huffing and puffing my 320-pound frame up to a top bunk.

After making my bed and putting my belongings in my assigned locker, I surveyed my surroundings. It was the first time I'd had even a minute to stop and think all day. This was my life now. This was my world. The cubicle—or "cube," as everybody called them—was sixteen feet long and seven feet wide. It was designed to hold four prisoners, but thanks to my former aggressive Justice Department there were too many inmates for the space, so it had been retrofitted for six. It occurred to me that my office at Justice was at least four times that size. And within that tight space were three bunk beds and six three-foot-high lockers. Plus five suspicious young black men and an overweight middle-aged white lawyer who used to play golf at the Country Club of Little Rock with the President.

Each wing of each dormitory held eight cubicles identical to mine. There were identical sinks, toilets, urinals, and showers at the end of each hall. I glanced at them on my way to supper, but I didn't stop. I didn't want to do anything to call more attention to myself. The evening meal, served from 4:45 to 5:30, was announced over a loudspeaker: "Main line is open. Unit A report to main line." Soon everybody shuffled out of the dorms and across the compound toward the dining hall. It was like prison movies you've seen a thousand times. There were cliques you could spot easily—groups of men who hung together, laughing with one another, smirking when they looked your way. I felt very, very alone. I wondered how Suzy was doing. I thought about my kids. This had to be a terrible time for all of them—maybe worse than it was for me.

In the compound and the dining hall, the inmates were polite but guarded. Later I would learn that every one of them had been just like me at one time, and they were letting me adjust. I have no idea what I ate for supper that first night. I just went through the motions, watching the men in front of me and doing what they did. I got my tray, got my tea, went down the cafeteria line and to a table. It was a blur. Later, back in my cube, my cubemates tried to explain how the phone system worked, how you got mail, how visits were arranged. (The latter took weeks—except for family, visitors had to be mailed a form, had to fill it out and send it back, and then had to be put on an approved list.) It all went over my head. I didn't have the context yet. I tried to read, tried to think, but mainly just tried not to break down. No matter how prepared I thought I was, I wasn't. Nobody is. It would get better, but I didn't know it then.

At lights-out, my cubemates were all in the TV room down the hall. I got in my bunk and lay there staring at the darkness. Soon I heard voices calling softly from the other cubes: "Don't sleep too well, Hubbell," said one. Then from a different direction: "We'll be there to get you later." Finally: "Don't bother to keep your underwear on." After that, the giggling started. I was afraid to even get up and walk to the bathroom, much less roll over and shut my eyes. I tried to keep one eye open and to avoid snoring. It was a long night. Nothing happened—including sleep.

*   *   *

The next morning I was up before the lights came on at six. The voice from the speaker droned again: "Main line is now open." Everyone began to move. I would come to know that disembodied voice well over the next year and a half. After breakfast, the voice would say, "Work call, work call," and everyone would move in a different direction. Throughout the day, the voice directed various individuals from on high: "Hubbell report to Unit A counselor's office." Every building was equipped with speakers. You could never get away from the voice.

My first few days were consumed with trying to learn how to use the phone system, getting my visitors list started, filling out forms, and taking every possible kind of physical. Once you're in prison you're the Bureau of Prisons' health problem. You aren't allowed to see a personal physician or to bring in your own prescriptions.

I also began to take daily walks. Among my goals for this forced sabbatical was to lose all the extra weight I had put on. Before I reported, I had tried to look at this experience in the best possible light: I had long said I wanted to go to a monastery, and this was as close as I had ever gotten. Some of the differences were hard to ignore—instead of brown sackcloth, my brothers and I wore green khakis; instead of Gregorian chants, the air was filled with rap. But there were similarities, too. This was a place for me to repent of my worldly ways and become a new man. I wanted to improve both my physical and spiritual beings. I wanted to read, write, think, pray. I wanted to shed pounds and gain wisdom.

I had been told that I could expect to testify before Congress just a few days after I arrived. My lawyers thought they had reached an agreement with the independent counsel that when this happened, I would simply be furloughed back to Washington. Suzy would pick me up, drive me to D.C., and after testifying, I would return to Cumberland. But that wasn't consistent with how inmates are normally transported, and I was to be given no special treatment. Now the administrators told me I would be transported by U.S. marshals. The evening before I was to testify, I mentioned the new arrangements to a buddy I had made during my daily walks. His name was George, and he was in for lying before a grand jury. We had struck up a conversation on my second day or so. He shook his head when I told him about the U.S. marshals. "Nothing can prepare you for that, Webb," he said. "Just get ready—the shame will overwhelm you."

The next morning at five-thirty a guard shook me awake. He said I was to get dressed, empty my locker, and report to Receiving and Discharge, known as R and D. I tried to explain that I would be back that night, but he said those were the rules. Every time you left the prison, you had to empty your locker and the contents were inventoried. I put on my khakis and carried my stuff to R and D, where I changed into a suit I had been allowed to bring in for these occasions (later, a member of Congress wrote to the Bureau of Prisons complaining that I had appeared in a suit instead of an orange jumpsuit. The BOP replied that every inmate is given the right to appear in court in a suit or street clothes. I'm sure the congressman wasn't satisfied by that response).

Two marshals were waiting for me, and my friend was right. They wrapped a chain around my waist and then clamped cuffs on each of my wrists. The cuffs were attached by chain to the chain around my waist. Then they put leg irons around each ankle. Nothing in the prison experience underscores the reality of your situation quite the way shackles do. The weight of the iron feels like guilt and shame. You waddle like a duck not just to keep the leg irons from cutting, but because you're less than human. You're a convicted felon.

Our drive to Washington was uneventful. The marshals were civil but businesslike. Once I got to the hearing, my daughter Caroline and my friend Marsha were allowed to be with me before my testimony and during breaks. Suzy stayed at work while I testified—we didn't need a congressional inquiry into why she took time off from the Department of Interior to visit her husband. Before I went to prison, I had agreed to do one interview, with CBS News. The piece had just run, and Marsha told me it had been well received. I had used that opportunity to apologize to the nation. During the hearing, Congressman Joe Kennedy complimented me on my statement that I had done wrong and was ready to take my medicine.

The testimony was before Chairman Jim Leach's House Banking Committee, and the purported focus of the hearing was on the hiring of the Rose Law Firm by the FDIC in the *Madison* v. *Frost* litigation. But soon I was being questioned about the RTC's referral to Justice and what role I played in the investigation. Every question seemed to imply that somehow the Clintons were using me at the Justice Department to prevent this matter from ever coming to light. The congressmen refused to accept my explanation that I had early on recused from any decisions involving Madison or McDougal.

Since the hearing didn't end until 8:30 P.M., the marshals decided it was too late to drive back to Cumberland that night. Suddenly I felt a gripping fear—was I going to spend the night in the D.C. jail? I thought Cumberland was bad, but a big-city jail would be life threatening. If the people in there found out who was locked up with them, I might not survive the night. The marshals must have had the same thought, because they decided to take me to one of their safe houses. They put me in a closed-panel van and drove me somewhere in the D.C. area. I tried to imagine the route from the movement of the van, but there was no way. Over the next eighteen months, I took this trip often, but I never had a clue as to where the safe house was.

The trip back to Cumberland was okay, but I kept having this strange fantasy: Suddenly the marshals were going to pull over and say, "Webb, it's all been a joke!" My friends and family were going to pop out of the woods laughing and we would all go home. Soon, though, I was back at Cumberland. I took off my suit and changed into my green khakis and then walked out into the compound toward my cube. The other inmates were surprised to see me. Several came up to talk. One said people had sworn they saw me leave the day before in a long, black limousine. So the rumor mill had it, the congressional hearing was just a ruse to give me special treatment—a weekend at home with Suzy and the kids. Any day now I was supposed to be pardoned. A few inmates had seen me get out of the U.S. marshals' car, waddling to the administration building in shackles. That had burst a few preconceived notions, but it would take months for all the rumors of furloughs and special big-shot treatment to die down.

Suzy's first visit was that Saturday. It had been only five days since we'd seen each other, but it seemed like a year. I kept expecting something to happen to prevent her from coming. Then the voice summoned me: "Inmate Hubbell, report to visitation." Before you see a visitor, you first have to be searched. Then you're led into a large room full of straight-backed chairs. I'd already read the rules of visitation—the one that jumped out at me was "no displays of affection except upon greeting." Suzy was as frightened and as fragile as I had ever seen her. Prison isn't a place where people go out of their way to be nice and helpful, even if you're a visitor. No one had told her what to do, where to go, how she was supposed to act. She had driven up by herself. When she last saw me, I was wearing street clothes. Now here the two of us were in this room full of sad, quiet men in green khaki trying to talk with their vacant-faced families. This was Suzy's first shock into our new reality. This was her shackle and chains.

She told me what everyone had been doing, and I told her what my week had been like. She was nervous, edgy. I hated to see her so devastated. A good many friends had called her, and she was grateful for that. The kids were doing okay. After an hour or two, there wasn't much more to say. It was time for her to head back home.

That afternoon I talked with a fellow inmate about how hard the visit had been. More than my own situation, I hated how tough this was on my family. He said his mother and father had moved in with his wife to help her take care of the kids and the family business. I imagined how the Wards would do, moving in with Suzy, Caroline, and Kelley. Seth and Vonnie wanted Suzy to move to Hot Springs and live at the lake house, but she told them her life was in Washington now.

The next day, Sunday, August 13, 1995, was Kelley's fourteenth birthday. I thought about her all day. Just one year before, she, Suzy, and I had been sailing with friends in the Greek islands.

*   *   *

The first week is the hardest, everybody says. I had made it. Now I only had eighty-three to go.

During that first month, I actually had a good bit of free time between all the physicals and interviews. My job assignment hadn't come through yet (there was great speculation that whatever I got, it would be very cushy), so I spent my days reading books, writing letters, making notes in my journal, and taking walks. I was determined to come out of this experience a wiser, better, healthier man.

I first read the books that I'd brought with me. Some of them, like my Bible and my Book of Common Prayer, would be ongoing companions. But from a list I had drawn up, people sent me scores of books I wanted to get through while I was in prison. When would I ever have more time? My intention was to use the books not just for my own enjoyment and education, but also as the basis for letters to and from friends. I knew that soon the boredom would set in on both sides, and I tried to head that off. You can only say, "I'm fine. How are you?" so many times. I asked my friends and family to send me quotes they liked, and I would send them the ones I'd found particularly provocative. One of my first letters was from Rebecca, who began by telling me her new college address. Then she included these:

"The road uphill and the road downhill are one and the same" (Heraclitus).

"I'd rather be the man who bought the Brooklyn Bridge than the man who sold it" (Will Rogers).

I collected quotes with a passion. It gave me a mission within my mission. I'd always enjoyed reading quote books, in which so much of life's wisdom was boiled down to a few pithy words. I'd had good intentions of collecting them before, but I hadn't taken the time. Now I could. As Coco Chanel said, "How many cares one loses when one decides not to be something, but to be someone."

My book of quotes became wonderfully, richly eclectic, including entries by Maya Angelou ("History, despite its wrenching pain, cannot be unlived. But if faced with courage need not be lived again"); George Wallace ("I would have wasted myself away if I had been hating all these years"); and Oscar Wilde ("[A pessimist is] one who, when faced with the choice between two evils, chooses both"). For twenty-one months in 1995 and 1996, my friends and family scoured the world's literature for great and true words. I think it made us better readers. I think the search became a comfort to all of us.

I enlisted other letter writers to help me with other goals. I read the entire Bible following a program sent me by my Episcopalian rector. A Connecticut friend from the Justice Department wrote a series of letters on her North, and I wrote letters to her about my South. I also corresponded with one of my and Suzy's oldest friends, Cricket Hicks (her husband, Basil, was in law school with me), on a project that I wouldn't have dared if I hadn't had almost two years for it—reading and comprehending James Joyce's *Ulysses*. Cricket, an English teacher, exchanged letters with me about each part. I think it was Cricket who sent me the following: "Proust wrote, 'The real voyage of discovery consists not in seeking new lands, but in seeing with new eyes.'" I imagined he was talking about me.

I found great comfort in the prison's Monday night Catholic Mass, given by Father Milton Hipsley. Even though I wasn't Catholic, he allowed me to take mass, anyway. "It's okay," he said. "You're a good Democrat." Some friends I talked with regularly in addition to corresponding with them. Every Wednesday night I talked with Mike and Marty Schaufele, and everyone was gracious about accepting my necessarily collect phone calls when I needed a lift. I talked to Suzy almost every day. Many friends, even those from Arkansas, visited me at Cumberland, flying into Washington and making the long drive into the Maryland mountains to see an old friend who'd gone astray. They were disappointed in what I had done, but they forgave me for it. My friendships had survived my betrayal.

One of the ironies of prison is that the thing you lose is the very thing you gain. I'm talking about time. Time is different in prison than it is on the outside. In the outside world, time is a whirling blur of forces and temptations, choices and consequences. In prison, time stops. You finally have time to face who you are. My prison had no walls to barricade me in, but I couldn't escape from myself. I found a place I liked, the bleachers at the softball field. Sometimes I watched a game there, and sometimes I went there to read. On Sunday mornings I took my Walkman and stole away to the bleachers to lose myself in the lush choral programs broadcast by Frostburg State, a small college in the western tip of Maryland.

Word got around that I had once been drafted by the Chicago Bears, and once again football helped me earn respectability. Sports is the common denominator between the White House and the big house. I was invited by a young man nicknamed Razor to watch the exhibition game on *Monday Night Football* between the Bears and the Cleveland Browns. Many inmates were from the Cleveland area, and it was going to be crowded in the TV room. At Cumberland, certain cliques control the TV viewing. You don't just wander into the sanctity of that room uninvited. I was a little nervous about going, but Razor had saved me a seat in the front row. The Bears were clobbered 55–13, so I took a lot of ribbing. They liked that—my willingness to be good-natured about their jokes. That soon earned me a nickname of my own: "the Big Easy."

More important, my being accepted allowed me to leave the first stage of prison—shock—and progress to the second stage, apathy. The first weeks were filled with adjustments, forms, learning the language. Requests to the administration are submitted on a form called a "cop out." Meals are called "main line." Money from home is "yellow love." I learned that some of the many rules were based on a single incident: Dental floss is unwaxed because somewhere sometime a patient inmate imbedded sand in waxed dental floss and created a saw.

I didn't encounter the violence I feared, mainly because the punishment for the slightest altercation was the Hole. I was still waiting for my job assignment. In federal prison everybody has a job. I had requested education, hoping to teach and do some good for some of my fellow inmates. I was encouraged by my counselor's reaction to my request, but once again I ran up against the fact that "everybody's watching." Education is a plum job in prison. There was no way they could let me teach.

My first job assignment was in the powerhouse, the energy and maintenance center of the camp and the neighboring prison. My days were soon taken up with repairing—or attempting to repair—anything that was broken in camp, from latrines to kitchen equipment to the dentist's X-ray machine. Actually, I found the work challenging, even therapeutic. Sometimes, though, the supervisors enjoyed just fooling with me. Once I spent an entire day moving huge rolls of razor wire across the back of the warehouse. My powerhouse job lasted for seven long months. Then I became a window washer, spending five hours a day, seven days a week, spraying Windex on the dining hall panes and then cutting the film with my squeegee. Finally, I stepped up to the job of cook. I've got some great recipes, but they all serve three hundred.

As I was adjusting, so was my family. We had hoped to make as few changes as possible while I was gone—keeping the house, the kids staying in the same schools. Soon we realized that was impossible. Our financial situation was deteriorating. Once we decided to sell the house, Suzy began looking for a place to rent. She saw a town house in the paper that looked promising, but when she and Kelley went to see it, it turned out to be Vince and Lisa's old place.

Suzy continued to work at Interior and appreciated the strong support of our Washington friends. I learned how fortunate we were in that regard when I talked to other inmates who seemed to be losing their wives and were estranged from their friends and children. I would later come to understand that some of this was self-imposed. Some men simply severed all emotional ties just to avoid confronting the loneliness and pain of separation. Sometimes when I looked out my window at night I saw a solitary figure sitting under the light, smoking a cigarette. He looked lonely and miserable. He walked slowly—inmates called it "the prison shuffle." I made a note in my journal about how easy it was to give up while you're in prison.

One major adjustment for me was the noise. I was a forty-eight-year-old man among, mostly, a group of kids. At times, the noise level was unbelievable. I wore my radio headphones as a defense, trying to listen to the plaintive lyrics of the country-and-western station instead of the yelling and screaming of the kid life around me. Real violence did occur at times, and when it did, there was always injury—a broken collarbone caused by the single swing of a milk dispenser handle, a face smashed by a weight bar against the head of a man who argued with the wrong person. I was warned about padlocks swung in the bottom of socks as both a defensive and offensive weapon of choice in prison camp. I wasn't often frightened, but I still walked softly.

On Labor Day of 1995 I signed up for the over-forty softball game. People were surprised that I would play, but even more that I *could* play. That afternoon in a limited appearance I went two for two, played first base, and became one of the guys. Mickey and Walter were very impressed with my statistics when I told them. Suzy, on the other hand, blanched when I told her about all the injuries suffered by the over-forties and the medical treatment or lack thereof that they received. She hoped I wouldn't play the fall season. But playing ball made me feel better. It helped with one part of my goal—shedding the pounds I had put on. As I began to do that, I found myself also shedding some of the guilt and shame that was dragging me down even more than my weight.

By mid-September my days had taken on a definite pattern. Suzy came up about every other weekend. I wrote in my journal after one visit that her hair was growing longer, and that at one moment she pulled her hair back and it almost took my breath away. As she left, I sat on the bleachers listening to the Rotterdam Philharmonic and watching the sun set over the mountains. I was happy and lonely at the same time. The next day I was deeply depressed after I talked to her. The newness was wearing off and the reality that I would be gone for a long time was settling in.

When the O. J. Simpson criminal verdict came in, there was almost universal celebration in the camp. I saw that it was based on an antiestablishment, anticop sentiment, and on sexism. Few of the men at Cumberland had any real respect for women in general. In some part, that was due to the fact that the camp administrator was a woman, but there was also a common thread of anger, bitterness, and sexual degradation. It wasn't limited to African Americans. I discussed this later with a counselor. She was initially surprised at my observation, but several months later she said that the subject had actually come up at a staff meeting. My observation was now a universally held opinion among the staff.

In mid-October one of my roommates left and was replaced by a savings and loan president from Pennsylvania. He was my age and was scared to death. I asked someone if I had been that scared. "Big Easy," he said, "you were worse!" I tried to help this man through the first few hours. I got him to call his wife and told him not to worry about attacks in the night. He would become my good friend, the man who introduced me to the joys of country music. But that first night he was merely a picture of me just two short months before.

Several days later I was told once again to clean out my locker—I was leaving.

I didn't keep count, but I estimate I made ten to twenty trips to Washington to testify during my months at Cumberland. Sometimes the inquiries were on matters that had nothing to do with the independent counsel or Whitewater. For example, I believe this deposition involved explaining my role in defending the administration in the Health Care Task Force. Each time I made a trip like this, I was nervous. This one probably wouldn't last more than half a day, but in keeping with policy, nobody would tell me anything. I worried that I might be transferred. Sometimes I was actually relieved to get back to Cumberland. It was becoming home.

On Thanksgiving 1995, I reflected on all that had happened to me in a year. Twelve months before, I had received a call from the President and First Lady, and she told me CNN was reporting that I would be indicted the next week.

The next week I was back in Washington again. The independent counsel or Congress wanted to see me more frequently now.

This was a world I once belonged in, but when I got back to Cumberland that time, I wrote in my journal, "Return from the Twilight Zone. Coats and ties, smiling senators, news cameras. Yet reality for me is marshals following me to the bathroom, chains and leg irons. During the morning and evening I sit in a holding tank with urine-stained linoleum and the word 'Slick' written on the ceiling. I wonder how he wrote his name up there."

Early in December I got the disturbing news that the independent counsel wanted me to appear before the grand jury in Little Rock before Christmas. The bad news wasn't the testimony itself, but the transportation and what could happen along the way. I was comfortable at Cumberland. The thought of different prisons, county jails, shackles, and chains frightened me. I had been warned by other inmates about what they called "diesel therapy." My family was all going to be in Washington for Christmas. I told Suzy I knew it wasn't critical for them to have me testify before Christmas. This was just another way of putting pressure on me.

On Monday morning the voice called me to pack up and report to R and D. I called Suzy and told her I was on the road. I was driven by van to the Federal Correction Institution down the hill, where I was strip-searched, put in traveling khakis, and, with twenty inmates from behind the fence, transported by bus to the airport at Harrisburg, Pennsylvania.

At the airport, buses from all the federal prisons in the area meet to exchange prisoners and receive new ones from the plane about to land. This was the infamous "Con Air." I had heard about it from other inmates, but you have to see it to believe it. Armed guards surrounded the buses and the plane. Weapons were everywhere. Everyone averted their eyes, the prison way. Soon I heard my name called. I exited the bus to freezing cold, where my chains and leg irons were checked and my mouth and ears inspected to see if I was hiding something. Then we entered a large old airplane. We sat six abreast in tiny seats. Despite my weight loss, I was still a big man, and I'm sure the men on either side of me were as miserable as I was.

Several hours later we landed in Oklahoma City and were

transported to the Federal Transfer Facility there. The BOP has adopted the Federal Express approach to inmate transfer. They processed some 150 men in a few hours. Then I was escorted to my cell, a nine- by fifteen-foot room with a bunk bed, toilet, and sink. My roommate was a young kid with twelve more years to go on a twenty-year sentence. All the cells opened to a common area with TV, eating tables, and chairs. There was a rack of soft-bound books, so I occupied my time by reading and praying. My roommate told me that word was spreading about who I was, but not to worry—everybody thought I was "too damn big to try to hurt." Soon a group of skinheads were ushered in, and the tension mounted. I wasn't particularly worried. We were locked down most of the time, and my cellmate was fine. I was just depressed because it looked like my family would be in Washington for Christmas and I would be stuck here in Oklahoma. Later, I wrote in my journal that words could hardly describe the coldness and depression of that facility. The frustration and pain on everybody's face . . . I began to understand the "prison look," the ability to sit or stand for hours looking blankly into space.

After three days I was processed out, strip-searched again, given different clothes, and put in a van with five other inmates bound for Arkansas. There was almost no conversation. Late that afternoon we arrived in Conway, a college town thirty miles northwest of Little Rock. My new home for the next few days was to be the Faulkner County jail. For my protection, I was registered as a John Doe and taken to a closet that also served as the chaplain's storage area. A mattress was placed on the floor, which was fine with me. The cells were loud and crowded. This was better.

Soon I was joined by another man who was charged with a drug offense. He was a lawyer, and obviously depressed. I couldn't help noticing the razor tracks on his wrists. We were allowed to leave the closet during certain hours and go watch TV with the trustees, to eat our meals and use the facilities. Even the trustees' room was overcrowded, designed for twelve but housing twenty-seven. I missed Cumberland. I missed Suzy. I thought of the narrator's existence in *You Can't Go Home Again*. One night my roommate just started crying. As I waited to go to Little Rock to testify, I wrote in my journal that I was anxious. "People do not want the truth," I wrote. "They want destruction of people's lives. Vince was right about that."

Finally, eight days after leaving Cumberland, I was taken to the Little Rock Courthouse to testify. This was my first time in Little Rock since my sentencing. I was escorted down the halls in cuffs and chains. Courthouse friends stepped out to say hello—but seeing the chains, they ducked back behind closed doors. I saw one begin to cry. The testimony lasted less than a day and to my mind there was nothing urgent about it at all. The questions focused on Hillary's billings to Madison. I just hoped I had time to get back to Cumberland before Christmas. I had heard that they did not transfer prisoners the last two weeks of December.

Ultimately, I was driven back to Oklahoma City, reprocessed, and put in a waiting cell. I prayed that I would be able to go home. The next morning I heard guards waking other inmates, starting at 4 A.M. By six, almost everyone else was gone, and I assumed I was stuck for the duration. Then at 8 A.M., I was told I would be leaving on the last flight before the Christmas shutdown. I was processed and put on a small plane with five Cuban inmates. Though nobody would tell me where we were going, I gleaned from conversations that we were heading to Atlanta to pick up another inmate, and then flying straight to Baltimore. An old refrain came to mind: "I'll be home for Christmas."

Several hours later, we were circling Fulton County airport. The five Cubans were talking, but I sensed that something was wrong. I overheard the pilot say, "We're going to Hartsfield, the marshals are putting away loose luggage . . ." As we started our descent, I noticed the marshals had assumed the crash position. I looked out the window and the crash and fire trucks were lining the runway. My fellow inmates and I remained in chains and uninformed. I started praying. Fortunately, the landing gear held, and we landed safely.

When we were processed in Atlanta, I was again isolated. The only isolation cell at the facility was the suicide watch cell outside the office. After being processed, including getting a lice shampoo, I was placed in a five- by seven-foot cell with a concrete slab for box springs, a toilet, sink, and a hole in the door through which to slide me food. My prayers were long and sincere that evening.

The next morning we were told we were leaving. While we were being processed out and resuited in chains and handcuffs, the largest and toughest of the Cuban travelers gazed at the cell where I spent the previous evening. "Who are you?" he asked. I didn't want to answer. He didn't care. "If they made you stay in there," he said, "you must be *one bad dude*."

I smiled. "Yeah," I said. When I got back to Cumberland, I wanted to kiss the ground.

One evening in the early spring of 1996, two friends and I were sitting in the bleachers talking. We were a strange trio, a prison triptych—one middle-aged alleged mobster from Boston, one young black tough from the streets of Cleveland, and me. We were talking about getting out.

My middle-aged friend said it was always the same. He would go home wanting to go straight, to live a clean life. For a while they wouldn't touch him. They would just let him believe he was home free. Then one day two detectives would show up at his business. They would ask what he'd been up to. When he asked, Why? they would say, Don't get smart with us. And the next thing you knew, they would haul him downtown and grill him about all his friends. Afterward, he would look out his window at odd hours and see the detectives watching him. They were just waiting for him to make a mistake.

The young black man said a similar thing would happen to him. It always did. He would scratch around for work, trying to stay out of the clutches of the drug dealers and the pimps and the bad guys who hated to see a man get clean. But even if he escaped them, the cops would pick him up once a week and stand him in a lineup. He was a convicted felon, so he was fair game. He had made a mistake, and they wanted him to keep paying for it.

Then it was my turn. "That won't happen to me," I told them. "I did wrong and I've accepted that. I've stopped blaming anybody else for what I did. I've stopped looking for excuses. I've learned that redemption is in admitting your mistakes and asking for forgiveness. I'll serve my time. I'll pay my debt to society. After that, I want to get on with my life. No, that *won't* happen to me."

They laughed. Yes, Webb, they said, it will. And they were right, except for one thing. It started even before I got out.

I was eligible for a halfway house in August 1996, so that spring the administration started the paperwork. But no good news came my way. In May, I received notice that the Rose firm had sued me. They wanted me to agree to repay them more than the court had ordered. I wasn't prepared to deal with them. They knew I was in no position to hire a lawyer to defend a lawsuit. I had tried to postpone the lawsuit, to reach an agreement to resolve the matter after I got out of prison, but instead they sued. I began to understand the mentality of institutionalization. People say that in prison you only have to live in the present. The past is too painful, the future too uncertain. After a while, there's a certain comfort in prison's mindless existence.

The late spring and summer were terribly depressing. Many of the friends I'd made had left camp, the Rose firm had sued me, the Senate had sicced Kenneth Starr on my consulting contracts, and I had blown up when Mike Chertoff, counsel for the Senate Whitewater Committee, asked during one of my testimonies if I had "been paid hush money" to refrain from revealing crimes committed by the President or First Lady. I told him that his question was "sorry," that I "had answered every damn question that anybody had put to me," and that I had a right to feed and support my family. My lawyers, my friends and family, and my fellow inmates were glad that I had finally exploded. But I knew as I was answering Chertoff that the media would take this topic and run with it. And I knew, from my Inslaw experience, that Kenneth Starr would have no choice but to investigate it—even if he, personally, had been of a mind not to. In his position, you can't afford not to turn over every stone.

Word finally came that I wouldn't be released until November 18, 1996. I had hoped for six months in a halfway house, but I would get less than three. Suzy was devastated. She needed me home; she wanted us to begin our life over. People tried to buck us up. "As soon as the election is over, Webb, they'll leave you alone." I hoped that was right. I finally settled financially with the firm. I agreed to pay them a total of $325,000, in quarterly installments, over a period of years. No matter how much it cost, I had to get closure. I couldn't start a new life with a lawsuit hanging over my head.

Suzy came to pick me up the day I was released from Cumberland to the halfway house. It is a tradition in prison that you leave everything you brought except the clothes on your back. I donated all my books—I had read eighty during my eighteen months at Cumberland—distributed several extra-large pairs of sweats and shorts to inmates who'd asked for them, and walked out carrying only my Bible, my Book of Common Prayer, and one treasure I had been given in prison. After I had worked for weeks with Father Hipsley to learn to pray the rosary, one night after mass he said, "Webb, I want to give you something." Nobody's supposed to give anybody anything in prison, but the father said he didn't care. He showed me his rosary. "I've had this for years," he said. "I took it to Auschwitz and prayed there. I don't understand it, Webb, but I'm moved to give it to you. You are supposed to have this rosary." It's a gift I'll treasure always.

Suzy and I embraced in the parking lot, hugging each other for a long time. We both hoped this would be the last we would see of this place.

In Washington, she drove me to an area of the city that I had carefully avoided in the past. Multiple housing projects, abandoned cars, streets that took on the aura of a battle zone once the sun set. That was my home for the next few months. There I was required to attend classes called "life skills," covering subjects like AIDS, how to open a bank account, and coping as we reentered society.

Two days before Valentine's Day, 1997, I finally came home to Suzy and my kids. I was lucky for that, and I knew it. In prison I sat with many a friend whose wife—or wife's lawyer—had just sent a letter saying she was leaving. Usually it happened just about the time the man was about to get out. There was something about that—they could stick by him while he was gone, but once he was free, the anger returned. They couldn't take the chance on going through it all again. My wife had stuck by me; my children hadn't turned away; my friends had forgiven me. Never mind that I was ruined financially. I had lost my law license. We now lived in a rented town house paid for by my sister Terry. Still, I knew I was a lucky man.

On the day we got home, a crowd of reporters was waiting for us in front of our town house. It would have been nice to think they were there for a story on Webb Hubbell's happy homecoming, the end of his long ordeal. But that wasn't to be. "Are you being paid hush money, Mr. Hubbell?"

"Tell us about Lippo!"

"Why didn't you cooperate with the independent counsel?"

I got out of the car and said, "I'm not going to talk to you."

"Why not, Mr. Hubbell?"

I issued a statement. "Because I've answered every question that's been put to me for more than two years, and look where it's gotten me. I have nothing more to say." Within two weeks of that homecoming, the independent counsel subpoenaed the White House for any documents surrounding my consulting contract with the Lippo Group. Soon investigators were looking into how Suzy got her job at Interior and Walter got his job with Fannie Mae. Walter's college records were subpoenaed three times to see who had been paying for his tuition.

A month later, in Little Rock, my friend Breda Turner called me in tears. She had gotten a call from a reporter at the *Los Angeles Times* saying he was doing a sympathetic piece on Webb Hubbell's release from prison. He wanted to talk with her about her contacts with me while I was away. The day she called me was the day her divorce was final. She was already a wreck. Then the article had appeared that morning, and it was a smear, a pack of lies. He quoted Breda as saying that Marsha Scott and I had met many times in her pool house to exchange messages to and from the White House while I was being questioned by the independent counsel before I went to prison. "I didn't say any of that, Webb," Breda said, sobbing. It was *Suzy* I was staying with at Breda's pool house. By noon, two FBI agents were knocking at Breda's door, demanding an interview. She was subpoenaed, pressured to take a lie detector test, and later made to testify before the grand jury. She is from Ireland, and they threatened to deport her if she didn't tell them all about me. The FBI knew that it was Suzy, not Marsha, who had stayed with me at Breda's house. They had interviewed Breda's husband, Te, and Marsha, so they knew what the truth was. Yet Breda felt that unless she said it was Marsha, she was going to be deported or go to jail. She kept telling them, "I'm a good Catholic. I'm not going to lie. Webb wouldn't want me to lie."

"Mrs. Turner," the FBI agents said, "why would a respected reporter for the *Los Angeles Times* not write the truth?"

Soon after that, another friend—actually, a friend of Suzy's at Interior—was subpoenaed to "talk about Webb Hubbell." This was Bob Hattoy, the well-known AIDS activist and Clinton supporter. When he received the subpoena, I had met Bob only one time. The FBI got him in the room and said, "You used to work in White House personnel, didn't you?"

Bob didn't understand what that had to do with me, but he answered the question. "Yes, I did."

"One of your jobs at the White House was to place gays and lesbians in the administration, wasn't it?" At that point, Bob understood. This wasn't about Webb Hubbell at all. He was incensed, and he didn't take it.

"Yes," he said. "Very successfully, as a matter of fact. And I also placed a lot of them in the FBI." I wish I could be that quick-witted.

These stories, about Breda and Bob, are just two of *many* I've heard about the FBI's conduct as a part of the independent counsel's investigation in Arkansas. I really don't believe that Judge Starr and Director Freeh have any idea how their agents have used lies and intimidation to pressure potential witnesses.

It didn't take long for me to become a pariah. I spoke with a man about my job prospects. "Webb," he said, "anybody who hired you would have to spend $100,000 in legal fees to explain it." My friends kidded me. "You're not just radioactive, Webb—you're Chernobyl!"

Nobody, it seems, can afford to be involved with me. While I was at Cumberland, Vernon Jordan wrote to me saying he couldn't wait till I got out so we could play golf again. As I write these words, I've been out of the halfway house for eight months, and Vernon hasn't called. Even Mickey can't afford to talk to me right now. Neither can Mike and Harolyn Cardozo. Mike is Director of the President's Legal Defense Fund. Occasionally Harolyn writes a note to Suzy saying she wishes we could see one another again. To each of them, and to all my friends who have been questioned, investigated, and hurt by their friendship with me, I want to say that I understand. I know it's too dangerous for them to be in touch with me or Suzy. They have suffered enough already, and I also recognize that some are so hurt that our relationship is damaged forever. I am not the victim here—they are. All I can do is apologize.

Suzy talks with her mother by phone every couple of weeks, but she no longer has any relationship with her father. Seth wanted her to move to Hot Springs and sell real estate, but she wouldn't do it. Neither Seth nor Vonnie visited Suzy (much less me) while I was in prison. They did attend Walter's wedding in Dallas in June 1997, but otherwise they've had no relationship with my children since all of this began. I regret this most for the Wards—they're missing out on four wonderful grandchildren who still love them unconditionally, and who remember better days.

There are a lot of people in my home state who have lived through similar nightmares over the past four years. Jim Guy Tucker, who became governor when Bill Clinton went to Washington, had to resign the governorship, has lost his law license, is seriously ill after liver surgery, and still faces another trial. Susan McDougal languishes in prison. Her diesel therapy, if press accounts are anything approaching accurate, makes mine look like a cakewalk. She hasn't even started serving her sentence yet. I'm sure it's no solace to her that she's considered a pinup in prison—not so much for her looks as for her stand-up attitude. Jim McDougal thought he had won when he was acquitted of defrauding Madison. Then he talked with Sheffield Nelson because

Jim thought Clinton should have helped him more. He ended up in prison taking his codefendants with him.

When we saw our friends moving to the White House, many Arkansans had a dream—that our state would become the next Georgia after Jimmy Carter, or Texas after Lyndon Johnson. Our image was supposed to be benefited by the elevation of our governor, the Rhodes scholar. But whatever we've gained has been tainted by the image of Paula Jones, the McDougals, and state troopers "telling all." Many people who were friends of Bill, Hillary, or Webb have paid a huge price for the dream.

I ran into a woman at the airport the other day. She had had minimal involvement with all of us over the years, but she wanted to say, "Hi," and that she was praying for me. As with others I've left out of this book, I'm afraid that by merely naming her I would cause her to be hurt more than she already has. She's just one of the many, many stories. When I visited with her a few minutes, she revealed that she was now broke from paying lawyers, and the press had broken her spirit questioning every aspect of her past. Still, she wanted to say, "I feel for you and your family."

As for my friends in prison, I've heard that the ex-S and L president is still sacking groceries. A bank president I knew still works at a dry cleaners. A young man from the coal mines of West Virginia is scraping by with odd jobs and trying to avoid falling back into crime. All of those men have been out for a year or more. Now this is the best they can get.

There is something terribly wrong here, but my thoughts about that are for another book. In prison, I lost seventy pounds, wrote more than a thousand letters, and read eighty books. I believe I achieved my goal of facing my failures and taking sole responsibility for them. I did wrong, and I paid for it. But every day now I think of something I read in one of those books. It was about what happens to people who go to prison. Everybody goes through three phases. The first is shock. The second is apathy. And the third is getting out.

I went through the first two, but the third is still a mystery to me. In some ways, I haven't been released yet.

Epilogue

Starting Over

Fort Marcy Park is a quiet, secluded place, the kind of park Vince Foster would have been drawn to. I went to see it on an unseasonably cool August day last summer. It was just over four years after Vince's death. This was the first time I had felt myself able to go.

Suzy drove me there. From the George Washington Parkway, heading north, there is a road that curves off to the right. In August, the trees were heavy and the shade was dense. We wound our way along the drive and soon came to a gravel parking area. This was where they had found Vince's car, with his jacket folded neatly on the passenger seat, his White House pass placed perfectly in the center of his coat.

We got out and walked, going left around the parking area, then back right toward the river. There was a clearing with a plaque, telling about Fort Marcy's role in the Civil War. I glanced at it, but couldn't absorb the words. Then we went down an embankment and up the other side. We came into a large open area, a grassy meadow. To our right past dense foliage flowed the Potomac. Far forward was a forest. And to our left, about midway to the end of the slightly rising meadow, a hundred-year-old cannon aimed into the brush where some enemy might have hidden. By that cannon, Vince lay down on a summer day and shot himself.

I came to this place for several reasons. In writing this book I've thought long and hard about all that has happened to my friends and me on our journey from Little Rock to Washington. It didn't turn out quite the way we hoped. Instead of achieving great things, we lost who we were. At least Vince and I did. Vince lost his life, and I lost my way. For both of us, I suppose it occurred long before we even got to Washington.

I've written earlier what I think happened to Vince. He was sick. Somehow, he thought he was helping us by killing himself. I suspect Lisa, and perhaps Sheila, will be upset by the story I've told here. They hoped to put all the speculation behind them and let Vince finally rest in peace. I respect that. It hurts *me* when I read articles and books about Vince Foster's suicide. And now here I am, writing about him, too. But nobody has written about him from the perspective I have. Vince was my friend. Now he's almost developed an aura of darkness, like me. I wanted to show him here the way he was—good, kind, fragile, human. I miss him terribly. He would have been disappointed in what I did, but I know he wouldn't have abandoned me.

My own missteps started long, long ago—before I actually started taking money. When I was sentenced, I told the judge that I had lost my way. It was true—I had felt it happening for years. I began my adult life as an idealistic young man, but as I acquired the trappings of success, they began to smother that idealistic young man who I had once been. It's curious, but lately I've been thinking a lot about my seven months in Mena, Arkansas, after I failed to pass the football physical. I was starting over then, just as I am now. I was making $900 a month at the phone company then. I had dreams. The road lay before me, and I had no idea where it would lead. In many ways I'm in that exact spot again.

Mena was a small town, and so is D.C. I work at the National Center on Institutions and Alternatives, and I make about $900 a month. I bear great regret for what I did, but I'm not bitter about going to prison—I'm grateful. Writing the last part of this book, rereading my prison journal, reflecting on all of this has had a profound effect on me. To see your life and associations, friendships and family, mistakes and mishaps in print is a sobering experience. Once again, my prayers have increased. I would like one day to help others in prison. Judge Howard ordered me to speak in prisons once a month. I hope I can continue past the court's order. I think I get more out of it than the inmates do. Once you've been there, you understand. If you haven't, then there's no way you can. I hope to teach, write, and someday renew the friendships I've lost through my misdeeds. Many people will not like this book, but it is written from my heart, to tell the way things were. I have to do that now. I can never again allow myself to live a lie.

Prison helped me rekindle my idealism. There is something about what you experience there that can transform you like nothing else I know. Maybe you have to hit bottom, lose your selfishness, before you can be reshaped and made right. I still think about those words from *The Natural,* but now with a hopeful difference. Before, I dwelled on Hobbs's line about there being some mistakes you just keep paying for. Now I can see the beauty in his girlfriend's response. "I believe we live two lives," she says, "the one we learn with, and the one we live with after we've learned." Believe me, I've learned. That's the life ahead of me now.

Suzy and I stood in the spot where Vince's journey ended, and then I walked to the river. Fort Marcy Park sits on a bluff, but this wasn't what I imagined when I thought of friends in high places. Across the Potomac, Bill and Hillary were somewhere in that Washington haze. I have conflicted feelings about them. Next to my family, Bill and Hillary have suffered the most from my crimes. I owed it to them not to come to Washington, to tell them the truth. I couldn't do that. Yes, I feel a great loss at our not being able to see one another. I don't know how they feel about me right now, and I can't find out. I suspect their feelings are mixed, too. My task is to apologize and to go on with my life, hoping someday for forgiveness and the friendship I once had. Somebody asked before I went to prison if I thought the President could forgive me. "Yes," I said. "He just has too big a heart." Probably the greatest criticism Bill Clinton's *friends* have of him is that he always forgives his enemies. I don't see this as a fault, even though others do. That may be a trait that they'll never understand in Washington, but I know Bill has retained that. It's too deeply ingrained in him. He had a lot of pain growing up, and though the joke is that he "feels your pain," I know it's true. I know he feels mine. And if I know he forgives his enemies, why would I think he could never forgive me?

Bill alone among us has achieved what he set out to do, but the price has been high. All of us found ourselves in prisons of one kind or another—Vince to his perfectionism, me to my materialism and the mistakes it caused, Hillary to the public persona she was forced to live in. But Bill is in a prison, too. He lives with guards and constant attention the way I did at Cumberland. You lose your privacy in prison. I know both Bill and Hillary hate that aspect of the life they have now.

I hope, especially for Hillary, that the next stage of her life will bring her the freedom to be who she really is. For almost twenty years, she's had to be a First Lady first, although she's certainly had her share of accomplishments. She's been Bill Clinton's wife. I know that that narrow image has been a painful sacrifice for her—not because she didn't want Bill to succeed as he has, or because she didn't want to be married to him. But because she— like so many other women—wants to show that a woman can love a man and still have her own identity, her own independence, her own important role in society.

I have no idea what Bill will do next, but I do know that he's very, very good at "refocusing" himself far ahead of the field. After he's out of the White House, I imagine he'll play golf for a while. And then he'll begin to assemble his vast network of advisers. "What should I do next?" he'll ask, and he'll listen to all their varied answers, testing himself against them. Whatever he does, I can't imagine that it'll force Hillary to continue playing the role she's played for so long. She'll no longer be constrained by his political ambitions. Hillary, I predict, will finally get the chance to be the person I've always known she was destined to be. I predict she'll have a big impact on the national discourse. (I can already hear the Republicans scrambling to their telephones, beating the bushes, getting ready to try to stop her.)

I told Suzy I was ready to go. We walked back through the meadow, up the embankment, down the path. On the way to the car, we passed a couple. The man turned and looked at me and then said something to his friend. I'm sure he thought he knew who I was. But he had no idea.

Acknowledgments

My special thanks to James Morgan, without whom this book would still be a dream. Jim is a gifted writer, probing journalist, insightful analyst, and now a good friend. His belief in this project from the start made it possible. His hard work made it a reality. To his gracious wife, Beth, thanks for sharing so much of Jim's time.

Michael V. Carlisle of the William Morris Agency believed in me and this project from the first time we met. He trusted me when many others had lost faith. He encouraged, prodded, and pushed, never giving up. He has endured subpoenas, lawyers, media, and skepticism with humor and aplomb. He is more than an agent—he is a friend to my whole family in the best meaning of the word. Jerry McGuire could take lessons from this guy. Thanks also to his assistant Mary Beth Brown. Michael and I would be lost without her.

William Morrow and Company stood up for all authors and publishers and the First Amendment when they opposed the independent counsel's subpoena for early drafts of the manuscript. They have my thanks and the appreciation of writers everywhere. I thank Paul Fedorko, my publisher, and Henry Ferris, my editor, for their trust that this book would meet William Morrow's standards of excellence. Henry Ferris went above and beyond to get this book completed—every author should be lucky enough to have Henry as his editor. I also thank Eric Steel for his hard work and patience in particularly difficult circumstances.

Nobody could have better lawyers than John Nields and Laura Shores who have always given me good counsel. They have never wavered in their loyalty to me and my family. Thank you is hardly sufficient for these two. Jack Lassiter and Charles Owen have provided me with the same good advice in Little Rock.

I am blessed with so many friends around the country, especially in Little Rock. They have stuck with me, written and visited me in prison, looked after my family, and supported me over the years in countless ways. This book would double in length if I tried to mention them all. More important, I don't want any of them to receive a subpoena. My friends Marty and Mike Schaufele stand as examples of unconditional love that each of you have given me and my family. To my friends in Cumberland present and past, inmates and administration, I thank you for the kindness you showed "the Big Easy" (my nickname there) and for what I have learned from you.

My sisters, Patty Sharp and Terry Collins, have given me so much, each in her own way. They define family. Terry was there for my family every time—never judging, only loving. My children have learned what family means from their Aunt Terry.

This book is dedicated to my wife and children. No man is more fortunate than I. Thank you Suzy, Walter and Missy, Rebecca, Caroline and Kelley.

Index